D1598751

What Is China?

WHAT IS

China?

Territory, Ethnicity, Culture, and History

GE ZHAOGUANG

Translated by

MICHAEL GIBBS HILL

THE BELKNAP PRESS OF
HARVARD UNIVERSITY PRESS

Cambridge, Massachusetts
London, England
2018

First printing

Publication of this book was aided by a grant from the Chiang Ching-kuo Foundation
for International Scholarly Exchange.

First published in Chinese as *He wei Zhongguo: Jiangyu, minzu,
wenhua yu lishi* (何為中 國 : 疆域, 民族, 文化與歷史)
by Oxford University Press (China) Ltd.,
Hong Kong, 2014.

Library of Congress Cataloging-in-Publication Data

Names: Ge, Zhaoguang, 1950– author. | Hill, Michael
(Michael Gibbs), translator.
Title: What is China? : territory, ethnicity, culture, and history /
Ge Zhaoguang ; translated by Michael Gibbs Hill.
Other titles: He wei Zhongguo. English
Description: Cambridge, Massachusetts : The Belknap Press of Harvard
University Press, 2018. | Includes bibliographical references and index.
Identifiers: LCCN 2017035842 | ISBN 9780674737143 (alk. paper)
Subjects: LCSH: China—History. | National characteristics, Chinese. |
Chinese—Attitudes. | China—Civilization. | China—Boundaries. |
China—Foreign relations.
Classification: LCC DS735 .G44913 2018 | DDC 951—dc23
LC record available at https://lccn.loc.gov/2017035842

CONTENTS

PREFACE

This short book discusses several questions: What is "China"? How did modern China emerge from ancient China? What challenges does this "Middle Kingdom," with its many national groups, complex cultures, and vast territories, now face? (Here I should point out that, with the exception of Chapter 3, a Japanese version of this book was published in February 2014 by Iwanami Shoten under the title *Chūgoku saikō: Sono ryōiki, minzoku, bunka* [Rethinking China: Its territories, peoples, and cultures] as part of their Iwanami gendai bunko series.)

A discussion of these questions must also take up several important keywords related to "China." They include *worldviews, borders, ethnicity, history, peripheries,* and *practical questions.* The questions related to each keyword can be summarized as follows: First, did ideas from ancient China about "All-under-Heaven" become the worldview of modern China? If not, how might that happen? This problem involves how China in the present day understands the traditional tribute system and how it approaches the modern international order. Second, did the "frontiers" become the borders of modern China? If not, how might that happen? This discussion can help us to understand a wide variety of debates about national territories. Third, as China has moved since the early modern period from the worldview of "All-under-Heaven" to a view that recognized the myriad states (*wanguo*) across the globe, how has it brought the "Four Barbarians" (*si Yi*) (a discussion of the translation of this term is contained in the Translator's Introduction) into China and worked to bring a structure to a vast China and Chinese nation? This discussion can help us to understand why Chinese people still hold ideas about a so-called greater China. It can also help us to understand why many scholars feel forced to discuss the history of various national groups in China solely in terms of Sinicization or acculturation. Fourth, how did what we now call Chinese culture take shape across history? Is this Chinese culture singular or multiple? Fifth, when in the early modern era did the sense of mutual trust between China and its peripheries—especially other countries in East Asia—disappear? How did the states of East Asia begin to grow apart from one another? This discussion will help us to gain a new understanding of international relations against the backdrop of the larger transformations of early modern East Asia. Sixth, I ask, from the perspective of cultural conflicts: Will the cultural resources of traditional China become a force for reason that will bring global peace and regional stability?

Although all of these questions are discussed in relation to "China," it is also the case that, when we discuss China, we also touch on its neighbors in Asia, such as Japan and South Korea (as well as North Korea and Vietnam), and even, at times, the Western world. Living in this mutually connected and interdependent world, we hope that reflections on history will lead to rational thinking that will restrain deeply felt nationalism and lead to mutual accommodation and respect. I hope that this book will allow me to discuss with readers some of the great questions that affect us all.

Of course, I must also say that, as a historian, my discussion of these issues will always begin from a historical perspective. This is because I hope to achieve what I mention in the Introduction: to apply a knowledge of history to understand oneself and to apply a knowledge of history to arrive at common ground with neighbors on our borders.

TRANSLATOR'S INTRODUCTION

The question raised by this short book, *What Is China?*, matters more each day. The lines dividing what or who is or is not part of China or Chinese culture or civilization have anchored politics and ordered history in East Asia for centuries.

This last statement draws a simple, pointed question: How do we define "China" and "Chinese"? Since the boundaries of the People's Republic of China, the largest of the states that lay claim to a shared history with imperial China or to what is called Chinese culture, draw together numerous peoples of different ethnicities, faiths, and mother tongues, how do we make sense of this combination of different groups in the twenty-first century? Ge Zhaoguang argues that the meanings of China and Chinese culture regularly change and avoid a single definition, and that honest discussion of these different meanings and how they arose gives us a better route to understanding both historical and contemporary China. He puts forward his solution as an alternative to what he sees as writings that are too eager to deconstruct and perhaps dismiss the idea of China as a historical entity altogether. Ge's wide-ranging discussion will appeal to readers interested not only in Chinese history or Asian studies but also international relations, global history, and current affairs. *What*

Is China? is the third book by Ge that has been translated in English; the present book and other writings have also been translated into Japanese. *What Is China?* takes up many of the points Ge discussed in *Here in "China" I Dwell* (*Zhai zi Zhongguo*, 2011) but addresses a wider audience.[1] Several of the chapters began as lectures and take a more conversational tone.

The political sensitivity of the questions taken up in *What Is China?*—even in historical scholarship—made headlines in the spring of 2015, when a long article published in an official journal of the Chinese Academy of Social Sciences attacked the so-called New Qing History, taking particular aim at scholars from the United States who have written histories of the Qing dynasty (1644–1911) that emphasized the interplay of ethnicity, language, and politics during the roughly two and a half centuries of Qing rule.[2] Many of these researchers used not only Chinese-language archival sources but also sources in Manchu, Mongolian, and other languages. Their scholarship challenged many received truths about China from the seventeenth century down to the present, including the idea that the Manchu rulers of the Qing dynasty had assimilated into Chinese culture—or, more to the point, were assimilated *by* Chinese culture—to a high degree. The debate over the New Qing History shows how the legacy of Qing rule continues to touch on sensitive political issues, especially the status of Xinjiang, Mongolia, and Tibet, and the connections between the people who live there and the countries of Central Asia and the Middle East. As the PRC moves to increase trade and interaction with Central Asia and the Middle East, these issues will persist.

Ge Zhaoguang answers the question *What Is China?* through the same means that have made him a renowned and widely read historian, namely, his use of an astonishing range of sources that go beyond the usual confines of intellectual history (or *sixiang shi*) as it was practiced in China from the time it emerged in the first half of the twentieth century as a freestanding category of scholarly work. Ge has argued for some time that intellectual history in China should take greater account of writings and other materials that fall outside the established canon, such as imperial almanacs and calendars, manuals for builders and the trades, and especially visual materials and historical documents written in languages other than Chinese.[3]

What Is China? also makes no secret of Ge's impatience with the way so-called Western theory, especially histories and critiques of the nation-state, have been used in studies of China written in English, Chinese, and other languages. The arrival of different waves of theory and conceptual frameworks in Sinophone academic institutions has been discussed extensively.[4] Here it is enough to say that Ge focuses on writing histories of China that engage with North American, Western European, Japanese, and other theories and conceptual categories but do not necessarily need to take those ideas as a starting point. Nonetheless, his work demonstrates a strong familiarity with North American, Western European, and Japanese scholarship on China, East Asia, and Central Asia, which Ge acknowledges and borrows from freely. At the same time, Ge's discussion of Gu Jiegang (1893–1980), Feng Youlan (1895–1990), Li Chi (also Li Ji, 1896–1979), and other scholars active in the 1930s and 1940s pointedly shows how earlier generations of thinkers in China approached the problems of nation, state, and race well before new theoretical models gained popularity in the 1980s and 1990s.

The introductory chapter to *What Is China?* offers an overview of schools of thought that have challenged the consensus on the meaning of "China" as a state, collection of national groups, and even a fundamental historical category. Ge rebuts some of what he sees as excessive arguments about the imagined or constructed nature of China or *Zhongguo* and puts forward alternatives that he hopes will balance out some possible objections to histories of China as a single historical formation.

Chapter 1 traces the transformation of ideas about the place of China or the Middle Kingdom in relation to the larger world. Ge details the elaborate worldview of "All-under Heaven" (*Tianxia*), which held that China occupied the center of civilization. The chapter draws on a huge range of materials, including maps, archaeological findings, legends and tales, and Buddhist texts that are often neglected in Confucian-oriented intellectual history. Although we eventually return to the often-told story of China's transition from All-under-Heaven to one state among many, Ge also points out other possibilities within Chinese history—in particular, the worldview of Buddhism, which took India as the center of the religious world—that might have pushed ideas about China as the center of All-under-Heaven in new directions.

In Chapter 2 Ge takes up the problem of territory and sovereignty in Chinese history. Ge argues that, within Chinese history, the idea of China as one state among many has substantial historical precedent in the Northern and Southern Song dynasties (960–1279), which repeatedly faced challenges at its borders from groups such as the Jurchens, who eventually overran much of the territory of the Northern Song. This new sense that China, the Central Land (*Zhongguo*), was fundamentally different from other groups, in terms of both its state structure and the characteristics of the people who lived there, arose much earlier than ideas about the nation-state that can be traced to early modern Europe. While Ge acknowledges the historical dilemmas that have faced the Qing, the Republic of China, and the People's Republic as a result of the massive territorial expansion that took place under Qing rule, he also points out that scholarly disputation in the first half of the twentieth century about China's peripheral territories cannot be untangled from imperial and colonial designs—particularly from Japan—on the lands and peoples within the borders of the Chinese state. Attempts made in the 1930s and 1940s by scholars in Japan to raise questions about China's status as a truly modern nation-state and the legitimacy of its claims to places such as Manchuria, Mongolia, and Tibet related directly to the Japanese state's desire either to exercise influence on these places or take possession of them.

Chapter 3 takes on the question of different *minzu* (national or ethnic groups) in modern China. Ge is keen to point out the ways that scholars within China approached this question in the first half of the twentieth century. Scholarship and opinion on this matter included calls to foment revolution and drive out the supposedly foreign Manchus; the slogan of "Five Nations under One Republic" (*Wu zu gonghe*) put forward by Sun Yat-sen (1866–1925); and attempts by later scholars to conduct research on the history of Chinese borderlands while trying to find the proper distance—if possible—between their work and the very practical concerns of maintaining the integrity of the Chinese state from encroachment by other powers. This tension reached its height as the places they researched often came under threat during the Second Sino-Japanese War (1937–1945).

Ge pays particular attention to publications such as *Yu Gong*, a journal founded by Gu Jiegang that adopted the English title *Chinese Historical*

Geography, treating them both as historical documents and as resources for dealing with the challenges to national history that he describes throughout the book. The careers of the scholars and intellectuals who wrote for the publications show how the persistent pull of politics and world events of the 1930s and 1940s affected the direction of their work. For example, academic researchers such as Fei Xiaotong (1910–2005) faced sharp criticism from their peers for suggesting that the minority groups who lived in areas that had been seized or were under threat from Japan might not be part of the larger Chinese state and nation. Although he does not say so directly, in my view Ge's approach suggests the need to view China's minority policy within a historical framework and to acknowledge earlier attempts to think through this problem when discussing the present.

Chapter 4 argues for an understanding of the multiplicity of Chinese culture across history. While he lays out a set of characteristics that broadly define the culture of China that is centered on the Han people, Ge points out the many foreign influences that regularly changed the characteristics of Han communities, especially in terms of religion and material culture. Ge's argument that we should understand China as a "(multi) national state" also pushes back against new traditionalist assertions about the importance of reviving a version of Chinese culture that forgets the diversity of China's dynastic history and easily devolves into Han chauvinism and even Han-chauvinist nationalism. For Ge, the imposition of this Han nationalism is as much an error of historical interpretation as are misapplications of theories of the nation-state.

Chapter 5 draws from sources in Japanese and Korean writings in classical Chinese to pose the question of how historical writings from China's neighbors can illuminate its history. The message from some of these sources is clear: after the fall of the Ming dynasty, prominent educated people in Japan and Korea who had encountered the Qing thought that China had changed so much that it could no longer claim to be the center of All-under-Heaven. In some cases, people in Japan and Korea saw themselves as the bearers of traditions that could be traced back to the Tang and Song dynasties, especially in their articulations of neo-Confucian thought. Ge argues that the seventeenth century marked a crucial turning point in East Asian history because the fall of the Ming and the growing influence of the West in the region began to push Japan and Korea away from identifying with China culturally and politically. In our present moment, the story of these changing viewpoints in Japan and Korea also poses difficult questions for versions of history, both popular and scholarly, that argue for a single, unchanging Chinese culture across history.

Chapter 6 discusses the implications of the questions raised throughout the book for the growing role of the People's Republic in global politics, economy, and culture. Ge argues that aspects of religious life in China, particularly the relatively peaceful coexistence between Confucian, Taoist, and Buddhist institutions in traditional China, may offer new alternatives for the world. At the same time, Ge cautions against reviving other ideas to suit China's new position in the world. For example, a revival or retooling of All-under-Heaven as a concept for understanding China's foreign relations may be a useful framework for understanding some aspects of the current moment, but it might also lend credence to a new kind of PRC exceptionalism that brushes off current norms (however unsatisfactory they might be) in favor of a new set of priorities that are dangerously unclear.

Many of the key ideas in *What Is China?* raise questions about translation, equivalence, and the modes by which languages and sets of ideas interact with one another. For the translator, even the word "China," despite being used in many languages, does not always have an exact correspondence in the written and spoken languages used by China's imperial rulers. The Qing dynasty, for example, referred to itself in writing as the Great Qing State (*Da Qing guo*), not China or *Zhongguo*.[5] Ge Zhaoguang regularly places the term with which "China" is translated, *Zhongguo*, in quotation marks to draw attention to its possible meanings and disputes over those meanings. His usage forces the translator to choose the best term to approximate his approach. When I deviate from the term "China" and use "Middle Kingdom" or "Central Land" to translate *Zhongguo*, I give the pinyin in parentheses to guide the reader.

Ge also regularly uses the term *si Yi*, which often is translated as "Four Barbarians" of the four cardinal directions but also may refer in a more neutral way to non-Han peoples; the translation of *Yi* as "barbarian" was even the subject of diplomatic disputes between the Qing and British Empires.[6] Alternate translations include "foreign peoples" or "people of the four directions." I translate this term as "Four Barbarians" because, in my view, *What Is China?* uses the term *si Yi* with full knowledge of this historical baggage: part of the work to understand China's borderlands included moving away from these earlier terms used in Chinese-language discourse (and their implied hierarchies of culture) toward a new set of standards for researching these places and the people who lived there.

Where possible, quotations of canonical writings draw from existing English translations, especially when those translations might provide more information and context to readers who do not read Chinese. I added translator's notes only to elaborate on terminology or references that might not be familiar to nonspecialist readers, or to indicate other sources used in preparing this translation.

I am grateful for the hospitality of the John W. Kluge Center at the Library of Congress, where I put the final touches on the translation. Wu Xin offered advice on translation questions, and Mark Kellner provided many of the Japanese translations and transliterations in the book, especially of historical materials. Ge Zhaoguang graciously answered many questions, especially concerning historical sources. I also thank an anonymous reviewer for Harvard University Press who offered many suggestions for improvement. Any errors or omissions in the translation are my responsibility.

What Is China?

INTRODUCTION

On the Historical Formation of "China"
and the Dilemma of Chinese Identity

In this chapter, I want to discuss with readers a few historical problems, some of which may involve (1) "Asia" and "China"; (2) scholarship, politics, and identity; and (3) global history, national history, and regional history.

As a professional historian, I originally had no desire to discuss these problems. In recent years, however, I have felt more and more that the study of Chinese history cannot avoid these problems, just as we cannot avoid them when we observe China's reality today. Recently, as China continues to expand (I dislike the word "rise" or *jueqi*), one of the problems it faces is how China will get along with Asia and the rest of the world in terms of culture, politics, and economics. I recognize that China has already run into a number of difficulties, including questions related to the Goguryeo Kingdom, the East China Sea and Diaoyu Island, the South China Sea and the Paracel Islands, the Spratly Islands, Outer Mongolia and Inner Mongolia, the Eastern Turkestan movement in Xinjiang and issues concerning Islam, problems in Tibet and with Tibetan Buddhism, problems with the borders between China and India, the Taiwan question, the Hong Kong question, and even the question of the Ryukyu Islands, which might catch fire once again.

Undoubtedly, political difficulties should be resolved by politicians according to international political norms, but there also exist certain historical questions that have not been fully addressed by historians themselves. As a result, some political figures are not only unable to separate questions of historical lands and territorial domains and actual territory but are also unable to apply a knowledge of history to arrive at common ground with their neighbors on their borders. A number of scholars have sensed the importance of these questions, but if they simply jump into the discussion without having obtained sufficient historical knowledge, then, on the one hand, they fall into debates that have predetermined positions and are loaded down with political ideology and engage in discussions that are neither rational nor scholarly, or, on the other hand, they jump into patterns laid out by fashionable Western theories and engage in empty talk about huge theoretical terms and concepts such as empires, nation-states, or the postmodern or the postcolonial.

Topics such as territory, nation, religion, the state, and identity have already received substantial attention from scholars in China. As a historian, then, I want to ask readers: From a historical perspective, what is "China," after all? I also took up the question in my book *Here in "China" I Dwell* (*Zhai zi Zhongguo*), which was published in Beijing and Taipei in 2011. This little book I have prepared here not only revisits many of the same questions from *Here in "China" I Dwell* but also presents new ideas I have developed as I continue to think through the "China" question.[1]

How Did the Interpretation of "China" Become Open to Question? What Dilemmas Are Found There?

What is "China"? Many difficult historical problems lie behind what looks to be a commonsense question.

On the one hand, from 1895 on, the Great Qing Empire (*Da Qing diguo*) was brought into the world and into Asia and forced to take on challenges posed by Western culture and new elements in East Asian culture. During this time, traditional Chinese ideas about All-under-Heaven (*Tianxia*) and the tribute system were challenged by the modern world order, while the traditional Chinese political system came under attack from Western democratic systems, resulting in changes not seen in the previous two thousand years.[2] The change within tradition so commonly seen in ancient China was forced to become change *without* tradition. When we discuss China from a historical perspective, then, we must also include Asia or even the entire world, because from this point forward "China" is no longer a self-contained historical world, and all discussions of history must involve the world or Asia; at the very least, they must be set against the backdrop of Asia.

On the other hand, these changes that occurred in the early modern world and in Asia have worked with ever greater force to stimulate the writing of global histories and regional histories that emphasize interconnection and mutual influence. In the past few decades, postmodern theories of history have gained popularity as they have called for critiques of historical narratives of the nation-state. As scholars have warmed to the idea of Asian history or global history, they have also promoted a new trend in the international scholarly domain that questions whether "China" really exists as a political state or as a state with a high degree of cultural unity. Some people ask, Why is it acceptable for "China" to be treated as a historical world that can be narrated and with which one can identify? This type of question has made its way into domestic discussions in China and has gained influence in a number of scholarly fields.

We should be grateful for this sharp questioning. It is only because of this questioning that we can discuss and consider anew the question of "what is China." I believe that these historical problems concerning "China" have both resulted in a number of political and cultural dilemmas for China and have given the scholarly world—especially historians—an area of research with global significance. Why? Because, as a state, the true nature of China can be understood neither through a simple application of the European concept of empire nor through the use of definitions or theories of the early modern European nation-state. Questions concerning China's territories, nations and peoples, faiths, territorial boundaries, and identities are far more complicated than for any other country in the world.

If we look back on the history of "China," we can, putting it simply, say that a China with political and cultural continuity was established very early. From the third century BCE, when the Qin Shi Huangdi established a unified empire and used its official power to ensure that "all weights and measures were standardized, the gauge of wheeled vehicles was made uniform, and the writing system was standardized,"[3] down to the second century BCE, when the Han dynasty "admired nothing other than Confucianism" in its philosophy but, in terms of its institutions, "took variously from the ways of the Lords Protector and the [ideal] Kings"[4] in its political system, a Chinese empire (*Zhonghua diguo*), relatively unified in terms of politics, culture, and language, had formed. Over the long medieval period, China underwent numerous wars and territorial divisions, was the site of the intermingling of different national groups, and was ruled by a long line of leaders from various clans and national groups. Nonetheless, all the way down to the times of the Sui and Tang dynasties, China still maintained an empire that reached across much of East Asia and exercised a substantial degree of control over the various peoples within its territories. We should remember that, from the Han dynasty through the Tang dynasty, the world of ideas did not really have a sense of foreign lands (*waiguo*) or of an international order (*guoji zhixu*). Even if a number of foreign peoples across history, such as the Xiongnu, the Xianbei, the Turkic peoples, or the Tubo, was able to put up strong resistance to this empire, generally speaking the world of ideas also did not really recognize enemy states of equal status, much less foreign countries of such status.[5]

It was not until the Song dynasty (that is, the tenth century through the fourteenth century) that major changes occurred in China's relations with its neighbors.[6] Song-dynasty China found itself in a multistate, international environment and began to produce a sense of the "Middle Kingdom" that has extended to the present day. One needs only a basic knowledge of Chinese history to realize that this era was indeed quite different from those that came before it. In modern scholarship, why do so many people agree with the thesis of the Tang-Song transformation, which emphasizes that the Tang dynasty is an era of tradition, while the Song dynasty marks the beginning of the early modern period for China? Japanese scholars such as Naitō Konan (1866–1934) and Miyazaki Ichisada

(1901–1995) have put forward this argument, and Chinese scholars such as Fu Sinian, Chen Yinke, Qian Mu, and Fu Lecheng have all reached similar conclusions. I believe that the Song dynasty can be seen as "early modern" for a number of reasons: in addition to a number of aspects of the Song dynasty that have been discussed by previous scholars—such as urbanization and the rise of urban populations, the decline of aristocratic clans and the centralization of imperial power, the formation of the examination system, gentry elites, and rural culture, and changes in literary and artistic styles—the gradual development of a self-conscious nation (*minzu*) and state (*guojia*) is also an important marker of the "early modern." For these reasons, I emphasize that the Song dynasty was an essential period in the formation of a consciousness of "China."[7]

It must be pointed out, however, that once the prototype for this state had been formed, the political borders of the state and the international environment were still in a constant state of change. Even a diminished China continued to subscribe to the traditional view of an expansive, limitless All-under-Heaven and a "self-centered" tribute system. From the Song dynasty onward this "China," which gradually gained cultural unity and political unification, encountered even more difficulties. Aside from the cases of the Mongol Yuan dynasty and the Manchu Qing dynasty, which resulted in rule by foreign peoples and the creation of an expansive empire, China also encountered three very particular types of dilemmas that rendered "China" as a state unable to resolve problems of recognition and identity associated with the inner or domestic (*nei*) and the outer or foreign (*wai*). These problems eventually evolved into dilemmas faced by modern China, and I believe that they will extend into the future.

What are the three dilemmas?

The first concerns an orientation toward one's native state that appeared in neighboring states (including Japan, Korea, Vietnam, and so on) since the Song dynasty. From the time that China lost the cultural attractiveness and radiance of the Han dynasty and Tang dynasty, these neighboring countries were, at the very least, no longer willing to be culturally dependent or subordinate to China and were no longer willing in political terms to recognize the idea that barbarians from the north, south, east, and west surrounded the "central state" of "China" (*Zhongguo*). For example, since at least the times of the Sui and Tang dynasties, Japan has had a consciousness of itself as occupying a position of parity with China, but it would probably not be until the Yuan dynasty,[8] when the military forces of the Mongols, Jiangnan China, and the Goryeo dynasty of Korea joined together to attack Japan (which saw itself as a "divine land" [*shinkoku*]), that a true orientation toward one's own state began to develop in political, economic, and cultural terms. From this time on, Japan began to see itself as a divine land and devoted conscious effort to developing its own culture, eventually giving rise to a Japanese version of the "order of relations between Chinese and the barbarian."[9] Even though Ashikaga Yoshimitsu (1358–1408) attempted to relax this posture at the beginning of the fifteenth century (1401) by joining the tribute system of the Ming dynasty,[10] most of the subsequent Ashikaga, Hideyoshi, and Tokugawa samurai did not identify with his actions and even looked down on the tribute system centered around China.

A series of political changes occurred in East Asia following the collapse of the Mongol Yuan dynasty: Yi Seong-gye (1335–1408) established the Joseon dynasty, claiming the mantle of the Goryeo dynasty. Even though the new state still fell within the Ming-dynasty tribute system, it still exhibited a clear orientation toward one's own native state. In 1392, Zhu Yuanzhang (1328–1398), the founder of the Ming dynasty, gave a warning to ambassadors from Korea not to attempt to form an independent kingdom: "No matter where it rises or where it sets, there is only one sun above All-under-Heaven. This fact cannot be concealed."[11] Bowing one's head to the political hierarchy, however, is not the same as admitting to subservience in the cultural realm. Korea under the Joseon dynasty gradually made its way down the path of building its own cultural center, creating its own myths of origins, substituting the mythical Jizi (Gija) with Dangun, and adopting a strategy of feigned compliance and subservience while, in the arena of culture, instilling a sense of self-confidence through its education of gentry elites. Interestingly, the main support that they used for this cultural self-confidence was the neo-Confucian thought of Zhu Xi (1130–1200), which was derived from China.

Another neighboring state, Annam (or Đại Việt), did not identify with the Yuan dynasty from the very beginning, and neither the Song nor the Yuan were able to take territorial control of this state. The Trần dynasty defeated the forces of the Mongol Yuan three times, most notably when they turned back an invasion attempt in 1257. The two sides reached an agreement by which Annam would pay tribute once every three years, but in fact, according to a historical commentary by Pan Hui, it was "difficult to summon emissaries or conduct ceremonies for conferring titles of nobility, and after the fall of the Yuan, these tributes were not revived." Trần Thánh Tông (1240–1290) adopted a new name for his reign, Thiệu Long, and set himself in opposition to the authority of the Yuan dynasty. By the time of the Ming dynasty, the situation went unchanged as the Ming admitted that Annam was "set apart by seas and mountains, by the design of Heaven and Earth." Although the Yongle emperor (r. 1402–1424) attempted to bring them under the Ming's system of centralized administration (a move similar to the conversion of peripheral territories into regular administrative regions [*gaitu guiliu*] under the Qing), they were not successful, especially when the Later Lê dynasty established itself in 1428 and defeated the Ming armies yet again. Following these events, trends leading to an orientation toward one's own state grew ever stronger in Annam.[12]

Generally speaking, when the nation and the state become unified, the sense of self and self-worth will grow strong. When countries on China's borders such as Annam, Ryukyu, Korea, and Japan formed a sense of separate statehood, they gradually reached political independence and began to assert a cultural status that was separate from China. These developments resulted in an international scene that was different from the East Asia of the Han dynasty and Tang dynasty, enough so that a China-centered international order established on the worldview of All-under-Heaven and ritual order had to change. China, in turn, was forced to gradually accept the new political and cultural state of affairs brought about by these changes.

This is the first type of challenge that came from the periphery: those states that previously had been under China's influence gradually began to stand up as China's equals.

The second dilemma took shape only after Westerners came to East Asia during the middle part of the Ming dynasty.[13] Although Chinese territory was reduced after the founding of the Ming dynasty and China returned to being an empire established on the traditional basis of Han territory, ethnic groups, and culture, in the eleventh year of the reign of Ming emperor Wuzong (1516), a Portuguese man named Rafael Perestrello arrived by boat to China, opening the curtain on the long drama of the Western world's journey to the East. From this point on, the Great Ming Empire was drawn into an even greater world order, and the writing of Chinese history became a part of the writing of global history. Chinese culture, too, began to face the challenges posed by Western civilization. Even if this challenge was not particularly obvious in the middle and late periods the Ming dynasty, this historical trend of so-called early globalization grew ever stronger. From the Opium Wars to the late Qing dynasty, Westerners used ships and cannons to force their way in and demand that China agree to all varieties of unequal treaties. These developments caused All-under-Heaven to gradually become an "international" view of the world: a huge part of the world that, in terms of geography, history, and culture, had never had much contact with China suddenly became significant. Whose values, then, would come to dominate this world? Whose version of order would be able to guide this international world?

This is the second predicament faced by China: the challenge posed by the culture and political order of another world.

The third dilemma lies in the domestic questions that gradually arose from the expansion of the territory of Great Qing Empire. Many people have noted that the territory of Ming-dynasty China was basically the same as the fifteen provinces of so-called China proper.[14] The majority of people from that time recognized that Jiuquan was "an important defensive post on China's frontier" and that "those lands beyond Jiayu Pass (Jiayuguan) do not belong to us."[15] In this territory, which traditionally had belonged to the Han ethnic group, few prominent questions arose concerning ethnic groups or territorial regions. By the Qing dynasty, however, the situation was quite different. In 1635, before the Manchus had entered the territory of the Ming dynasty, the Mongol Eight Banners had already been established, and the Han Chinese Eight Banners were established in 1642. We should say, then, that before its forces entered Ming territory, the Later Jin dynasty was already a hybrid empire made up of Manchu, Mongol, and Han peoples. In 1644, the first year of the reign of Shunzhi emperor (r. 1644–1661), the Manchus entered the borders of the Ming and established the Great Qing dynasty

(*Da Qing wangchao*); in 1683, the twenty-second year of the reign of Emperor Kangxi (r. 1661–1722), the Qing reclaimed Taiwan; and Khalkha Mongols of the northern Gobi came back under Qing control in 1688. After these events, the "Middle Kingdom" that was largely made up of the Han ethnicity during the Ming dynasty became an empire that held the territories of the Mongols, Manchu, and Han. In 1759, the twenty-fourth year of the reign of Emperor Qianlong (r. 1735–1796), the Dzungar region and the area south of Tian Shan was pacified, and thus with the addition of Xinjiang (or the "Hui Region," or *Hui bu*), China became a super-empire that brought together the Mongols, Manchus, Han, and Hui peoples.[16] From the beginning of the Great Ming dynasty until the conversion of peripheral territories into regular administrative regions (*gaitu guiliu*) during the Yongzheng era of the Qing dynasty (r. 1722–1735), the Miao people and the Yi people in the southeast saw their territories converted from areas controlled by local chieftains to provinces, prefectures, counties, and subprefectures, all controlled by the central state. By this time China had become an empire collectively made up of the Manchu, Mongol, Han, Hui, Uighur, and Miao peoples. From the time of the Shunzhi reign (1644–1661) to the Qianlong reign (1735–1796), titles of nobility were conferred upon the Panchen Lama and Dalai Lama. The Dalai Lama went to Chengde for an audience with the emperor, and in 1792, the fifty-seventh year of the Qianlong reign, the Qing court dispatched Fuk'anggan (1753–1796) to Tibet, establishing the "Golden Urn" system of choosing Tibetan lamas, after which China became a country of either "five nations" (Manchu, Mongolian, Hui, Tibetan, and Han) or "six nations" (Manchu, Mongol, Hui, Tibetan, Han, and Miao). China could no longer be said to be a single people (the Han) overlapping with a single state (China).

Although a massive empire is certainly something to be proud of—an empire that stretched from Sakhalin in the east to Shule County (in Xinjiang) to the west and from the Stanovoy mountain range in the north and to Hainan Island in the south[17]—serious problems related to identity came along with this empire. At the time of the 1911 revolution that overthrew the Qing court, the China that had existed under the imperial system became a state modeled after the republican system. Although revolutionaries like Zhang Taiyan (1868–1936), Sun Yat-sen (1866–1925), Chen

Tianhua (1875–1905), and others mobilized the people with nationalist revolutionary slogans that promised to "drive out the barbarians and re-store China,"[18] the revolution that started under the banner of a so-called anti-Manchu restoration of Han political power was eventually forced to compromise, because no one was willing to be blamed for dividing the territory of the state. These anti-Manchu revolutionaries were forced to compromise and to accept ideas about nation and ethnicity advocated by Liang Qichao (1873–1929) and Kang Youwei (1858–1927) and assent to the idea of "Five Nations under One Union" that was described in the imperial edict with which the final Qing emperor abdicated the throne. However, the Republic of China and the People's Republic of China, which both inherited the legacy of the Qing dynasty, also inherited the problems that came along with the vast numbers of ethnic groups and massive territorial regions within it. In other words, the successors to the Qing dynasty faced the problem of how the Manchu, Mongol, Han, Hui, Tibetan, and Miao could reach consensus over having just one state and how each could understand its cultural identity.

These issues constitute the third dilemma for "China": How to manage each ethnic group's identification with the state?

Modern China inherited the Song dynasty's shifting relations with the periphery, the international environment that had existed since the Ming dynasty, and also the complex internal relations between nations and state that had been reached by the Qing dynasty. In *Here in "China" I Dwell*, I emphasize that across history, "China" is a shifting "China." Even if China continued to think of itself as a great, unified celestial kingdom, it would continue to face the three complicated historical questions of what constitutes the domestic, the periphery, and the outer.[19] For these reasons, "China" is a special kind of "state." It is essential that now we understand that this China "did not evolve into a nation-state [as in Europe]. While the idea of a limited state was contained within the notion of the empire without borders, this limited state also con-tinued to imagine an empire without borders. The modern nation-state is the product of the traditional centralized empire, preserving remnants of the ideology of empire, from which we can see that the histories of both were intertwined."[20]

For these reasons, then, the European idea of the early modern nation-state is perhaps not all that well suited to China, while China, this particular state, can only be understood by going back into history.

Questioning "China": The Inspiration and Challenge of New Theories and Methods in the Study of History

How, then, should we understand this vast and complicated "China" or "Middle Kingdom"?[21] Without a doubt, we will no longer be bound by arguments that hold that the political territory of the People's Republic of China should equal "historical China."[22] Should we then, however, follow some of those early Japanese historians of China who argued that "*Shina* [China] had no borders"[23] or that "China is not a state," and conclude that China should be limited to the area south of the Great Wall and become a purely Han state? Or should we follow the modern scholarly model borrowed from the standards of the European nation-state, and see China as an empire without any real unity? Or should we follow postmodern theory and see "China" as a community that is not only without unity but also is established by being "imagined"?

These are not groundless concerns. In the international field of "China" studies, the following theories and methods have come to challenge and question the traditional narrative of "China" as a historical world.

1. *Regional Studies.* Since 1982, when the American scholar Robert Hartwell published an article on "Demographic, Political, and Social Transformation of China, 750–1150,"[24] an emphasis on researching geographic regions has stimulated and influenced scholarship on the Song dynasty in the United States. This emphasis is found in work by Robert Hymes, Richard Davis, Paul Smith, and Peter Bol on regions such as Fuzhou, Sichuan, Mingzhou, and Wuzhou. Of course, scholarship on regional studies or local history did not begin here; it had already begun by 1977, with William Skinner's scholarship on cities in early modern China.[25] The work of Hartwell and those who followed him, however, contributed to the growth of regional studies on China in the United States and in Japan. From 1990 on, the China studies field in Japan

developed a notable new trend in scholarship on regions. This regional perspective in research in many ways constituted a narrowing of very broad studies on "China." It is fair to say that these works constituted a deepening of historical research and scholarship, as China studies had in fact overlooked regional differences and emphasized unity and completeness for quite some time. To a significant degree, however, the methods of regional studies unexpectedly raised the question of whether a single or unified Chinese history, Chinese civilization, or Chinese thought ever existed. Some scholars even believe that it is impossible to discuss a historical world called "China" in broad terms, and argue that China should be broken down and researched separately as different localities or regions.

2. *Asian Studies or East Asian Studies.* On the one hand, research models that take Asia or East Asia as a historical world were influenced by Europe and North American world geography and ideas about world civilizations that take Asia (or East Asia) as a discrete whole. On the other hand, they are also related to discourses about Asia and so-called oriental studies (*Tōyōgaku*) that appeared in Meiji-era Japan—a complicated period of history. Simply put, the questioning that took place about whether "China" could be a nation-state or historical world had begun during the Meiji era, and Meiji-era oriental studies, following Western ideas about the nation-state and trends in Western studies of China, gradually developed into an oriental studies that paid outsized attention to Korea, Mongolia, Manchuria, Tibet, and Xinjiang. Scholars who worked in this vein no longer considered "China" to be a unified whole that extended over large swaths of territory and a variety of peoples. What had originally been a new trend in scholarly research, however, gradually became politicized, turning into ideas about how to understand China and even becoming policies directed toward China. Even after World War II, these issues gained wide attention in the academic study of history in Japan.

I have discussed this issue of Japanese historiography of China in an essay titled "Where Are the Borders?"[26] Beginning in the Meiji period, and especially after the First Sino-Japanese War (1894), Japan made ever stronger demands on China and on the territory in its own periphery. Some Japanese scholars no longer saw the "Qing Empire" as one "China," and instead misapplied new ideas about the nation-state that were popular in Europe to interpret what in the past was called "China" as different "dynasties" (*wangchao*). These dynasties, in turn, are merely seen to be traditional empires, while the real "China" should only be understood as a state that is majority Han, located to the south of the Great Wall and to the east of Tibet and Xinjiang. At the same time, according to this line of argument, the national groups on the peripheries constituted different communities, all with different cultures, politics, and ethnicities. More-over, Manchuria, Mongolia, Xinjiang, Tibet, and Korea were merely part of the "periphery" outside China. If these ideas were put forward from a historical or scholarly perspective, then there would be no problem dis-cussing them, but they became both an intellectual trend and part of for-eign policy, resulting in arguments being made in the Japanese cultural and political sphere that "China should strengthen its geographically cen-tral areas and relinquish control over the 'Four Barbarians,' while Japan should join together with Western powers to seize China's right to exer-cise control over its periphery."[27] This trend also resulted in sentiments in Japan that held that Manchuria, Mongolia, Xinjiang, Tibet, and Korea were like part of their own country. In 1923, before the beginning of World War II, the renowned Japanese scholar Yano Jin'ichi argued that China could not be considered a so-called nation-state, and that Manchuria, Mongolia, Tibet, and other places originally were never part of Chinese territory. In 1943, he argued in a series of talks at Hiroshima University for a theory of historical narrative that went beyond China and focused on Asia as a single unit.[28]

Of course, these events are far in the past. In recent years, however, as a result of a sense of cautiousness toward "Western" (that is, European and American) discourses, scholars in Japan, Korea, and China have often been open to influence from postcolonial theory and theories of Orientalism. With the hope of avoiding universal history based on the European and American experience, this discourse on Asia has gained more attention, with its supporters arguing for East Asian history,[29] "thinking through Asia,"[30] and "Asian communities of knowledge" as ways to allow Asia or East Asia to be considered as a historical world. We should recognize that the revival of the idea of Asia is a significant way of moving beyond the political borders of individual nation-states so as to construct an imagined political space that dispels state-centered biases from within and resists "Western hegemony" from without. From a historical perspective, however, some questions still need clarification. First, how did Asia become or when will it be able to become a community of culture, knowledge, history, and even politics that makes a claim to a shared identity, shared historical origins, and a shared "Other" (Europe and America or the West)? Second, if or when Asia becomes a "history," when it strengthens and emphasizes the connectedness and unity of this space of East Asia, will that then also consciously or unconsciously weaken the centrifugal forces and the sense of differences between China, Japan, and Korea? Third, from the perspective of Chinese researchers, will an excessive emphasis on "beginning by thinking through Asia" dilute the role of "China" within Asia?

3. *"Concentric" Theory from Taiwan.* Political questions constitute a great difficulty when discussing the history of Taiwan. Here I want to make every effort to engage in the scholarly discussion and not a judgment based on political values. Scholars in Taiwan have always been relatively cautious concerning the "China" question, putting forward many criticisms of attempts to use the current political territory of China to define a historical China. They avoid definitions of "China" that include Taiwan and avoid a discourse of Chinese history that includes Taiwan. Instead, some scholars attempt to go beyond the political territory of contemporary China and redefine Taiwan's position.

Borrowing the style of regional and area studies that go beyond the nation-state, these scholars reexamine the scope of Chinese history. Some Taiwan scholars put forward the "concentric circle" theory, the most representative of which is, of course, from Tu Cheng-sheng.[31] In one essay that sums up many of his arguments he said, "By the 1990s . . . our ideas about a history based on concentric circles reversed a mode of understanding that could be called 'China as the principal body, and Taiwan as the auxiliary dependent.' "[32] Tu argued that this was a way to combat cultural hegemony, and thus he attempted to break apart traditional discourses of "China," arguing that this new "concentric circle" takes Taiwan as the center. As it expands outward, the first circle includes local and rural history, the second circle is Taiwan history, the third circle is Chinese history, the fourth circle is Asian history, while the fifth expands outward toward world history. The narrative he puts forward is based on aspirations to rescue "Taiwan" from "Chinese" identity. Tu argues that, in the past, Taiwan has been forcibly written into discussions about China, and if one wants to strengthen a Taiwan group identity, then, of course, one must smash the myth of Chinese cultural unity, because this so-called unity is realized only through the "coercion" made possible by political hegemony.

In terms of historical narrative, the prominence of Taiwan highlights a sense of China's incompleteness. When such "centrifugal" force is attributed to China, ways of describing China that once went unquestioned can be seen as quite problematic. At a ceremony held in late 2003 to celebrate the seventy-fifth anniversary of the Institute of History and Philology at Academia Sinica, Tu Cheng-sheng called both for a "history of China that goes beyond China" and for a "historical perspective that examines All-under-Heaven (*Tianxia*) from Taiwan's point of view." Here we can mention a well-known example of a fiery debate that took place in the same year. When designing a new map, Tu Cheng-sheng suggested giving less weight to the old vertical and horizontal lines of longitude and latitude and instead shifting the map counterclockwise by ninety degrees, so that Taiwan would be at the center of the map. This way, Taiwan would no longer be on China's southeastern "frontier"; instead, China's coast would be on the top of the map where Taiwan is in the center, while the Ryukyu Islands and Japan are on the side to the right of Taiwan and the Philippines are on the left.

In this narrative of history and space, then, has "China" been removed? These same types of narratives and problems seem to have the potential to emerge in historical discourses concerning regions such as Xinjiang, Tibet, Inner Mongolia, Northeastern China, and even Yunnan.

4. *"History of the Mongol Era" and "The New Qing History."* In earlier common narratives about the history of "China," what was most difficult to include in "Chinese history" in an orderly way was the two empires of the Mongol Yuan dynasty and the Manchu Qing dynasty. The difficulty that these two great empires brought to the historiography of "China" was that they demanded that historians go beyond history centered on Han China and collect a richer set of documents and materials, many of which came from different perspectives and different languages, and work to describe a much broader geographical space, a greater number of nations

and ethnicities, and more complicated sets of international relations. These practices made it impossible for a traditional "Chinese history" based solely on Han-ethnicity dynasties to address these dynasties that stretched beyond the Yin Mountains in the north, the arid regions in the west, Liaodong in the east, and Lingnan in the south. For these reasons, the Japanese historians Honda Minobu and Sugiyama Masaki put forward the idea of the "history of the Mongol era," which argued that it was this framework, and not the history of the Yuan dynasty (*Yuan shi*), that altered the writing of both world history and of Chinese history, because this version of history belongs neither to "Chinese history" nor to "world history." This model, they argued, went beyond narratives of Chinese history that were centered on the Yuan dynasty and instead viewed history from a larger, global space. Their approach gained the support of many scholars.

A similar example can be found in the history of the Qing dynasty, where in recent years a new trend, called the New Qing History, has developed in the United States. The New Qing History emphasizes that the Qing Empire was not the same as the dynasties found in the twenty-four canonical histories (*Ershisi shi*). The Manchu Qing ruler was a Khan whose subjects included Manchus, Mongols, Uighurs, Tibetans, Han Chinese, and central Asian ethnic groups, and was not a Chinese emperor in the traditional sense. The Manchus made use of parts of Confucianism, but, in essence, preserved unique aspects of Manchu culture and cultural identity. The Manchu Qing Empire, therefore, is not a synonym for "China," but rather as an empire that exceeded what we consider to be "China."[33] The current fashion in so-called New Qing studies in Europe, North America, and Japan has extended this emphasis on the independent nature of Manchuria or of Manchu culture.[34] Scholars working in this vein all emphasize that the history of the Qing is not the history of Qing-dynasty China, especially not of Han China. We can say that their discussions, on the one hand, extend debates that took place in the past among Japanese scholars about "foreign rulers" in China or "conquest dynasties"; on the other hand, they also show the influence of contemporary theoretical interest in going beyond the nation-state and emphasizing identities of marginal ethnic groups. This scholarship has deep significance: First, it preserves a historical narrative of dual or plural national identities. Second, it emphasizes the historical processes by which minority or foreign ethnic groups influenced Han peoples. Third, it refuses to use a notion of "China" that is based on contemporary borders or on the Han ethnicity to look at the past. This is because, from the perspective of the New Qing History, to look at the past through the lens of China's territory, peoples, and culture as they are now would mean making history subservient to "China."

Both the perspective of the "history of the Mongol era" and the methods of the New Qing History have real scholarly value. The problem they share lies in whether, in their rejection of "Sinification" or of "China," they might also go to another extreme, one that ignores the continuing significance and influence of Han culture during the Mongol era and during the Manchu Qing dynasty and fails to address whether or not Han culture still had major significance for the entire Great Qing Empire.

5. *Postmodern Historiography*. Lastly, one other challenge to "China" can be found in postmodern theories of history, which also come from Europe and North America. The critique of modernity (*xiandaixing*) undertaken by postmodern historiography also involves a questioning of the legitimacy of the modern nation-state that emerged in the early modern period. In particular, since the arrival of theories about the nation as an "imagined community," attempts to question histories that are rooted in the perspective of the modern nation-state have revealed in profound ways how historical studies have misunderstood the nation and the state, and have pointed out the ways in which we customarily use the modern nation-state to imagine, understand, and tell the story of ancient states. These studies show that historical states often shift across time. The space they occupy grows or shrinks, and the peoples within them sometimes unite and sometimes separate from one another.

On the one hand, postmodern historiography's views on and ways of discussing the modern nation-state emerge from the colonial experience in places such as (in Asia) India, Pakistan, Malaysia, Indonesia, and from the peoples and states in the African Great Lakes region.[35] On the other hand, these perspectives also arise from early modern European history, during which time the reorganization of nations and states was a universal phenomenon. It should be pointed out, however, that, first of all, although China in ancient times went through periods of division, it was also covered by a much larger "Han culture." Second, following the unification that took place under the Qin dynasty and the Han dynasty, people became accustomed to identifying with the early version of the geographic and cultural region of Hua-Xia, which they believed to be the civilized part of the world.[36] Third, because of the differences in size between the center and the margin and between Han and non-Han groups, Han politics, culture, and tradition enjoyed a high degree of continuity. For these reasons, then, neither a "Renaissance" nor a period in which the "empire" broke apart and reformed into a "nation-state" came to pass. Therefore, we must ask the following questions. First, should historians give consideration to those unique aspects of Chinese history that are different from European history? Second, can we say that the unity of Chinese and especially Han civilization, the overlap between where the Han people lived and the space of dynasties across history, the continuity of Han traditions, and the history of identification with Han political power are all coincidental and debatable? Third, is China a nation-state that only came to be established (according to Western divisions of history) in the early modern period?

We should recognize that local and regional narratives, Asian or East Asian narratives, Taiwan-centered narratives or "Great Khanate" narratives, or even narratives of bifurcated history all give us a new, multipoint perspective for researching Chinese history that leads us to recognize the complexity of the history of "China" and the real importance of those narratives.[37] These are theoretical issues that can be approached in an evenhanded way as scholars take up these challenges, move beyond these individual theories, and work to reestablish a narrative of Chinese history.

Historical China, Cultural China, and Political China: The Challenges "China" Poses to Western Theories of the Nation-State

The perspectives, theories, and methods in Chinese studies that were just discussed made for strong medicine for the Chinese scholarly world, forcing us to reflect on whether "China" could serve as an unspoken, commonsense concept, and leading us to reconsider whether or not a culturally unified "China" actually exists.

As a Chinese historian, I want to explain again that this "China" did exist from the time of the Qin and Han dynasty onward, despite a variety of divisions and changes. I make this argument because:

1. Even though China's borders have often changed, the central region has been relatively stable, becoming very early on a place with commonly recognized territory and a unified politics, nationality, and culture; this region also comprised a historical world.

2. Even though there were periods of so-called conquest dynasties or foreign rule (for example, the Northern and Southern dynasties, the Five dynasties, the Mongol Yuan dynasty, the Manchu Qing dynasty, and so on), the cultures of foreign nationalities were continuously coming into and overlapping with China, just as the culture based largely on the Han ethnicity continuously melded with other cultures and underwent changes. The cultural tradition based on Han culture, however, extended across time in this region,[38] forming into a clear and distinct cultural identity and cultural mainstream. For these reasons, this culture also constitutes a civilization.

3. Regardless of how dynasties were established, they all believed that they were "China" or the "Middle Kingdom" and argued for the legitimacy of the dynasty in terms of the traditional Chinese world of ideas, such as the Five Elements or the use of a calendar based on imperial reigns. At the same time, the twenty-four dynastic histories and Chinese-language historical writings such as the *Comprehensive Mirror in Aid of Governance* (*Zizhi tongjian*) and the *Ten Comprehensive Encyclopedias* (*Shi tong*) also strengthened this idea of a state with cultural continuity.

4. The notion of All-under-Heaven, through which traditional culture imagined itself as the center of the world, and the tribute system, which depended on courtly ritual, also helped build up

a consciousness of the Middle Kingdom (*Zhongguo*) among
Chinese rulers, government ministers, the highly educated,
and the common people.

Previously I mentioned the formation of a Chinese identity during the
Song dynasty. What I would like to describe here is how the prosperous
reigns of the Han and Tang dynasties were succeeded by a consciousness
of the state that gradually emerged during the Song dynasty, not only in
terms of culture but also in terms of politics and economics. For the following four key reasons, China formed a preliminary idea of "the state"
in terms of its international environment, territorial borders, trade and
economy, and national identity. First, with the continuous presence of the
Liao dynasty, Xixia dynasty, Jin dynasty, and the Mongol Empire, a sense
of the existence of countries equivalent to "enemy states" had already
taken shape by the Song dynasty. The official *History of the Song* (*Song
shi*) was the first such history to have separate chapters on "Biographies
of Foreign States" (*Wai guo zhuan*) and "Biographies of Foreigners and
Barbarians" (*Man Yi zhuan*), which shows evidence of ideas about international distinctions between inner and outer. Second, work undertaken
at this time to "demarcate borders" (*kan jie*) demonstrated that clear ideas
about borders and territory existed. Third, the emergence of designated
centers of cross-border trade and the Maritime Trade Supervisorate (Shi
bo si) demonstrate that ideas about borders had also come into the
economy. Fourth, the Song dynasty's well-known ideas about the proper
way of handling state affairs (*guo shi*), as well as their rejection of foreign
peoples and cultures and attempts to strengthen their native culture, gradually formed into an early modern sense of the state and of identity. Despite our previous discussion of how "China" from the Song dynasty on
faced three major dilemmas that caused it many problems, it nonetheless
had a cultural identity, a shared history, a unified set of ideas about ethics,
and highly organized state institutions and political systems, in addition
to a space under its control whose location was basically clear. For these
reasons, the formation of the early modern Chinese state is not necessarily
related to European-style "early modernity."

This last point is especially true in terms of culture. The state territory centered around Han areas and a consciousness of the state led the

Chinese "state" to mature relatively early. Neo-Confucianism (*lixue*) achieved a high level of systemization, popularization, and acceptance as common sense because of support from the state, elites at the center, and the landed gentry. As a result, the sense of civilization that came from Confucian ethics expanded during the Song dynasty from urban to rural areas, from the center to the margin, and from the upper strata of society to the lower strata. These developments led China to have a civilizational unity at an early time. For these reasons, this virtually unspoken "state" became the Han Chinese people's basis for their historical memory, discursive space, and identification with their nation and state.

It is also for these reasons that the path taken in the formation of the Chinese nation is quite particular—or, put another way, the formation of the early modern nation-state in Europe is quite particular. I believe that there are problems with using European concepts and definitions such as empire or the nation-state directly and in a simple way to define and explain China in history. At least since the Song dynasty, "China" has had both the characteristics of a traditional imperial state and aspects that resemble early modern nation-states; it has resembled *both* a modern nation-state and a traditional civilizational community. For these reasons, theories that argue that traditional empires and modern nation-states belong to different historical eras not only do not accord with Chinese history but also do not fit with China's consciousness of itself as a state and its formation as a state. These same theories offer even fewer means to understand aspects of modern China such its territory, its peoples, and the state.

Many people treat theory like fashion—the newer, the better—and thus, as Western theories of moving beyond the nation-state gain ever more influence, scholars wrongly look down on national histories in the belief that it is backward and even nationalist to insist on writing national histories in this day and age. I ask in response: Can European history be understood this way, and can the history of Asia or China be understood this way? Why must we "rescue history from the nation" and not understand the nation within history?

Is East Asian History Possible? Do National
Histories Still Have Meaning?

For European scholars, the writing of national histories may be related to the rise of the modern nation-states and attempts to use history to manufacture national identities. For them, therefore, "writing history beyond modernity" against the backdrop of a postmodern, globalized world has revolutionary significance. For countries in Asia and Africa that have experienced the history of colonization, the writing of national history undoubtedly confirms the idea of the state left over from the colonial era. For them, too, historical writing that goes beyond the nation-state is, of course, of great significance. For East Asian states, and especially for China, however, it still seems necessary to emphasize national histories even while recognizing the importance of global history.

Why is this the case? The reason is simple: history is not simply a history of civilizations but should also be the history of politics. Across history, the mutual connections and influences between civilizations exist at the same time as actions taken between states to exercise political control and divide territories. Whether in terms of the process of state formation or the influence of the state on culture, the history of nations and states in East Asia may in fact be different from Europe.

First, East Asia lacks a universal religion (like Catholicism) that exceeds the boundaries of the state or of the emperor's rule and functions as a platform or medium for communication and self-identification within communities. The various peoples spread across different states, therefore, lack a basis for communication and mutual identification through culture or faith.

Second, although the blending of different national groups occurred in China during such times as the Wei-Jin dynasties, Northern and Southern dynasties, the Mongol era, and the Qing dynasty, because there was not a great deal of mobility and movement of populations or overlap of political powers between Japan, Korea, and China, the divisions of territory, national groups, and culture between the three countries are largely stable and clear. Moreover, those major historical events that influenced politics, created culture, and formed identity in these three countries were guided in large part by the state or ruling dynasty, and the state played a major role in shaping politics, religion, and culture.

Third, before the nineteenth century, this region lacked an educated elite whose influence transcended individual states and national groups. As a result, the lines between national perspectives are sharply drawn, as are ideas about differences between these countries.

Fourth, although China across history has occupied the position of a metropolitan state with a powerful emperor, in fact China did not have the ability to achieve absolute dominance over all states on its periphery. Ideas about the differences between Chinese and foreigner (racial differences) existed between these states, and since the early modern period each has gradually established a sense of agency based on its own intellectual traditions (as in "National Learning" [*Kokugaku*] in Japan and neo-Confucian learning [*Jujahak*] in Korea); each country has gradually strengthened its linguistic independence (as in the development of Japanese and Korean syllabaries and glossing systems); and, even more so each country has established a sense of its own independent history (as, in Japan's case, the writing of histories of the age of the gods and the focus on an uninterrupted line of succession, and, in Korea's case, legends of Dangun).

For these reasons, I believe that, at least in the near term, it would be very difficult for East Asia simply to become a "community" that would go beyond individual states, and thus national distinctions are still important for the way we think about history. This is because we must always remember that, in East Asian history after the Song and Yuan dynasties, China, Japan, and Korea had in fact already drifted in different directions. In particular, from the sixteenth and seventeenth centuries onward, the differences between the three countries grew ever larger as they took varying paths and achieved differing results in politics, economics, and culture.[39] This is why, even with the growing popularity of narratives of global or East Asian history, I still emphasize the importance of national histories.

In fact, my argument is not an expansion of nationalist (or statist) historiography, but rather is a sign of caution toward nationalist (and statist) historiography. My agenda has a particular goal in mind: to achieve a sense of caution toward placing excessive emphasis on state (or governmental) power or placing excessive emphasis on national (or ethnic) consciousness in the histories of East Asian countries, especially ancient China. Even if we say that the sense of caution is largely directed toward China today, the high level of centralization of power in China today and the excessive strength and size of the government also have their sources in history, and the sources in history must still be traced back to and clarified through the study of the history of ancient China.

   In the Chinese scholarly world, in recent years there have been a number of discussions of concepts such as "autocracy" (*zhuanzhi*), "sovereign power" (*wangquan*), and "enfeoffment" (*fengjian*).[40] The goal of these discussions is to understand how "China" and its dynasties in history may or may not have been different from other "states" in terms of politics, economics, and culture. Beginning with the debate between Qian Mu (also Ch'ien Mu 1895–1990) and K. C. Hsiao (also Xiao Gongquan, 1897–1981), these discussions have continued down to the present day. The problem, however, is that if we only continue to "rectify names" (*zheng ming*) at the level of concepts and investigate issues through theory, then we may never reach a real conclusion. I believe, then, that people should keep the following phenomena about Chinese history in mind:

1. *The relationship between religion and imperial power.* Ever since the debates that began in the Eastern Jin dynasty about whether it was acceptable to say that "monks do not pay obeisance to kings" ended in a victory for imperial power, Buddhist and local religions (*daojiao*) gradually came under the management of officials. Confucian ideas about loyalty and filial piety combined with Buddhist ideas about karma and retribution, and thus Chinese religions, regardless of whether it was Buddhism, local religions, or other religions, were basically under imperial control. This situation was different from the status of religion in Japan and Europe.

2. *Relationships between localities and the center.* From the Qin dynasty onward, the state transformed from a system of enfeoffment (*fengjian zhi*) to a system of centralized administration (*junxian zhi*); from the Tang dynasty onward, the military moved from the control of local commanders to the central government, and Chinese culture tended to move from regional and local differences toward unity. Although local areas at times pulled away

from the center, they largely remained within a unified state. This state of affairs was also different from the Japanese *Han* domain system and the various states of the European Middle Ages.

3. *China's international relations with the outside world.* China's sense of self-centeredness, which was influenced by ideas about the distinctions between Chinese and foreigner, along with its sense of excessive pride (which was shaped by the tribute system), led to the notion that the emperor was not only the Son of Heaven who ruled over the officials and commoners of the Middle Kingdom but also the ruler of all the peoples of the myriad states. This idea that "All-under-Heaven is ruled by one ruler" was strengthened and even made mythical by the forms of ritual sacrifices to heaven on Mount Tai and to earth at Fenyin. In the East, traditional ideas that "under the skies, no land is not ruled by the king" and "just as there are no two suns in the sky, the state cannot have two rulers," were more deeply rooted than in the West, and therefore China's "imperial state" exerted even greater control over territory, officials, and the common people than what was found in the West.[41]

4. *China's internal national or ethnic relations.* Across history, ethnic groups that had originally been distinct from one another gradually melded together, especially by the time of the Qing dynasty, which eventually brought the Manchus, Mongolians, Hui, Tibetans, and Miao into the same territory, resulting in a multiethnic empire. This empire extends down to the present, which makes the imperial memory of traditional China continue to exist within the nation-state of modern China.

Compared with the Japanese concept of uninterrupted imperial succession, on the surface it may appear that Chinese history cannot be cleanly linked together through each dynasty. We should see, however, that although since ancient times China has been through periods of dissolution or separation, this "state" seemingly has already been narrated by one "history," one that does not resemble a mere imagined community described by postmodern theory.[42] This history proceeds from the time that the formation of a strong, central political power was made possible by the unification achieved by the Qin and Han dynasties to the cultural unity that was established from the Tang and Song dynasties onward, down to the unified dynasty based on the Han people that was reestablished by the Ming, and finally down through the Great Qing Empire, during which the Manchus entered China proper; brought Mongolia into the dynasty's territory; converted peripheral territories into regular administrative regions; established control over Xinjiang; stationed military forces in Tibet and established the Golden Urn process for selecting lamas; and brought together Manchu, Mongolian, Hui, Tibetan, Miao, and Han into one vast empire, thereby defining the territory of modern China. In China, then, we often hear statements that begin with, "From the time that Pangu created the earth and sky, down from the times of the Three Kings and Five Emperors of antiquity (*san huang wu di*), down to the present day" and "Where does one start reading in the twenty-five dynastic histories?" Of course we feel they are too linear and overemphasize Han Chinese dynasties, but should we not also consider why this "state" is always narrated by one "history"?

I support the writing of global history, but I see no need to throw the baby out with the bathwater and treat national histories as if they were modes of narrating history that are outdated, conservative, or useless, especially when rewriting the history of politics. Of course, I want to be careful to point out that, in narratives of Chinese history, although the narrative space occupied by "national history" is the "nation-state," it need not take the current borders, ethnic groups, and politics of the modern nation-state and read that back into "history." For these reasons, it does not necessarily resemble the situation that Prasenjit Duara has described in which we need to "rescue history from the nation."[43] This can be achieved if the "nation" described in this type of national history does not doggedly maintain a narrative with unchanging boundaries, and does not limit "history" so that it remains within boundaries and borders that are traced backward into the past from the modern nation. Regarding the "China" in Chinese history, for example, I have said many times that "China is a dynamic entity within history, dividing and recombining with various dynasties, and with borders changing even more often, set as they are by the central governments of successive dynasties."[44] More important, the dynasties, ethnic groups, and borders of this "China" were always shifting, overlapping, and blending together across history.

I believe that if those who write national histories recognize the historical changes that took place within the nation and the state themselves, then they will not fall into the trap of allowing the "nation" to kidnap "history" in its original form. In this way, the writing of national histories will continue to have significance in China.

Conclusion: Understanding "China" and Chinese History from Different Historical, Cultural, and Political Perspectives

In *Here in "China" I Dwell,* I argued that three points needed to be observed in the work of reestablishing historical narratives of "China." Allow me to repeat them here.

First, in terms of its historical significance, "China" is a shifting China, not only because of the many cases of dissolution and unifications that occurred across the dynasties but also because the territory and borders controlled by the central governments of the dynasties across history changed even more frequently. We absolutely must not make simple claims that a place "has been a part of Chinese territory across history."[45]

Second, in terms of its cultural significance, China is a relatively stable cultural community, one that forms the basis of the "nation" of "China," especially in the central territories of Han-ethnicity China. This is a relatively distinct and stable China, a civilization where "carriages all have wheels of the same size, all writing is in the same characters, for conduct there are the same rules," and that possesses a cultural unity.[46] It makes no sense to place excessive emphasis on deconstructing (the nation-state of) China.[47]

Third, in terms of its political significance, "China" often cannot be equated with a dynasty and also does not refer to a certain government. Can the government (that is, political power) be equated with the state? And can the state be directly equated with the "motherland" (*zuguo*)? These are concepts that still need to be clarified. Political identities often influence cultural identities, and they can even wipe out historical identities. Even today, some people still unthinkingly take the government to be the same as the state, or take the state that formed across history to be the motherland that must always be the object of their loyalty, creating, in turn, many misunderstandings, animosities, and biases.

❧ 1 ❧

WORLDVIEWS

From "All-under-Heaven" in Ancient China
to the "Myriad States" in the Modern World

Introduction: *A Map of the Myriad Countries of the World* and Ancient China's Entry into the Early Modern World

In the fall of 2001, I went to the Italian embassy in Beijing to see an exhibition about missionaries and China. I stood for a long time in the modest exhibition room, staring at a map of the world titled *A Map of the Myriad Countries of the World* (*Kunyu wanguo quantu*). On the map there were five great continents, four oceans, and strange creatures and fishes. For a moment, it was like I had gone back in time.[1] We should not underestimate this little map, for it is an important historical marker that symbolizes a major change in the worldview of ancient China. What was that change? Under the influence of this map, the idea of All-under-Heaven, which was part of Chinese people's long-standing view of themselves as the center of the world, gradually changed from a view that "the center was everywhere" to the "myriad states" (*wanguo*, also "ten thousand states"). From this time on, China was to live in this world (*shijie*) among the myriad states. If we should say that we now live in the era of globalization, then we might say that globalization was already in its early stages from the time that this map of the world provided Chinese people with a view of the myriad states.

Originally this map was mounted on six panels. Over the years, the original frame for the panels was lost, and the separate panels were reassembled into one giant map, roughly five feet tall and twelve feet across. Experts believe that these panels were painted four hundred years ago, after a world map titled *Map of Mountains and Seas (Shan hai yudi tu)* by a missionary named Matteo Ricci (1552–1610). Ricci, a member of the Jesuit order from Italy, was not a cartographer; some researchers have argued that this map followed another world map that had been made by a European named Abraham Ortelius (1527–1598), and thus it was still very clear and accurate. In 2000 I made a special trip to Antwerp to visit the workshop that had printed Ortelius's map back in those times, where I also saw other maps that had been published then. I realized that, four or five centuries ago, Europeans' knowledge of the world, which followed along with the routes of their ships, was already relatively advanced; even missionaries had learned this new knowledge and information. The fact that missionaries who had lived in that world of learning brought such knowledge to China was something of a coincidence. In those days, Matteo Ricci did not have any particularly deep intentions but thought that the map was a way to gain favor with curious educated elites and officials and to make it easier for other Catholic missionaries to come into China and enjoy greater freedom to spread their faith. He also wanted to use this map of the myriad states to challenge Chinese people's self-regard. He did not consider these questions much further, however, and absolutely did not imagine that his map would have such a deep and lasting influence on Chinese thought.

When Chinese people look at world maps, they may think of those people from earlier times, who began to realize that All-under-Heaven was much larger than they had originally thought—with many more countries—and that China was not as big as had previously been imagined.

Early Modern Western Views of the World
and Ancient Chinese Views of All-under-Heaven

By this point you may want to ask me: Before Matteo Ricci's map of the world, how did Chinese people see the world?

I should explain first that, before the Han and Wei dynasties, people in ancient China did not normally use the words "the world" (*shijie*). This word is a Buddhist term. Over a long period in ancient China, Han Chinese people used the phrase "All-under-Heaven," which comes from the saying, "Under the whole Heaven, every spot is the sovereign's ground" (*pu tian zhi xia, mo fei wang tu*). All-under-Heaven is the world beneath the sky or Heaven.

Of course, nowadays anyone with any knowledge knows that the world is big, that the Earth is round, that China is in Asia, that there is an Eastern Hemisphere and Western Hemisphere, that there are other countries on the other side of the ocean, and that you will need a passport and visa to go to other countries. These are all facts of modern times, however, facts that came into being after Christopher Columbus (1451–1506) discovered the New World and after Ferdinand Magellan (1480–1521) circumnavigated the globe. Early modern ideas about "states" and maps of the "world" took shape very late in history. Chinese people of the fourteenth or fifteenth centuries (and many others) did not understand states and the world in this way. When we speak of Europeans like Columbus discovering the New World or of Magellan circumnavigating the globe, some people say that this was imperialism; others say that this was the advance of civilization; others say that these were geographical discoveries. Still others will ask: Since these parts of the world were already there, with people living there, what was the great discovery? Of course it sounds a little bit like postcolonial theory to say that these events amounted to no more than Europeans just showing up in these places. Nonetheless, whatever debates we may have in the present day, a few hundred years ago these events were among the most celebrated in history, because they symbolized the fact that human beings had finally gained a complete knowledge of this Earth on which they lived, this world (*shijie*). Moreover, particularly for Westerners, these events also meant discovering that the world had so many different types of cultures and traditions and so many different types of peoples and places.

For a number of reasons, these developments were important for Westerners. First, their system of knowledge about the world finally had a complete image of the globe, which was crucial for arriving at a complete understanding about the planet on which they lived. Second, as they undertook comparisons of the nations and cultures of people in foreign places, Westerners established a sense of their own centrality or relative superiority. In their system of knowledge, especially in the set of values that enabled the universal pursuit of wealth, prosperity, and civilization, the existence of others such as "undeveloped peoples and nations," "Oriental people," and "barbarians" established the position of Westerners at the center of the world, at the pinnacle of status. Third, this definition of the position of their own place and culture gave the West confidence about its ability to master the world. We know that people cannot observe themselves independently, just as we know the other person looks into the mirror, he or she must look at other things in order to define his or her position and image. So, too, when we look into the mirror, even the mirror itself must use that layer of opaque materials to reflect the image of an object. When the West was expanding, the discovery of other civilizations was for them much like finding a mirror. By looking at other peoples and civilizations, and then looking again at themselves, they gained an understanding of how they looked—whether they were ugly or beautiful. Before they had seen other people, they could not have known as much about themselves. The development of anthropology in the West took place for precisely this reason. For these reasons, then, these three points are all important for the definition of values and meaning in the history of knowledge in the West.

It is also fascinating to see China looking back in the mirror. People in ancient China also had a worldview that made Chinese people quite proud. Two or three thousand years ago, people in ancient China had not traveled to every corner of the world, but Chinese people nonetheless had formed an image of All-under-Heaven based on their experiences and imagination. This imagination of All-under-Heaven can be broken into three components. First, where they were was the center of the world.

Second, the Earth resembled a chessboard or was shaped like the Chinese character *hui* 回, extending outward in four directions from the center. The first circle (in the center) was the capital, which was occupied by the ruler; the second circle was the land of the Chinese (Hua-Xia); the third circle was occupied by barbarians (*Yi Di*). It was in roughly the Spring and Autumn and Warring States periods that the concept of a "Middle Kingdom" (or China, *Zhongguo*), surrounded by barbarians to the north and south, emerged. Third, within this All-under-Heaven, geographical spaces that were farther away from the margins were considered less cultivated, and the people who lived there were more barbaric, with a lower level of civilization. Those people were called the barbarians of the south, north, east, and west (*Nan Man, Bei Di, Xi Rong,* and *Dong Yi*).[2]

This leads to another question: How did the image of All-under-Heaven come into being?

The Nine Provinces and Five Zones

The "Tribute of Yu" (*Yu Gong*) chapter in the *Book of Documents* refers to the "Nine Provinces" (*jiu zhou*), while the "Discourses of Zhou" (*Zhou yu*) chapter in the *Discourses of the States* (*Guo yu*) chapter refers to the "Five Zones" (*wu fu*). The "Nine Provinces" were Ji (冀), Yan (兖), Qing (青), Xu (徐), Yang (揚), Jing (荆), Yu (豫), Liang (梁), and Yong (雍). Generally speaking, if we look at the map moving clockwise from north to south, from north to east, and then south, and then toward the west, we draw the outlines of a region that more or less includes the modern-day provinces of Hebei, Shandong, Jiangsu, Hubei, Hunan, Henan, Sichuan, Shaanxi, and Shanxi. This area is "All-under-Heaven" as understood by people in ancient China, places that now are, by and large, purely Han regions.[3] According to legend, when Yu the Great brought the floodwaters under control, the space that he was concerned about largely overlapped with "Hua-Xia." What was Hua-Xia? It was the part of the world that people in ancient China believed to be relatively civilized: All-under-Heaven.[4]

The "Five Zones" refers to areas that center around the territory occupied by the king in Luoyang during the Eastern Zhou dynasty. In addition to the "center" occupied by the Eastern Zhou king in Luoyang, the area that surrounded this center (or "Kingly Domain," *wang ji*) was a Central Zone (*dian fu*) under direct of the rule of the king. The Central Zone, a circle of five hundred *li,* was on the outskirts surrounding the Kingly Domain. (In ancient capitals, *jiao* or "outskirts" referred to the area one hundred *li* outside the city walls. That which was outside the *jiao* was called the Central Zone.) Beyond that, for five hundred *li,* was the Lords' Zone (*Hou fu*), which was the land controlled by the enfeoffed feudal lords, such as the state of Song in Shangqiu (in Henan) and the state of Zheng (also in Henan), or the state of Qi in Shandong. Five hundred *li* beyond the Lords' Zone was the Pacified Zone (*Sui fu*). The character *sui* originally referred to a rope on a cart that would prevent passengers from falling off. Here it is used in the sense of pacifying someone, as in the word *suijing,* "to pacify or appease"; the *sui* is a rope that can be held on to but not leaned on. The next five hundred *li* is the Controlled Zone (*Yao fu*). Here the character *yao* means to arrange or agree on, in the sense that this domain can only be ruled by alliances or mutual agreements between different parties. Most rulers would pay only partial attention and even turn a blind eye to this area. The outermost area was five hundred *li* of the Wild Zone (*Huang fu*); *huang* or "wild" refers to a wild and barbarous place whose people can probably be left to their own devices because they are so far away.[5] In this sense, expanding out from five hundred square *li* of territory outward, there are named regions encompassing five thousand square *li,* we see how people in ancient China imagined the Earth as if it were shaped like the character *hui* 回.

The *Tribute of Yu* dates roughly to the Warring States period, and the *Discourses of the States* is probably also from that period. In these works we see that ideas about the Nine Provinces and Five Zones were very common during the Warring States era; we also see the beginnings of a shared or common geographical space for the Han people. The "Summer Offices" (*Xia guan*) referred to in the *Rites of Zhou* (*Zhou li*), which came slightly later, complicated this vision even further, referring to an organization that was dedicated to managing the territory of the state, and expanding number of the Five Zones to the Nine Zones.[6] These additions did not change the structure of space that gradually extended outward from the center and did not change the idea that the level of civilization gradually fell as one traveled farther away from the center.

Many readers have probably heard of books from ancient China such as the *Songs of the South (Chu ci)*, the *Zhuangzi, The Tale of King Mu, the Son of Heaven (Mu Tianzi zhuan)*, and the *Classic of Mountains and Seas*. These works often imagine the world at China's edges, with the Kunlun Mountains to the west and Mount Penglai to the east. They tell of how King Mu of Zhou went to the Kunlun Mountains to meet the Queen Mother of the West (*Xi wang mu*), or of how people traveled to the Island of Immortals on Mount Penglai to obtain the elixir of immortality. What is most interesting here is that many people have heard something about the *Classic of Mountains and Seas,* a book that records how people imagined the world in ancient times. Each place in the *Classic of Mountains and Seas* has a strange creature or story: the flying chariots of the Country of Singlearm (*Qi gong guo*), the flying fish of Mount Blueroanhorse (*Gui shan*), or the animal named Awestruck (*Kui*) on Mount Flowwave in the East Sea.[7] These stories appeared again and again, all the way through works such as the *Pictorial Encyclopedia of the Three Powers (San cai tu hui)*, an encyclopedia that dates from the Ming dynasty, to *Flowers in the Mirror,* a novel by Lu Ruzhen (ca. 1763–ca. 1830) of the Qing dynasty. Both of these books referred to the Country of Gentlemen, the Country of Giants, the Country of Hairy People, and the Country of People with Deep-Set Eyes.

If we read closely, the vision of the world found in these books is still based on a civilized center that extends out in the four cardinal directions. According to legend, the *Classic of Mountains and Seas* originally included maps and pictures, and the text was meant to be an explication of them. A poem by Tao Yuanming (365–427) says, "I skim through the *Story of King Mu* / And view the pictures in the *Classic of Mountains and Seas*."[8] The book records information about mountains (the Southern Mountains, Western Mountains, Northern Mountains, Eastern Mountains, and Central Mountains); the southern, western, northern, and eastern parts of the "Regions within the Seas" (*hai nei*); the southern, western, northern, and eastern parts of the "Regions beyond the Seas" (*hai wai*); and the southern, western, northern, and eastern parts of the "Great Wilderness" (*da huang*). In other words, if we were able to look at the pictures or maps that accompanied the *Classic of Mountains and Seas* today, we would see a square-shaped universe with the Central Mountains in the middle, surrounded by the mountains of the four cardinal directions, which in turn are surrounded by the regions within the seas, the regions beyond the seas, and the Great Wilderness at the edges.

The people on the edges—the barbarians of the north, west, east, and south—are all barbarians in the eyes of the Chinese, who are at the center of this world.

Round Heaven, Square Earth: Imagining Space

Did Chinese people from those times never travel anywhere beyond the so-called Great Wilderness? We do not know. Although some people say it happened, we have no records to prove it. If no one traveled beyond these boundaries, however, how did they know that the world reflected what was in the map? My guess is that this view of the world came from how people in ancient China imagined the relationship between Heaven and Earth. People in ancient China believed that "Heaven [corresponds to] a circle, and Earth [corresponds to] a square (*Tian yuan di fang*)." In other words, Heaven was believed to be rounded like a basket turned upside down, covering the Earth, with the North Pole and South Pole at its midpoint. The Earth was square, like a chessboard, with the area around Luoyang at the center. These explanation of the universe are found in the *Mathematical Classic of Zhou Gnomon* (*Zhou bi suan jing*) and in the *Lü Commentary to the Spring and Autumn Annals* (*Lü shi Chunqiu*),[9] which refers to circular shapes above and square shapes below. In the pictorial stones of the famed Wu Liang Shrine, which date back to the Han dynasty, there is a scene that depicts the mythical figures Fuxi and Nüwa. Fuxi holds a carpenter's square, while Nüwa holds a compass; Fuxi is drawing the Earth in a square shape, while Nüwa lays out Heaven in a round shape.[10] The square Earth and round sky do not quite seem to fit together—so much so that some people might ask: If Heaven is smaller than Earth, then wouldn't the four corners of the Earth might stick out and not be covered by the sky? Or, if Heaven is bigger than Earth, would there be some places where there is no Earth and only sky? Nonetheless, people believed this idea for a long time.

But why? The reason is simple: it came from their experience of looking at Heaven and from what they inferred about Earth. If you look at the sun during the day and at the moon and stars at night, they all move from east to west (or from right to left), revolving around a "spool" or axis to the north. Doesn't it look as if Heaven is like a broad hat covering over us? Many things in ancient China imitated this mystical space. To give a few examples: the "shi" boards (*shi pan*), a divination tool used in ancient times, had an upper half with a round disc shaped like Heaven and a lower half with a square disc shaped like the Earth. Ancient Chinese chessboards had similar shapes, and the center of the chessboard for Go (or *Weiqi*) is still called the "center of Heaven" (*Tian yuan*). The Luminous Hall (*Ming tang*) and Round Mound (*Yuan qiu*), where sacrifices were performed to Earth and Heaven, also imitated these shapes. Even kings' palaces in ancient times extended out from the center toward the four directions, just as ancient cities were designed with a clear center and outlying suburbs in the four directions. For these reasons, people in ancient China always believed that the place they lived was the center; that their civilizational status was higher that of the people who lived in one of the four directions away from them; and that the lands that extended out in the four directions were always on lesser footing when compared with the center, whether in terms of wealth or the level of civilization. According to this line of thinking, the periphery should be governed and administered by the center. People in ancient China believed that All-under-Heaven was right here, and that the people of the "Middle Kingdom" (that is, China) should look down on the "Four Barbarians" (*si Yi*), and that Chinese civilization should radiate outward in all directions and educate and civilize the barbarians.

This is not strange; Westerners say that "the center is everywhere." Everyone must look at the world through their own eyes, and thus where they stand is the starting point for their understanding of things, and is also the reference point for north, south, east, and west. What is far from themselves is on the margin, what is behind the focus of their attention is the background; I may be in your view, just as you might be what I am focusing on. The core ethnic groups of ancient China were located in the central plains, between the Yellow River in the north and the Yangtze River in the south. Of course, they understood this area to be the center of the vast space they imagined as All-under-Heaven and regarded Hua-Xia civilization as superior to the peoples on their periphery.

The Four Directions and Beyond: From "Yan Who Spoke of Heaven" to the Journeys of Zhang Qian

To return to the subject at hand, some people in ancient China who were not convinced by this map of the world. Some even courageously asked, "Is there an even larger world beyond?" According to legend, during the Warring States era there was a man from the state of Qi named Zou Yan, who later came to be known as "Yan Who Spoke of Heaven." In the days after he would have been alive, people often said that because the state of Qi was on the seacoast, the great vastness of the waters made for a greater sense of space in his imagination, and therefore he put forward the idea of the "Nine Great Provinces."[11] According to Zou Yan, the Nine Provinces of China were only 1/81 of All-under-Heaven, and China's real name was the "Spiritual Country of the Red Region." Beyond its borders lie eight other provinces, which, together with China, comprised one of the nine great continents. This continent was surrounded by an ocean, beyond which lie eight other great continents, each of which was surrounded by an ocean. Taken together, these nine continents comprise what was really All-under-Heaven.

Was there any basis to these speculations? Were they imagined by Zou Yan, or were they simply tall tales? We cannot be sure. It is likely that, from very early on, ancient China had all kinds of interactions with the outside world. A chapter on "Meetings of Feudal Lords with the King" (*Wang jian*) from the *Leftover Zhou Documents* (*Yi Zhou shu*) describes a gathering of foreign groups from the four directions.[12] *The Tale of King Mu, the Son of Heaven,* which was recorded on bamboo slips from the Western Jin dynasty (roughly the middle period of the Warring States era) and recovered from the tomb of King Xiang of Wei (d. 296 BCE) in Ji County, also records a story of King Mu of Zhou traveling to the western frontier to meet the Queen Mother of the West.[13] Could there be any background to the stories that entailed actual meetings or interactions? Indeed, it is difficult to say. It is strange, however, that these imaginings did not change Chinese people's ideas about All-under-Heaven. From the pre-Qin period down through the Qin dynasty and Han dynasty, people in ancient China continued to believe that they occupied the center of All-under-Heaven and looked down from the commanding heights on the barbarians who lived in the four directions of the periphery.

By the Han dynasty, an important opportunity appeared for the situation to transform. From 138 BCE to 126 BCE, during the reign of Han Wudi, a man named Zhang Qian, under orders from the emperor, set out for the Western frontier (*Xi yu*), eventually returning to the Han Empire after thousands of miles of travels. He was said to have described for the Han court and emperor what he saw in Dawan (an area near contemporary Afghanistan), Kangju (an area covering contemporary Pakistan, Azerbaijan, Uzbekistan, and southern Kazakhstan), Dayueshi (an area from part the Pamir Mountains westward, now in contemporary Afghanistan), Daxia (now contemporary northwest India and Pakistan, near Kashmir), as well as what he had heard about Wusun and Anxi (now within the borders of contemporary Iran), Tiaozhi (near Syria), and Yuandu (India).[14]

This was a critical event in history. First, this journey expanded Chinese people's concrete knowledge of the world on the periphery. To the East, this knowledge now extended to Japan and Korea. To the north, it extended to Mongolia and Siberia. To the south, it extended to the South China Sea and to Southeast Asia. To the west, it extended to the area of Pakistan, Afghanistan, Syria, India, and Iran. In other words, Chinese people during the Han dynasty already had an understanding of what today is the entirety of Asia and regions beyond. What they had known about prior to Zhang Qian's journey was limited to what is now the East Asia region, such as Japan and Korea. (The famous gold seal from the Han dynasty excavated in Kyushu in Japan shows contact between these two places from early times.)

Second, Zhang Qian's journey stimulated desire among Chinese people to explore and interact with the outside world. After Zhang Qian traveled to the Western frontier, other explorations took place, including Zhang Qian's journey to the southeast, journeys by Ban Chao and Ban Yong of the Eastern Han to promote exchange with Western regions, and Gan

Ying's travels to the Persian Gulf. Third, people in the Han dynasty and later were able to encounter and observe cultures and economies from different backgrounds. The opening of the Silk Road and, in the wake of these events, the arrival of Buddhism in China, all took place in this historical context. From this time forward, China's history was a part of world history, or, at the very least, Asia's history.

Unfortunately, however, for reasons we can't explain, these events did not result in real changes to deeply held beliefs in ancient China about All-under-Heaven. From the Han dynasty onward, even though Zhang Qian, Ban Chao, Gan Ying, and many others traveled to faraway places, China stayed at the center of All-under-Heaven in the imagination of Chinese people. At most, they contributed to a sense of a growing number of "barbarians" in all four directions. In this map of the world, however, the center was clear, while the edges were blurry and indistinct. This was Chinese people's map of the world: even though, taken together, Central Asian and west Asian countries like India, Afghanistan, Iran, and Pakistan, along with Japan, Southeast Asia, Korea, and the grasslands to the north all added up to vast territories that were much bigger than China, from the Han dynasty through the Tang dynasty, people in medieval China continued to believe that people in these places had no culture to speak of and, therefore, there was no other "world" (*shijie*) outside.

The Separation of Ideas from Knowledge: The Persistence of the Chinese View of All-under-Heaven

Why did people in ancient China cling to this idea of "All-under-Heaven" for so long? I believe it is because, aside from Buddhism, China never faced a serious challenge from another civilization. Chinese people continued to believe, then, that they were the center of All-under-Heaven; that Han civilization was the peak of human civilization; that the people on the periphery were barbaric; and that people who did not follow the moral system of the Han needed to be saved. Those who could be saved were considered Chinese (*Hua-Xia zhi min*), while those who could not be saved were to be cut off and kept away from the center.

Generally speaking, Chinese people were not inclined to use military means to bring All-under-Heaven under their control, but rather believed that their civilization could "pacify foreign lands" (*wei fu yi bang*) by what came to be known as "conciliating" or "cherishing men from afar" (*huai rou yuan ren*). At times, however, the Chinese were unable to control the situation, resulting in tensions that grew into outbursts of anger. In the Western Jin, for example, Jiang Tong (?–310) wrote an essay titled "Discourse on Moving the Rong" (*Xi Rong lun*), which called for separating the living space occupied by the Han from other nationalities,[15] but this argument for separating out the Chinese from foreigners did not seem to carry much influence at the time. We need to realize that, for people in ancient China, *Zhongguo* (China, or the Middle Kingdom) often referred to a civilizational space, not a modern state with clearly drawn borders. Chinese people believed, therefore, that all of the countries on their periphery occupied a lower rung on the hierarchy of civilizations and should study, pay tribute, and make obeisance to China. As in the *Illustrations of Tributaries* (*Zhi gong tu*) that was so frequently painted in ancient China, which depicts the peoples of the periphery making a tribute to the dynasty of the Central Lands, the Chinese emperor is always painted in a way so that he is very large, while the foreign envoys are distinctly petite. In various kinds of maps from ancient times, such as those from the Song dynasty, we have the *Map of Chinese and Barbarian Lands* (*Hua Yi tu*), which shows the lands of China and the barbarians of the four directions, and the *Map of Territories* (*Yu di tu*), which shows all of the places that can be reached by a wheeled cart, and also the *Geographical Map* (*Di li tu*), which shows the geography of the known world. If you look at these maps, you will see that they all place China in the center, and when they do include surrounding countries, they are so small that they look like little parasites on the body of the great state of China.

These images have no relationship to Chinese people's actual knowledge of the world. We know that after Zhang Qian of the Han dynasty, routes of exchange between continental Europe and Asia had already been opened, with groups of traders and Buddhist monks traveling great distances between East and West.[16] By the time of the Tang dynasty, China had even greater interactions with the outside world, with roughly 150,000 "foreigners from the north" (*Hu ren*) living in the capital, Chang'an, where people recorded seeing "Kunlun slaves" (*Kunlun nu,* dark-skinned slaves), foreign dances and music, and fashionable foreign clothes. In later times, the territories of the Mongol Yuan dynasty seemed to extend on forever. At that time, a Persian named Jamal al-Din created a globe with vertical and horizontal lines that depicted "three continents and seven oceans."[17] By the time of the Yongle emperor (r. 1402–1424) in the early years of the Ming dynasty, the eunuch admiral Zheng He (1371–1433) led a fleet of ships across the oceans. Although scholars do not believe the theory put forward by Gavin Menzies, an English amateur historian, that Zheng He discovered the New World,[18] we do know that he went as far as the east coast of Africa, that the distance he covered in his travels was far greater than the entire territory of China, and that people in China already knew of many other civilizations.

It is interesting, however, that despite these events, the ancient Chinese ideas and imaginings of All-under-Heaven, "China," and the "Four Barbarians" never changed.

Buddhism Did Not Conquer China, but It Did Give China an Opportunity

Historians are not supposed to imagine replaying history, but they, too, are ordinary people, and sometimes they will imagine, "What if . . ." Of course, looking back on history of ancient China, they might also think that there was an opportunity for thoroughgoing change in the ancient Chinese idea of All-under-Heaven.

We know that there are internationally recognized territorial boundaries, that there are ideas about the sovereignty of the state, as well as ideas about the nation-state; all of these ideas have to do with early modern and modern times. In ancient China, the word *guojia* (now translated as "country" or "the state") was seen frequently. On the back of copper mirrors from the Han dynasty, we often see inscriptions that express wishes for "the state (*guojia*) and the people to be at peace and without trouble," and for "the northern barbarians to be wiped out and the lands of the four directions to submit and obey."[19] As we mentioned before, however, generally speaking the state in ancient China was a cultural concept that had a clear center and blurry edges. "If he is of our kin, he is sure to have the same mind." This statement means that anyone who comes from the same culture can be part of the same state, even though the notions of the state or All-under-Heaven are not particularly clear. "If he is not my kin, he is sure to have a different mind."[20] Anyone who is culturally different from me is one of the Four Barbarians; he does not belong to the same state as me, and is not even part of All-under-Heaven; we refer to him as someone with whom "we cannot live under the same sky." The standard used for whether or not people identify with one another lies in whether or not their "mind is the same." According to the philosopher Lu Jiuyuan (1139–1192), "Within the four seas, minds are the same, and principle (*li*) is the same."[21] This statement expresses a type of universalism that argues that All-under-Heaven is one family; its standard of identification is culture. From this point of view, then, legally defined borders are not particularly important. According to the "Royal Regulations" chapter of the *Book of Rites,* which was completed in the early part of the Han dynasty, "the people of those five regions—the Middle Kingdom, the Rong, the Yi (and other wild tribes among them)—had all their various natures, which they could not be made to alter."[22] Any group of people who shares the same cultural identification can be included as vassals of China and as part of All-under-Heaven, because "under the whole Heaven, every spot is the sovereign's ground; to the borders of the land, every individual is the sovereign's minister." A group of people who, in terms of culture, are not compliant, are then considered to be from different lands with different customs, and, in the end, are not a part of All-under-Heaven. In ancient China, therefore, the state, civilization, and truth all overlap. We can say, then, that behind statements such as "All-under-Heaven are one family," "within the four seas, we have those who truly know us," and "all men within the four seas are brothers," there lies a China-centric particularism. On the other hand, however, it is also a universalist worldview, a worldview that argues that there is one center of civilization and that argues for a universal application of the idea of civilization throughout the world.

Despite the fact that, from the Han dynasty onward, a great deal of cultural materials, knowledge, and material goods entered China, and despite the fact that a great deal of strange-looking foreigners also came to China, neither goods nor people presented a fundamental challenge to the civilization that was already established. The reasons for this are quite complicated, but to put it simply: on the one hand, although the territory of historical "China" underwent many significant changes, it remained by and large centered on the Nine Provinces occupied by the Han people, with the ocean to the east, the high plains and mountains to the west, ice-capped mountains and snowy plains to the north (along with the Xiongnu, Tukric peoples, Khitans, and Jurchens), and with lush forests to the south. It was quite easy under these circumstances for a closed view of All-under-Heaven to form. On the other hand, it is usually the case that, for a state such as China that possesses a long history of civilization, it is only when another highly developed civilization that can rival it appears that we begin to see fundamental influences on its tradition.

Buddhism, which began to arrive in China in the Eastern Han dynasty, brought a deep shock to Chinese culture by showing that there were at least two centers of civilization in the world. Three aspects of Buddhists teachings simply could not be accepted in Chinese civilization at that time. First, Buddhism taught that the power of religion could stand alongside the secular power of the emperor, occupying a primary position in the social hierarchy and social values. Believers need not pay respect to the emperor or their parents, but they absolutely had to respect the Three Jewels of Buddhism: the Buddha (enlightened ones), the *dharma* (Buddhist teachings), and the *sangha* (Buddhist community). Second, Buddhism taught that, in terms of the religion, the center of All-under-Heaven was India, not China. Third, Buddhism taught that the highest truths, the most superior people, and the most correct ways of living were to be found not in Confucian teaching but in Buddhism. Buddhism was a higher level of "civilization," or at least was another viable culture and civilization that had established itself in the world.[23]

How could a China centered around the Han people accept these beliefs? If these beliefs had been accepted, then China would have been a different place, not the China that exists now.

Buddhist Views of the World and the Buddhist Worldview

As is well known, Buddhism later was "Sinified," not only through the
combination of "three teachings in one" (*san jiao he yi*) but also through
other developments in which Buddhism yielded to mainstream Chinese
ideology and Confucian teachings. We should remember, however, that
Buddhism posed a challenge to the idea that China was the only civilization in All-under-Heaven. As Buddhism made its way to China, some Chinese people were forced to admit that Hua-Xia civilization was not the
only civilization, and that China was not the center of All-under-Heaven.
This was an opportunity to rediscover the world, especially because Buddhism's ideas about the nature of the world were fundamentally different
from those previously held in China.

In the Buddhist system of knowledge, the world is not a piece of land
with China located at its center. Rather, it is divided into four great continents, and China is one among these continents. According to legend,
the center of the world is Mount Meru, which is surrounded by four great
continents. China is located on Jambudvīpa, one of the continents of
the Earthly Realm; there are also the continents of Pūrvavideha,
Aparagodānīya, and Uttarakaru. According to such works as the *Sutra
of the Great Conflagration* (*Da louyan jing*) and the *Precious Grove of the
Dharma Garden* (*Fa yuan zhu lin*),[24] the sun, moon, and stars all revolved
around Mount Meru, illuminating All-under-Heaven. Each of the four
great realms has two central continents and five hundred lesser continents;
the four great realms and the eight great continents are all occupied by
humans, while the two thousand lesser continents may or may not be occupied by humans. Among these places, it is said that the *phala* (fruit of
one's actions) is the most positive in the northern continent, where there
is much happiness and little bitterness and the people live for a thousand
years. In this place, however, no great leader like the Buddha would appear. The people of the southern continent are fierce and courageous,
with sharp minds. Because they have karmic activity and are able to learn
Sanskrit, Bodhisattvas will appear among them. The land of the eastern
continent is vast, while in the western continent there are many oxen,
goats, jewels, and gems. Buddhist documents also mention "Four Sons

of Heaven." The renowned French scholar Paul Pelliot (1878–1945) wrote an essay on these Four Sons of Heaven that discussed how, in the Buddhist imagination, there are eight princes in Jambudvīpa and four Sons of Heaven.[25] To the east is the Son of Heaven of Jin, who is the emperor of China; to the south is the Son of Heaven of Sindhu, who is the ruler of India; to the west is the ruler of Great Qin, which probably refers to the emperor of Rome; and to the northwest is the Son of Heaven of Yuezhi, who probably is the ruler of the Kushan Empire. At that time, followers of Buddhism in India believed that Jambudvīpa was "ruled by four kings. The land to the east was called Zhina (China) and was ruled by a man-king. The land to the west was called Persia, and was ruled by the treasure-king. The land to the south was India and was ruled by the elephant-king. The land to the north was called Xianyu and was ruled by the horse-king." These ideas probably made their way into China as well. The Tang-era *Supplement to the Biographies of Eminent Monks* (*Xu gaoseng zhuan*), compiled by Daoxuan, mentioned these stories when discussing Xuanzang, the famed monk who traveled to India to collect Buddhist scriptures.[26]

It is important to remember that religions have their own particular perspectives. Because Buddhism made its way to China from India via Central Asia or South Asia, generally speaking, believers in Buddhism will to varying degrees oppose the worldview that takes China to be the only center. The reason for this is simple. If China is the only center of the world, then what of India, where Buddhism began? Since these religious truths emerged from India, then India should be the center. It is not possible to say this, however, in China, and thus one can only say that there are two centers (India and China) or three centers (India, the Western frontier [that is, inner Asia], and China), while others say that there are four centers (Persia, India, China, and Xianyun [that is, the territories north and west of China]). This imagined map of the world is quite different from the traditional Chinese view of "All-under-Heaven," which is centered on China. Where once it had been said, "The state cannot have two rulers, and the sky cannot have two suns," this imagined map of the world is quite different. For these reasons, the only maps of the world that we know of today from ancient China in which China is not taken to be the only center of All-under-Heaven are found in three maps of the world from the Buddhist *Complete Records of the Buddha and the Patriarchs* (*Fo zu tongji*). Before the Song dynasty, it presented a vision of a diverse world that was extremely rare for its time. Its *Geographic Map of the Land of China to the East* (*Dong Zhendan dili tu*), *Map of the States of the Western Regions During the Han Dynasty* (*Han Xiyu zhu guo tu*), and *Map of the Five Indian States in the West* (*Xi tu wu Yin zhi tu*) depicted a world with three centers,[27] providing Chinese people with resources by which to transform their worldview.

We should pay attention to the fact that this worldview is quite different from China's idea of All-under-Heaven. In this worldview, China is no longer the center of All-under-Heaven. In this respect, it resembles the "Nine Provinces" described by Zou Yan. Much later, these discussions of four realms and Nine Provinces would indeed become a resource through which Chinese people would accept new imagined maps of the world. It is unfortunate, however, that although Buddhism brought these new resources for matching the world and that, following these events, Arabs during the Yuan dynasty brought maps of the world with an even larger vision, which led Chinese people's knowledge of neighboring lands to exceed by a great measure those ancient ideas about the "Five Zones" and "Nine Provinces" or so-called divisions between Chinese and barbarians,[28] these challenges did not bring about a fundamental change in Chinese people's views of the world. It was only several hundred years later that this change took place—during the globalized sixteenth century, when Westerners arrived in China.[29] It was only in the twelfth year of the reign of the Wanli emperor (1584), when Matteo Ricci's *Map of Mountains and Seas* appeared in Guangdong, that Chinese people finally got a glimpse of "the world." After this, a symbol that foreshadowed a collapse in Chinese thought appeared.

After Matteo Ricci's *Complete Map of the World:* The Transformation of China's View of All-under-Heaven

Let us return to the *Map of the Myriad Countries of the World* (*Kunyu wanguo quantu*) mentioned at the beginning of the chapter.

In 1584, the twelfth year of the reign of the Wanli emperor, the Italian missionary Matteo Ricci arrived in the city of Zhaoqing in Guangdong province. With the support of the city's prefect, Wang Pan (*jinshi* 1565), Matteo Ricci engraved and printed the *Complete Map of the World* (*Shanhai yudi quantu*), the first Western-style map of the world to be printed in China; this map was the predecessor to the *Map of the Myriad Countries of the World,* which was printed slightly later, in about 1602.[30]

From the latter half of the sixteenth century through the seventeenth century, all kinds of maps that had been based on this map from 1584 were produced, twelve of which survive today. At that time, even Matteo Ricci was concerned that if the emperor saw how small China was on this map, he would think it showed disdain for Chinese people and would take offense. (Indeed, many prominent conservatives attacked this view of the world. They argued that the maps deliberately exaggerated the size of foreign lands and offered an ungainly portrayal of China. Some officials even argued that the map combined the versions of the world imagined by the *Classic of Mountains and Seas* and by Zou Yan, resulting in nothing more than an absurd product rifled from ancient Chinese texts that "treated China's immense lands as one continent, full of absurdities that fall apart under the slightest examination."[31]) The worldview represented by the map was accepted by many key figures, however, including intellectuals such as Li Zhi (1507–1602), Fang Yizhi (1611–1671), Xie Zhaozhe (1567–1624), Li Zhizao (1565–1630), and Xu Guangqi (1562–1633). More important, the Wanli emperor himself was pleased with the map. Although he did not understand the significance of a change in the notion of All-under-Heaven, this emperor, who would later be buried in the ostentatious Ding Ling tomb outside Beijing, ordered the court eunuchs to have *Map of the Myriad Countries of the World* reproduced on the panels of a large screen. In this way, the map gained legitimacy; with official approval, it was seen as rational, and thus won the approval of the educated class.[32]

In fact, Matteo Ricci's map was crafted with certain goals in mind. He hoped to make China abandon its ideas about the superiority of Chinese culture and accept Catholicism. He said, "Once they see that their own country is much smaller by comparison then other countries, the barriers can be lowered a bit, and they will be willing to develop relationships with other countries."[33] Indeed, ancient China's relationships with other countries were always conducted in terms of "pilgrimage," "tribute," and "presentation" to the superior Chinese ruler, or in terms of China "pacifying foreigners," "pacifying men from afar," "nurturing barbarians," or "managing foreigners," none of which had much of a sense of equality or diversity. During the Sui dynasty, the Japanese ruler wrote "a letter to the Son of Heaven in the place where the sun sets, from the Son of Heaven in the place where the sun rises," which managed to offend Chinese people.[34] Much later, the English embassy to the Qianlong emperor, led by George Macartney (1737–1806), did not result in more open relations because of all the problems surrounding hierarchy and ritual that arose during the meeting.[35] Nonetheless, in terms of intellectual history, this map resulted in significant changes, because it told people in China the following:

1. The world in which humans lived was round, not flat.
2. The world was extremely large, and China occupied only one-tenth of Asia. Moreover, Asia occupied only one-fifth of the world, and thus China was not a massive country with limitless borders.
3. Ideas about "All-under-Heaven," "China," and the "Four Barbarians" handed down from ancient China were incorrect. China was not necessarily the center of the world, and the Four Barbarians might also come from civilized countries. In fact, in the eyes of these so-called barbarians, China may in fact be one of the "Four Barbarians."
4. Chinese people should accept the idea that "from the eastern sea to the western sea, minds and reason are the same." So, too, should they recognize that civilizations throughout the world are equal and have equal validity, and that there are in fact some universal truths that transcend the boundaries of the nation, the state, and their territories.

From All-under-Heaven (*Tianxia*) to the Myriad States (*Wanguo*)

If these ideas gained acceptance, then, fundamental assumptions that held that the Chinese Empire was the center of All-under-Heaven and that

China was superior to the Four Barbarians would be completely destroyed. For people in earlier times, however, these fundamental assumptions, with their long history and deep cultural background, were of paramount importance and could not be held up to serious scrutiny. In the world of traditional thought, they were a part of the foundation of Chinese civilization—if they were removed, wouldn't the Heavens collapse and the Earth be rent?

This so-called collapse extended over a relatively long period of time, across the centuries spanned by the Ming dynasty and Qing dynasty. Nonetheless, we see the fissures it created in the traditional Chinese view of the world. This is true not only for educated gentry elites but also for ordinary educated people, as seen in works such as the *Encyclopedia of Maps and Books* (*Tu shu bian*, 1613) by Zhang Huang, *Gleanings of the Terrestrial Landscape* (*Fangyu sheng lüe*, 1610) by Cheng Bai'er, *Draft for Investigating Things and Extending Knowledge* (*Gezhi cao*) by Xiong Mingyu (b. 1579), and *Woof of the Earth* (*Di wei*, 1624) by Xiong Renlin, all of which accepted new ideas about "the world" (*shijie*). These traces of textual evidence demonstrate that these maps and their worldviews had already begun to break apart this knowledge, thought, and faith of ancient China. Although real change would only become evident in the late Qing dynasty, and although the period of later times is also quite complicated,[36] from the late Ming onward, changes in the imagined map of the world foreshadowed the fact that China would be forced to accept the bitter truth that China was no longer the center of the world, and that China's view of the world would be forced to cross the distance from "All-under-Heaven" to the "myriad states."[37]

❧ 2 ❧

BORDERS

On "Chinese" Territory

Some years ago I accepted an invitation to take part in a small forum to discuss a number of issues, including China's borders, the environment on China's periphery, and China's diplomatic difficulties. The newspaper that organized the discussion sent me an e-mail that very deliberately used the phrase "China's borders / territories" (*Zhongguo jing/yu*), distinguishing between "borders" (*jing*) and "territory" (*yu*); it also made an interesting comment that "the borders are over there, while China is here," which implied what would really be discussed at the forum: as a modern state, China must deal with a certain tension between its borders as they are understood in political terms and its territory as it is understood in cultural terms. It did not take long, then, for me to understand the topic of the forum as follows: the differences between borders (the domain of lands, as defined by politics) and China (the space of cultural identity).

I was interested in this perspective, because I had previously written a few pieces that addressed this question. When I saw the invitation, two writings came to mind: first, the famous poem by Du Fu (712–770) that begins with the line, "The country is in ruins, but the hills and rivers remain";[1] and, second, the essay by the late Ming-dynasty writer Gu Yanwu that analyzed the differences between "losing the state" (*wang guo*) and "losing All-under-Heaven" (*wang Tianxia*).[2] It seemed to me that "hills and rivers," the state, and All-under-Heaven all have slight differences between them in the traditional Chinese world of ideas. It also occurred to me that debates about the borders, territories, and histories of China and the world on its periphery that have been going on since the early modern period all involved these questions of China's borders and "China," and that they are also questions of historical territories, cultural spaces, and political mappings.

With these questions in mind, then, I'll begin my discussion.

The Problem of Borders and the State: More Than Just the Diaoyu Islands, the Spratly Islands, and the Liancourt Rocks (or Dokdo)

Borders and states make for an enormous problem, one that involves far more than ongoing disagreements such as China's disputes with Japan over the Diaoyu (or Senkaku) Islands; the disputes between China and Vietnam, the Philippines, and Indonesia over the South China Sea Islands; China's dispute with India over the McMahon Line; and South Korea's dispute with Japan over the Liancourt Rocks (Dokdo). Moreover, for China, these questions may be traced back across history and may involve such questions as why "China" can have such an enormous territory, why "China" is not necessarily just a China made up of the Han ethnicity but in fact is a huge country made up of many nationalities, characterized by so-called diversity in unity (*duo yuan yi ti*).[3]

It would not hurt to begin by discussing history textbooks in South Korea. In recent years, history textbooks have often come under scrutiny, because materials used for teaching history nurture and forge young citizens' ideas about history and cultural identity. They cannot avoid discussing such questions as the origins of cultures and nations, religious faiths, as well as various aspects of the cultural mainstream, historical territories, and space of the nation. It is extremely easy, therefore, for history textbooks to draw out nationalist undercurrents and even much stronger forces between citizens of different countries who have different understandings of history. In recent years, a number of provocative statements have appeared in middle school history textbooks in South

Korea (especially those that contain historical maps of Korea). These statements point to intense nationalist sentiments in the intellectual field in
South Korea and also show that, among educated people in South Korea,
some conflicts exist between knowledge about Korean history and knowledge about Chinese history. Several examples of this phenomenon exist, as
in the argument that Korean history is longer than Chinese history; or the
story of Dangun, which is often taken as the origin of the Korean nation; or
exaggerations about the size of the territory of Goguryeo during the Tang
and Song dynasties. In fact, people noticed long ago that ever since China
began the Research Project on the History and Current State of the Northeast Borderland (also called the Northeast Project) and its application to
designate the Goguryeo Ruins within its borders as a UNESCO World
Heritage Site, South Korea began to take a number of positions on historical questions. For example, conferences and publications sponsored by the
Northeast Asian History Foundation demonstrate that the question of borders and states continue to be overshadowed by historical conflicts,[4] even
when they seem to have been determined in the modern era. As a result, the
modern exists within history, just as history exists within the modern.

Compared with Korea, Japan's questioning of the legitimacy of "Chinese" territory began earlier and was undertaken with greater rigor. Beginning in the Meiji period, during which time Japan was influenced by
early modern Western ideas of the nation-state, European Orientalism,
and, more important, the rise of Japanese militarism and so-called
Asianism, Japanese scholars of Asia developed a particular interest in the
"Four Barbarians" (*si Yi*) of traditional China, such as Korea, Mongolia,
Manchuria, Tibet, and Xinjiang, no longer accepting the idea that the
various historical Chinese dynasties constituted unified entities that
spread across multiple borders and different nations. They gradually developed what had originally been a purely scholarly area of research into
a conceptual justification for undermining the legitimacy of China as a
modern state, making this issue into a hot topic of discussion in Japanese
scholarship on history before, during, and after World War II.[5] I mentioned earlier that in 1923, Yano Jin'ichi published a book titled *History
of Modern China* (*Kindai Shina ron*), which began with essays titled
"China Does Not Have Borders" and "China Is Not a State." Yano argued that borders were a fundamental condition for the successful organ-

ization of states, and, among early modern national states, borders were essential. China, however, "not only does not have borders, but also does not have the result of borders, and may not even be a national state at all." For these reasons, he argued, China could not be called a nation-state, and places such as Manchuria, Mongolia, and Tibet were not a part of Chinese territory.[6] In 1943, a key point in World War II, Yano gave a series of lectures at Hiroshima University in which he argued for a theory of historical narrative that went beyond China and focused on Asia as a single unit; these lectures were published as a book titled *Imagining the History of Greater East Asia* (*Dai Tōa shi no kōsō*).[7] Although these ideas were suppressed after World War II, they still rise to the surface from time to time, leaving traces in scholarship on history and geography even today.

Of course, among modern Chinese intellectuals, we also see a number of not very good ideas put forward about the relationship between the territories of ancient dynasties and modern political territory. For example, some people argue that scholarship on Chinese history should not be based on "the territorial domains of historical dynasties," but rather should "trace backward through history based on the territory of today's People's Republic of China." These people also argue that this method has three advantages. First, it allows us to "free ourselves from old points of view," by which they mean the dominant role of previous dynasties' views of history. Second, such an approach is free of the biases of Han ethnic chauvinism. And third, this approach would allow us to "research history so as to understand contemporary social life."[8] As I pointed out in the Introduction, however, "China" is a particular kind of state. The scholars who speak from the ideological position of the state attempt to establish the legitimacy of the current political territory of this "China" *first*. They then turn back to retrace and narrate the various histories held within this space in the belief that that their methods can protect the legitimacy of state territory as it exists today.[9] These ideas, however, do not accord with historical thinking. As early as 1960, Sun Zhamin pointed out that historians should "consider the question of historical territory within the scope of the historical territories of Chinese dynasties, because the scope of the lands controlled by each dynasty was different, expanding and contracting across time." Sun offered even more direct criticism in the 1980s, arguing that methods of historical research that traced

backward in time according to the current territory of the People's Republic of China "were very clearly in error. The most misleading aspect of this method is that it blots out the historical process by which
China became a 'unified, multi-national state' and confuses the 'back then'
of history with the 'today' of contemporary times, which are two concepts of time that are utterly different from one another."[10] Sun's arguments are undoubtedly correct. We should both say that the historical
space of China possesses strong continuity and recognize that the "domains" of ancient times and the "territory" of modern times are not one
and the same; they often changed. Recognizing these changes in territory across history does not amount to denying the legitimacy of state
territory as it exists today.

We cannot use the borders of modern states to trace our way back to a
narrative of the domains of dynasties of the past; just as we cannot use
the territorial domains of dynasties in the past to make assertions about
the borders of modern states. Of course, history and politics have many
deep connections, but historical scholarship and political action have def-
inite, rational differences. There is no question that problems related to
Chinese territory and Chinese borders not only appear repeatedly in the
form of "history," but also that, when these questions are not handled
well, they appear in many different places, as in problems related to
Xinjiang, Tibet, Mongolia, and, of course, the Taiwan question. Clearly,
these "borders" come under all kinds of suspicion, just as "China" is
facing various kinds of challenges. As I noted in the Introduction, these
challenges come not only from territorial conflicts that arise between
actual states but also from various theories and methods for understanding
history, such as East Asian history, regional history, histories of conquest
dynasties, concentric circle theory, and postmodernist historiography.
These questions deserve serious discussion.

Borders, States, and Early Modern Nation-States: Is China Exceptional or Universal?

To discuss these issues, we must begin with the so-called nation-state and
how it came into being. The concept of so-called borders that surround

politically legitimate territory is said to be related to the formation of the modern nation-state, because traditional empires did not concern themselves with the legitimacy of their domains, because traditional empires imagined that the space they occupied was "vast and all-encompassing." In his famous study, *Inner Asian Frontiers of China,* Owen Lattimore was keen to point out that any discussion of the borders of China must distinguish between the "frontier" and "boundaries."[11] I can understand what he means by this distinction, because during the imperial era sometimes frontiers were just vague, transitional areas that historically had been determined according to nationality, custom, and culture. Under the circumstances, they were quite unlike what is found in the more recent era of the nation-state, in which borders were determined through political power (that is, through mutual recognition of neighboring states). Although sometimes aspects of history, ethnic groups, and culture are taken into consideration when making borders in the modern era, what is more important is that they are drawn by the treaty and mutual agreement between legitimate states. According to this theory, strictly speaking, ancient China had only frontiers and did not have borders, and it is only modern China that has "territory" and official borders. However, according to the way that this issue is treated by most theorists, the formation of the modern nation-state began in early modern Europe. But do these ideas apply to China?[12]

In the Introduction I argued that Chinese history does not necessarily need to be measured according to the history of Europe. The prototype for the early modern Chinese-style nation-state, what may be called a sense of a limited state, began to take shape during the Song dynasty, probably earlier than what had occurred and Europe. Morris Rossabi edited a volume of essays that discussed the international relations of the Song dynasty titled *China among Equals,* whose title points to the argument that, beginning in the Song dynasty, a China that was positioned among states with equal powers and capabilities had already encountered the problem of borders. As the subtitle of the book, "The Middle Kingdom and Its Neighbors, 10th–14th Centuries," indicates, great changes occurred between China and its neighbors in the period from the tenth century to the fourteenth century. During the Song dynasty, China was no longer like the Tang dynasty, which encompassed All-under-Heaven, and the Song emperor could no longer be called the "Heavenly Khan" in the same way that the Taizong emperor (r. 626–649) of the Tang dynasty held that title. The Liao dynasty to the north, the Xixia in the northwest, the Jurchens, and, later, the Mongolians, gradually forced the Song into its role as one state among many. The Song Taizu emperor (r. 960–976), then, lamented, "Beyond the four posts of my bed, the rest of the house belongs to other people."[13] By the time of the Chanyuan Treaty, which was agreed to during the reign of the Zhenzong emperor (r. 997–1022), the Song and Liao dynasties had already begun to refer to each other as the "Northern and Southern Dynasties" and to speak of the "Emperor of the Great Song composing a letter to the Emperor of the Great Khitan [Liao]." These statements show that there was no longer just one ruler of All-under-Heaven—there were at least two.[14]

The *Fragments of Collected Documents of the Song Dynasty* (*Song huiyao jigao*) records that in 1052 the Renzong emperor (r. 1022–1063) issued an edict to instruct the Institute of Academicians to discuss state letters (*guoshu*) that were exchanged between the Northern Song and the Liao dynasty. Generally speaking, the phrase "state letters" should refer to documents that represent the intent of the state. At that time, documents from the Liao dynasty referred to the Liao as the "Northern dynasty" (*Bei chao*) and referred to the Song dynasty as the "Southern dynasty" (*Nan chao*). After extensive discussion, however, Song-dynasty officials concluded that "ever since the previous [that is, Renzong] Emperor made peace [with the Liao], state letters have had a set format, and variation from them cannot permitted freely. All subsequent letters, then, should refer to the 'Khitan,' as had been done in the past." This statement indicates that, at that time, and on that particular land (which could claim continuity with the Han and Tang dynasties), the policy of "one China with different interpretations" (*yige Zhongguo, ge zi biaoshu*, that is, referring to each other as the Northern and Southern dynasties) had given way to "one country on each side" (*yi bian yi guo*, that is, requiring that each side referred to the "Great Song" and the "Great Khitan").[15] Tao Jinsheng has concluded, then, that people during the Song dynasty already had achieved two important aspects of a "multipolar international system." First, he argued, people of the Song dynasty "understood that the central plains (*zhongyuan*) region was a 'state,' and that the Liao, too, was a

'state.' Second, they recognized that boundaries between states existed."
The former is demonstrated by the fact that documents from this time
often referred to "neighboring states" (*lin guo*) and "brother states"
(*xiongdi zhi guo*), while the latter is demonstrated by the fact that "surveying boundaries" (*kan jie*) became an important activity in foreign
policy and politics. Tao concludes, "The importance placed on borders
by people during the Song dynasty is sufficient to refute arguments made
in recent years that 'clear laws and regulations and limits on power' did
not exist between traditional China and foreign powers."[16]

These events gave China clear borders for the first time and also gave
it an awareness of equal foreign relations between states.[17] In historical
documents from the Song dynasty, we see a number of terms that begin
to tell people about the existence of "others," some of which had very
rarely been seen in China before the Tang dynasty; these terms include
"surveying boundaries" (*kan jie*), which refers to drawing borders; "exchange markets" (*hu shi*), which refers to trading sites established on the
borders; and "ceremonial ritual" (*pin li*), which refers to diplomatic
rituals between states with reciprocal status.[18] A direct result of the formation of this awareness of differences between nations and of borders between states was that China (mainly Han scholar elites) from this time on
had to take other states and foreign lands seriously. Two results of this
can be seen: first, China began to place limitations on crossing borders.
In addition to surveying and setting borders, Chinese officials also wanted
to limit the areas in which so-called foreigners could reside and the extent to which "Chinese people" could leave the country. Such regulations
even touched on books containing technical knowledge and people who
were familiar with the type of knowledge they held, forbidding both books
and people from going to foreign regions so as to prevent the outflow of
valuable knowledge and technology. From extant documents we can see
that these strict measures were closely enforced throughout the Northern
and Southern Song dynasties. Just as with the modern nation-state, strict
boundaries existed for knowledge, people, and state lands.[19]

The second result was the determination of the meaning of the "proper
way of handling state affairs" (*guo shi*), which referred to a consensus between the ruler and officials and a common effort to create a sense of
identification with one's own country, people, and culture. Elites during

the Song dynasty, and especially the Southern Song dynasty, exhibited a particular caution, which was rooted in nationalism, toward foreign religions, customs, and other civilizations. Whereas many elites of the Tang dynasty gladly welcomed new and interesting things, Song-era elites were vigilant, fearful, and critical, adopting a relatively severe attitude toward foreign religions, faiths, customs, and practices. Their resistance to and suppression of foreign religions included almost anything that might be considered a part of foreign civilizations (such as cremation of the dead or the wearing of foreign-style "northern" clothing [*Hu fu*]). Clearly, these attitudes are related to the fact that the Song dynasty was always under the threat of foreign groups. Its most obvious efforts at resisting foreign civilizations can be found in its attempts to promote its own native culture and traditions. Ideas such as the discussions of orthodoxy (*zhengtong lun*) in the historiographical writings of the Northern Song, debates about casting out foreigners (*rang Yi lun*) in Confucian thought, and prominent discussions of Heavenly Principle (*tianli*) and Confucian orthodoxy (*daotong*) in neo-Confucianism (*lixue*) all worked from various perspectives to reassert the boundaries of Han-centered civilization and to drive out elements of foreign civilizations that had begun to permeate Han culture.[20]

For these reasons, we should say that if we do not take early modern Europe as the only standard by which to measure the formation of the nation-state, then we see that the limited early modern nation-state, or at least the rise of a consciousness of the early modern nation-state, occurred in China earlier than it did in Europe; just as the Japanese historians Naitō Konan (1866–1934) and Miyazaki Ichisada (1901–1995) argued that the Song dynasty represented China's "modern age." My view on this matter might seem to differ from commonly held views that Europe's "early modern period," including the "early modern nation-state," was prior to that of China. However, although the nation-state in Europe has only gradually taken shape since the early modern period, the various territories, ethnic groups, faiths, languages, and histories do not necessarily fully overlap. The boundaries between early modern European nation-states, then, were still just the spaces controlled by particular political powers, yet as borders of political power, they were only lines on a map.[21] The Chinese nation-state, however, is different in many ways from that of Europe, such that many of the key elements of the early modern European nation-state do not find an exact match in China. Why, then, is Europe the "universal" and China the "particular"?

Perhaps the history of the formation of the Chinese nation-state was an equally rational and natural process.[22]

What Is the Early Modern Nation-State?
Theories from Europe

Most theoretical approaches now argue that five major differences exist between nation-states and empires.

The first concerns the existence of clear borders: nation-states use borders to divide political, economic, and cultural spaces. Although ancient and medieval states did have centralized powers and political institutions, they did not have clear borders. The second difference concerns the consciousness of state sovereignty: the political space of the nation-state is the scope of state sovereignty, which has political sovereignty and the power of national self-determination that does not allow interference by other states. The third difference concerns the formation of the concept of the citizen and the dominant role of ideology that organizes the citizenry, that is, nationalism, which understands the state as a spatial unit. This concept includes not only citizens who are defined by a constitution, civil law, or laws of citizenship, but also ideologies such as patriotism, culture, history, and myth. The fourth difference concerns institutions of the state and systems that control politics, the economy, and cultural spaces (all of which go beyond the power of an emperor or king). The fifth difference concerns international relations that form between individual states: the existence of international relations affirms the independent sovereignty of the nation-state as well as the limitations placed on its space.[23]

All of these definitions are based on early modern Europe, however. The European definition of the nation-state comes from European history, especially early modern European history, and does not necessarily apply well to the various countries of the East, especially China. Unlike Europe, China's political domain and cultural space moved out slowly from the center. If not during the Three Dynasties of Antiquity, then

certainly during the Qin and Han eras, we see the beginning of a generally unified language, sense of ethics, customs, and politics, which
began to bring stability to a "(Han) nation" in this place that is called
"China" (*Zhongguo*). This is markedly different from the European situation, in which the nation is regarded as "a very recent newcomer in
human history."[24] For these reasons, theories that divide empires and
nation-states into two separate eras or time periods do not accord with
Chinese history in general or with the history of how ideas about the
consciousness of the state (*guojia yishi*) formed in China, or with the
history of the formation of the state itself in China. As I noted in *Here in
"China" I Dwell,* China did not simply change from a traditional empire
into a nation-state. While the idea of a limited state was contained within
the notion of the empire without borders, this limited state also continued to imagine an empire without borders. The modern nation-state
is the product of the traditional centralized empire, preserving remnants
of the ideology of empire, from which we can see that the histories of
both were intertwined.

Many people might think that ideas from ancient China such as All-
under-Heaven and the tribute system show that, in the world as imagined
by China under the tribute system, there was no clear consciousness of
boundaries between "states." From very early on, however, a Han civilization had become the mainstream in China, one centered around the regions in which Han people resided. The civilization used such means as
tribute, "bridling" of vassal states (*ji mi*), conferring of titles, and conquest to maintain distinctions between other peoples and regions, thereby
forming a vast empire in which "the center is clear, but the margins are
shifting."[25] By the time of the Song dynasty, in response to the rising power
and pressure generated by foreign peoples on the periphery, officially organized border surveys had already begun to show that a consciousness of a
limited "nation/state" was taking shape, just as clear borders/boundaries
were in fact appearing. As Zhang Guangda has said about awareness of
the state among the Jurchen and the Song, "the Song dynasty from this
time on chose to give up Yunnan outside of the Dadu River, and also
parted ways with the western frontier area (*Xi yu*). The western border
withdrew to Taizhou, and the western frontier area underwent a process
of Islamization. From this we can see that Zhao Kuangyin (Emperor Taizu

of Song, r. 960–976) sought to create a dynasty with self-defined borders and limits."[26]

In a certain sense, "self-defined borders and limits" refers to the gradual formation of a limited "state," and not seeing oneself as an "Empire" or All-under-Heaven. Therefore, if you examine history closely, you will discover that, in the traditional world of ideas, although All-under-Heaven was talked about at different times in history, it often was a vaguely imagined notion, and not necessarily an actual system or set of standards by which to manage "China" as a state or to address problems in international relations.[27]

Conclusion: Complex, Difficult Problems

I undoubtedly agree with the argument made by Gu Jiegang (1893–1980) that we should not believe that "the eighteen provinces where the Han people live have been as unified as they are now since ancient times. To do so would be to apply the perspective that arose after the Qin and Han dynasties to understand [Chinese] domains from before the Qin and Han."[28] I would also like to say, however, that the era for the type of great empire that did not require clear borders had probably come to an end by no later than the Song dynasty. If it had not been for certain reasons— such as the great empires such as the Mongol Yuan dynasty and the Manchu Qing—then China indeed would have made the transition from All-under-Heaven to the myriad states. If we can paint with such broad strokes, then, we might say that from the time that the Song and Liao dynasties designated the territories held by each side during the Jingde reign in the Song (1004–1007), down to the time of the Treaty of Nerchinsk, which was executed by the Qing empire and Russia during the Kangxi reign (1661–1722), aside from the period of the Mongol Yuan dynasty, China was gradually moving away from an expansive vision of the world based on All-under-Heaven and distinctions between "Chinese and foreign" (*Hua-Yi*) and entering a practical world of "myriad states" and beginning to establish borders and differences between you and me, self and other. For its relations with both its enormous neighbor, Russia, and with a tributary state like Korea, the Great Qing Empire ultimately had no

choice but to draw clear borders. Beginning in 1712, the Qing official Mu
Kedeng (1664–1735) began his border surveys, finally establishing the
borders between the Qing and Korea along Paektu Mountain (Mount
Changbai), the Tuman River, and the Yalu River.[29] After 1895, as it faced
external pressure from both Eastern and Western powers, the Great
Qing simply could no longer exist as a borderless empire. It had to move
into the role of a limited "state," using written agreements (conventions
or treaties) to set its borders. As a result, for early modern China, which
had been drawn into the larger world, those borders that had begun to
take on modern significance still retained aspects of a relatively stubborn
and traditional worldview, because they came from a time when the prosperous Great Qing Empire was expanding its borders out in all directions. China, then, still stubbornly held to a vision of All-under-Heaven
that stretched out over limitless domains.[30]

Of course, this is a complicated historical issue.[31] Allow me to offer a
simple summary of the preceding historical analysis, which, I believe, can
be divided into three main points. First, if China is centered around the
Han people, then its nation and state overlap in terms of geographical
space. As a result, clear "borders" of the nation and state of Han China
can be established with ease. The Song dynasty took action to clarify its
borders in response to pressure from the Liao, Xia, Jin, and Yuan states;
established a system for managing markets for foreign trade, which clearly
delineated boundaries between the dynasty and its neighbors in terms of
both wealth and knowledge; and engaged in diplomatic negotiations in
times of both peace and war. All of these actions brought the existence of
borders and a consciousness of state sovereignty to Song-dynasty China
at a very early time. Second, through the gradual establishment of a unified Han ethical system, the historical tradition, modes of thinking, and
cultural identity established since the Song dynasty have clearly given rise
to a self-affirming Han Chinese nationalist ideology. The debates about
"distinctions between Chinese and foreigners" (*Hua Yi zhi bian*), debates
about "orthodoxy" (*zhengtong*), and debates about the consciousness of
"loyal subjects" (*yimin*) all took shape from the Song dynasty onward and
originally were the products of this consciousness of the state. As for some
of those borderlands that had been (in the language of the imperial court)
"kept under the yoke," "pacified," or left under the jurisdiction of local

chieftains, they eventually became what was clearly part of the domain of the dynasty, both because of pressure from the court and decisions made by the leaders of these areas. As a result, the borders of Chinese territory gradually took shape. Third, China developed a complex set relations with the rest of Eastern world from the Song dynasty to the Qing dynasty.[32] This was particularly true from the Ming and Qing onward, as the relations between the states of the Great Ming (and later Qing), Korea, and Japan formed into an "international" field that, between one state and another, resulted in dividing lines between them, over which they conducted reciprocal relations. This international field had an order of its own, one that the Ming and Qing dynasties imagined in terms of a tribute system or an order of "conferring nobility" that could manage relations between states effectively through ritual. This "international" field, however, disintegrated under the challenges posed by another, new world order and was eventually replaced and forgotten.

However, this trend toward a Han nation-state that originally could have moved toward distinct borders, a clear-cut identity, and ethnic-national unity—all of the markers of the transition to a "nation-state"—was considerably complicated by the history of rule by foreign peoples under the Mongol Yuan dynasty and the Manchu Qing dynasty, both of which greatly expanded their domains, bringing into China vast territories and a multitude of ethnic groups. This history shows us a path of state building that is completely different from what is found in early modern Europe. These complications are especially relevant for the Great Qing Empire, which was built on the inclusion Manchu, Han, Mongolian, Uighur, Tibetan, and Miao peoples, and whose domains extended to "Sakhalin Island in the east, from Shule in Xinjiang to the Pamir Mountains in the west, to the Stanovoy Range in the north, to Mt. Ya (Yashan) in Guangdong in the south."[33] As China later inherited both this traditional idea of a "grand unification" (*da yitong*) and a state based on the Republic of China's "Five Nations Under One Union," both historical "domains" and modern "borders" became the subjects of extensive debates. These debates are also worthy of discussion.

❧ 3 ❧

ETHNICITY

Including the "Four Barbarians" in "China"?

How Early Modern China Became a "Nation"

In his *Confucian China and Its Modern Fate* (1958), the American scholar Joseph Levenson made a sweeping conclusion about China's transition into the early modern world: "In large part the intellectual history of modern China has been the process of making a *guojia* [nation] of *Tianxia* [All-under-Heaven]." This argument, which was later summarized as "from All-under-Heaven to nation," demonstrated that China was forced out of its traditional imperial order of All-under-Heaven and the tribute system (which took China as the center of the world) and into a new, modern international order in which the myriad states had parity with one another.[1] According to this argument, China was also forced to leave behind its Confucian civilizational ideals in favor of the universal standards of the early modern West. There is no question that the so-called arrival of the West was the most important factor in these changes. From the cultural influence of Western missionaries to the Western gunboats of the late Qing era, the early modern West's political institutions, science and technology, and ideas about culture gradually wrought vast changes on China and China's sense of itself.[2]

These changes resulting from "(Western) stimulus" and "(Chinese) response," however, are just one part of China's early modern transition. Indeed, China was a vast, traditional empire, but its transition to an early modern nation-state, which itself was fated by history, was different from all other countries, including its neighbors, such as Japan, Korea, and Vietnam. I believe that what sets China apart most clearly from other countries in its transition is not just the process of moving from All-under-Heaven to nation-state but also "bringing the Four Barbarians into China" (*na si Yi ru Zhonghua*), a process that in itself is worthy of discussion. In other words, with the territory inherited from the Qing Empire and the ethnic groups that lived there, modern China attempted to bring the many ethnic groups on its periphery into a single "Chinese nation" (*Zhonghua minzu*) and eventually became a (multi)national modern empire or nation-state.

If we do not pay adequate attention to the interrelatedness of the processes of "moving from All-under-Heaven to the myriad states" and "bringing the Four Barbarians into China," then we have no way to understand what this "China" is now. In this chapter, then, what I want to explain further is how that very complicated process by which modern China was simultaneously forced to move "from All-under-Heaven to the myriad states" and attempted to "bring the Four Barbarians into China" has a close relation to other important historical factors.

First, the sensibility concerning "unification" (*yi tong*) and the concept of "China" that came from the world of traditional Chinese thought unquestionably bore a great influence on how Chinese politicians and educated people attempted to rebuild "China."

Second, even if this sensibility concerning unification and the concept of "China" was influential, what is more important is that the expansion of the Great Qing Empire out toward the "Four Barbarians" was the key factor that later led to a host of problems. Because the Republic of China and the People's Republic of China inherited the Qing's national groups and domains, any discussion of "China's" territory, peoples, or identity must take into account the history of the Qing dynasty.

Third, in any discussion of "China's" nations, territories, or similar questions, the international background is crucial. The Japan factor may be more important than the West, however, because the challenges that came from Japan beginning in 1894 always served as the most important backdrop against which people came to understand questions related to "China's" territory, peoples, and identity.

Because of limited space in this chapter I can only attempt to look at modern China from the perspective of history, especially the history of scholarship. I examine how politicians, historians, archaeologists, and anthropologists from the late Qing period to the Republican period attempted to "bring the Four Barbarians into China" and establish discourses concerning "China" (*Zhongguo*) and the Chinese nation (*Zhonghua minzu*) at the same time as they faced the question of the transition from All-under-Heaven to the myriad states.[3]

"Five Nations under One Union" and "Driving Out the Barbarians": Debates about Rebuilding "China" in the Late Qing

Some of the events concerning the reconstruction of "China" during the late Qing and early Republic that I discuss here were already treated briefly in the Introduction. Some readers may be familiar with these events, but I will review them once more.[4]

After a series of upheavals that included the Opium Wars (1839–1842 and 1856–1860), the Taiping Rebellion (1850–1864), the First Sino-Japanese War (1894–1895), the Hundred Days' Reform (1898), and the Boxer Rebellion (1899–1901), by the beginning of the twentieth century the Great Qing Empire was battered by storm winds from all directions, as the great Western powers and Japan applied pressure from outside that would dismember the Qing state, and, in the domestic sphere, revolutionaries began to question the legitimacy of the Qing dynasty itself. Beginning in 1901, Zhang Taiyan (1868–1936) and others repeatedly made the point that China originally belonged to the descendants of the mythical Flame Emperor and Yellow Emperor. The "Eastern Hu," they argued, had "invaded the lands inside of the Great Wall, stolen the emperor's seal, and cast their poison throughout China (*Zhonghua*)."[5] The "Eastern Hu" that Zhang referred to were the Manchus. He argued that the Manchus and the Han were not of the same race, and that the Manchus' "language, political beliefs, food, drink, and dwellings were all different from those of China."[6] In his view, then, the overthrow of the Ming dynasty had made China a "lost state" (*wang guo*).[7] His views were an important line of thought at the time, as revolutionaries who were Zhang's contemporaries understood Han nationalism to be a key force for overthrowing the Qing dynasty. Examples of this thinking can be found in *The Revolutionary Army* (*Geming jun*, 1903) by Zou Rong (1885–1905) and *An Alarm to Awaken the World* (*Jing shi zhong*) by Chen Tianhua (1875–1905),[8] both of which promoted this type of nationalism.

Looking back across history, we see that this nationalism was a new form of thinking about distinctions between Chinese and foreigners that had been gradually taking shape since the Song dynasty. Unlike the Tang dynasty, which "mixed together all in one country, containing both Chinese and foreign," the people of the Song dynasty came to believe that Chinese and foreigners need not be involved with one another. According to the Song-dynasty scholar Fan Zuyu (1041–1098), the Tang dynasty's pursuit of a "massive and boundless" empire that "wished to make Chinese and foreign into one" could only "gain empty renown while encountering very real problems."[9] From this time on, aside from the Mongol Yuan dynasty and the Manchu Qing dynasty, Chinese empires from the Song through the Ming all followed the strategy of limiting China to a Han-ethnic dynasty. In the late Qing, this strategy transformed into Han nationalism. Following the global trends of their era, those anti-Qing revolutionaries who supported Han nationalism were certain that "today is undoubtedly the era of nationalism."[10] In establishing a new Republic of China, therefore, they believed that it was necessary to drive out foreign races. According to "The Meaning of the Republic of China" (*Zhonghua minguo jie*), an essay by Zhang Taiyan, that which is called "China" must stand apart from the "Four Barbarians,"[11] by which Zhang meant not only Manchuria but also Tibet, Mongolia, and Muslim-majority areas in the west (*Hui bu*)—he believed there was no need to include these places in the Republic of China. Following this line of thought, then, the Republic of China established after the revolution would be like the Song and Ming dynasties, a nation-state based on the Han ethnicity, while its territories would return to roughly that of the fifteen provinces of the Ming dynasty.

Another line of thought emerged, however, from people who were later called the Protect the Emperor group (*Baohuang pai*) or the conservative camp. Also in 1901, Liang Qichao published his "Overview of Chinese History" (*Zhongguo shi xulun*), which argued that the Miao, Tibetan, Mongolian, and Tungusic races should be included in Chinese history along with the Han, and thus should also be a part of "China." To keep readers from questioning the unique phenomenon of a multinational state, Liang Qichao was keen to point out that nations across history were constantly changing and merging with one another, and that the Han people were never originally a single unit. He also asked a rhetorical question: Although the Han people claim that they are the descendants of the Yellow Emperor, does this mean that "they are all from the same family lineage?"[12] In fact, it was not that Liang Qichao disapproved of nationalism, but that, unlike Zhang Taiyan, he did not see nationalism as a force for domestic, race-based revolution. Instead, he saw it as a comprehensive program that could be used to resist imperialist forces from outside.[13] In 1903, Jiang Zhiyou (1866–1929) published an essay titled "A History of Nations in Chinese Antiquity" (*Zhongguo shanggu jiu minzu zhi shiying*) in the thirty-first issue of *The New People's Miscellany* (*Xin min cong bao*), a journal edited by Liang Qichao. Jiang's essay drew from work by Japanese scholars and agreed with them that the Miao peoples were the earliest inhabitants of China, and that the Han were a foreign people who arrived later. Jiang Zhiyou was not really giving full support to this idea that the Miao came before the Han. He was more interested in supporting the idea of historical evolution and a model of survival of the fittest. He also implied that there was no need to cling stubbornly to the traditional idea of a Han-ethnic "China." Finally, he was trying to push people in modern China to summon up the rough-and-ready spirit of the ancient Han people and wash away the many humiliations that had befallen China.[14] In 1905, Liang Qichao also published "An Investigation of the Chinese Nation across History," which emphasized that the Han-ethnic group, which was commonly referred to as the "Chinese nation" (*Zhonghua minzu*), was not an individual national group with a single bloodline, but rather had been formed through the intermingling of many national groups. "From the beginning," Liang argued, "the Chinese nation that we see today was in fact formed through the intermingling of a great number of nations."[15] In the same year as Liang Qichao's essay, Jiang Zhiyou published another piece, "An Investigation of the Chinese Race," which praised the thesis put forward by the French scholar Terrien de Lacouperie (1844–1894) that the Chinese race had "come from the West." Jiang used this Western origins thesis to pick apart stubborn ideas held by Han Chinese and to call on them to bring back broad-minded thinking and restore an atmosphere of tolerance.[16] The version of "China" that Liang Qichao imagined would include both the original lands of the eighteen provinces as well as its dependent territories, such as Manchuria, Mongolia, Muslim-majority areas, and Tibet. Liang argued that "China is by nature a state made through grand unification, with the unification of races, languages, literatures, and morals and ethics."[17]

At the beginning of the twentieth century, these two ways of thinking that had emerged from the revolutionary camp and the conservative camp were locked in constant battle. It is of great significance that, less than ten years later, although the extreme Han nationalism of the revolutionary camp had to a certain degree helped the revolutionaries to overturn the Qing dynasty, no one who took the reins of political power in China was willing to risk being blamed for allowing the country to be broken up or have territories cut away. Even revolutionaries had no way to rely completely on military force to resolve the question of the transfer of political power, and therefore they could accept only certain compromises. For these reasons, the establishment of a new nation under the banner of the Republic of China adopted strategies put forward by the conservative camp. The abdication edict from the last Qing emperor in 1911 called for preserving the model of "Five Nations under One Republic" that "continued to preserve the complete territory of the five nations of Manchus, Han, Mongols, Hui, and Tibetans." When the Republic of China was established in January of 1912, and Sun Yat-sen assumed the role of provisional president, Sun declared that he accepted the program of "Five Nations under One Republic." In his inaugural speech he assumed responsibility for unifying Chinese territory, "combining the lands of the Han, Manchus, Mongolians, Hui, and Tibetans into one state." Thus the stance taken by the revolutionary camp had transformed from exclusion to inclusion.[18]

This debate finally came to an end. Why, however, did this state of affairs come to be? Here we have to mention the stimulus and influence that came from Japan.

In the Introduction I mentioned that Japan defeated China in the First Sino-Japanese War of 1894, which, in turn, resulted in the signing of the Treaty of Shimonoseki in 1895. As a result of this treaty, China ceded Taiwan and other territories to Japan. These events provoked an upheaval in Chinese thinking that had not been seen in thousands of years, leading a China that had sought to transform within tradition to turn toward transforming *without* tradition. In Japan, however, this victory led to debates about whether China really should remain whole or be split apart. Some of the writings from this debate that had the deepest influence on China were "A Plan for Dealing with China" (*Shina shobun'an*) by Ozaki Yukio and "Preserving the Integrity of China" by Ariga Nagao.[19] During the Hundred Days' Reform of 1898, the Chinese-language newspaper *The Reformer* (*Zhi xin bao*) published an article titled "On Preserving China" (*Cun Zhongguo shuo*), which had been translated from the Japanese newspaper *Chūgai jiron*. After the failure of these reforms, another translation, this one titled "Strategies to Carve Up China" (originally published in a Japanese newspaper), was printed in the November 1898 issue of the *East Asian Times* (*Yadong shibao*). These articles forced educated readers to recognize the extremely difficult questions that China was facing. This was especially true in the translation of an article by Ariga Nagao, "On the Preservation of China," printed on January 31, 1899, in the *East Asian Times*, which began by asking the following question: Should China be "kept whole" or "carved up"?[20]

This question was debated widely in political and scholarly fields in Japan since 1895. Japan at the time wanted to imagine itself as Asia's savior, expanding Japanese territory from Korea, of which it had already taken possession, into neighboring Manchuria and Mongolia. It also attempted to contain China within the Han-ethnic regions to the south of the Great Wall, turning China into a Han-ethnic state. At that time, the East Asia Society (Tō-A-kai) and the Common Culture Society (Dobunkai), with the support of Konoe Atsumaro (1863–1904), used the notion of "civilizational survival of the fittest" to explain Japan's dominance in Asia. They also discussed the close relationship between China and Japan as one of "the same writing and same race" (J. *dōbun dōshu,* Ch. *tongwen tong-zhong*).[21] This notion gave rise to the idea that China should see Japan as a leader with ambitions to rescue East Asia; but it also gave rise the argument that China should abandon its relationships with the so-called Four Barbarians. As Japanese scholars have noted, this trend developed "after war broke out between Japan and the Qing, as (Japanese) citizens showed ever greater interest in the Asian mainland. It also developed against the backdrop of Japan's dramatic rise among modern nation-states during the second decade of the Meiji era, as Japan's consciousness of its status as an Asian nation steadily grew and it worked to put on display a unique East Asian culture that stood in contrast Western culture."[22] These developments led them to see Korea, Manchuria, Mongolia, and even Xinjiang and Tibet as part of "their own" territory.[23]

Ariga Nagao, who supported "keeping China whole," argued that if China were in fact kept whole, "then two goals would be achieved: first, it would stay whole all on its own, and second, those people who depend on it would remain whole." Looking at the situation at that time, however, he believed that China was unable to remain whole on its own, because the great Western powers were looming around it, and because China was so weak and poor that it lacked the power to resist them. If those who depended on China remained whole, then what other strong states could they depend on? Ariga's analysis offered two possible solutions. The first was called "assistance from one source," in which China simply threw its lot in with one other powerful country; the other solution was "assistance from multiple sources," which would mean that "two or three strong countries would establish a confederation to support China in its areas of weakness."[24] Ozaki Yukio's *A Plan for Dealing with China,* however, called for Japan to completely absorb China, "just as the Yuan dynasty did to the Song dynasty, as the Qing dynasty did to the Ming dynasty, and as England did to India." Why? Because he believed that, for Chinese people, "outside of the Imperial court, there is no awareness of the state," and that "if the people do not have an understanding of ideas about the state, then even if their military is powerful, their state is certain to be lost," and therefore it made more sense to take the opportunity to carve up China immediately.[25] Both arguments for keeping China whole or for carving up China, then, in fact were already focusing on breaking up China from its then-current status as a multinational empire.

People in China had different ideas. Even though politicians such as Sun Yat-sen had once believed that China should exclude Manchuria and Mongolia, it was nonetheless the case that, as I mentioned earlier, no one was willing to assume responsibility for giving up territory, losing sovereignty, and shaming the nation. Political leaders of the Republic of China, then, whether it was Sun Yat-sen or Yuan Shikai, could only work to maintain a multinational state with vast territories. Even though scholars have agreed with theories about the nation-state that come from Europe, the traditional notion of the empire made by "grand unification" continued to exert a deep influence over them, and the Chinese scholarly world continued to use traditional ideas about "China" to which they were accustomed. It would be fair to say that it was Japan's imperialist political ambitions that gave Chinese scholars the impulse to reexamine their ideas about the nation and state and to develop new perspectives from which to work toward keeping China whole.

From the establishment of the Republic of China down to the time of the May Fourth movement, the idea of the "Chinese nation" (*Zhonghua minzu*) was widely accepted during these times of domestic turmoil and foreign interference.[26] By the 1920s and 1930s, new ways of thinking about how to "bring the Four Barbarians into China" were developed in the face of new emergencies, as scholars began to argue that "the Chinese nation encompasses all" not only in legal terms but also in terms of scholarship and thought.

"The Chinese Nation Encompasses All": New Directions in Scholarship in the 1920s and 1930s

In the 1920s serious differences lay beneath the surface of two the most important trends in scholarly thought and their attempts to define "China" and to establish a Chinese identity.

The first major scholarly trend was critical of theories that arrived in China via Japanese interpretations of Lacouperie that held that Chinese

culture came from the West, as well as arguments derived from this theory
that held that the Miao people were the original inhabitants of China prior
to the Han.[27] Scholars who disagreed with these interpretations of Lacouperie were also critical of Johann Gunnar Anderson's argument, derived
from his archaeological research, that Neolithic pottery culture came to
China via the West. Lacouperie's "Western origins thesis" was relatively
popular during the late Qing, while Anderson's archaeological discoveries
from the early 1920s, which he discussed in his 1923 book, *Early Chinese
Culture,* used comparisons of Yangshao and Central Asia to argue that
Neolithic pottery culture was transmitted from West to East. This argument seemed to prove the accuracy of Lacouperie's Western origins thesis.

The great majority of Chinese scholars believed that the Western origins thesis amounted to a challenge to the uniqueness and autonomy of
Chinese culture. Even if scholars in the late Qing were receptive to these
arguments, Chinese scholars such as Fu Sinian (1896–1950), Li Chi, and
He Bingsong (1890–1946) tried continuously to use historical arguments
and archaeological discoveries to prove both the local origins and diverse
nature of Chinese culture. This project reveals a highly "nationalist" historical perspective and agenda for archaeology. They clearly intended to
cultivate a new basis for the Chinese nation and its historical identity.

The second major scholarly trend was the "debating antiquity" (*gu shi
bian*) movement, which will be familiar to many readers. In the 1920s Gu
Jiegang and others called for new investigations into the Three Dynasties of Antiquity, the classical canon, and ancient legends. At a basic level,
this movement modernized and remade traditional historiography and
philology. Working with the modern standards of scientific inquiry, ob-
jectivity, and neutrality, these scholars reexamined ancient documents related to China's early history in a way that assumed they were guilty
until proven innocent: if a verdict could not be reached, then they were
suspended from the historical record until legends (and myths) were gradually driven from historical inquiry. Those figures who once had served
as symbols of the Chinese nation, such as the Flame Emperor, the Yellow
Emperor, and Emperors Yao, Shun, and Yu, as well as ancient documents
related to China's revered classical canon were all treated with thoroughgoing suspicion. Gu Jiegang's plan for debating antiquity was to "overturn unreliable histories." This project included (1) "dispelling the idea

that the nation has one origin," (2) "dispelling the idea that [China's] territory has always been unified," (3) "dispelling ideas that focus on individuals in ancient history," and (4) "dispelling the idea that antiquity was
a golden era."[28] It was precisely because of this agenda that this scholarly
movement was accused by people such as Cong Lianzhu and Dai Jitao
(1898–1949) of "attacking the roots of the nation."[29] Why? Because the
oft-repeated idea that the nation has one origin implies that the Chinese
nation has a shared ancestry, just as the idea that China's territory has
always been unified means that Chinese territory has been the same
since ancient times; the legendary figures from ancient history symbolize
the shared origins of the Chinese nation; and the idea that antiquity rep-
resents a golden age implies that culture should return to its traditions.
Symbols have the power to bolster identity and cohesion, and thus
casting any suspicion on these symbols meant casting suspicion on the
roots of history itself and attacking the basis of Chinese identity.

In the 1920s these two seemingly opposed scholarly orientations
achieved few new breakthroughs. In the late 1920s and early 1930s, however, crises at the level of the nation and the state led to subtle changes in
the perspectives of these two scholarly orientations, or at least the perspective of scholars who were positioned within these scholarly orientations. Let us take a look at the threats that China was facing during this
time: as early as 1921, Gong Debai had translated "A Letter Concerning
Absorbing China," an essay by Kawashima Naniwa (1865–1949) that provoked a strong reaction among Chinese students who were studying in
Japan.[30] In 1927, the infamous Tanaka Memorial, which called for Japan
to conquer China, was exposed. Regardless of its authenticity, the document was quickly translated and published in China,[31] where it elicited
outrage across the country. From 1928 onward, public opinion in China
was ever more influenced by Japan's ambitions to invade China and by
its actual behavior. Readers in China saw the publication of works such
as *Japan's Annexation of Manchuria and Mongolia* (*Riben bingtun Man
Meng lun*), a translation of work by Hosono Shigekatsu; *Looking at China
in Turmoil* (*Guan dongluande Zhongguo*) by Tsurumi Yūsuke; *The Situation in Manchuria* (*Manzhou xianzhuang*) by Nozawa Gennojō; and
Japan's Fundamental Views on China (*Riben dui Hua zhi jichu guannian*)
by Tada Shun,[32] as well as the translation and publication of studies on

the history and geography of Manchuria and Mongolia by Shiratori Kurakichi, Asano Risaburō, Inaba Iwakichi, Satō Yoshio, and Yanai Watari. There was also a steady stream of reports from magazines and newspapers that exposed information about Japanese scholars' and students' visits to Manchuria, Mongolia, and Tibet.[33] People were completely shocked by the way Japanese people were repeatedly traveling to Manchuria and Mongolia to excavate artifacts from northeastern China and using archaeology and studies of ancient documents to discuss the fate of Manchuria.

Even more shocking were the Mukden Incident of September 18, 1931; the conquering of the northeastern provinces by Japan and the establishment of the Manchurian puppet state (Manchukuo) in 1932; the establishment of the Islamic Republic of East Turkestan in 1933; and the appearance of a so-called autonomy movement for northeastern China. All of these events brought China into an unprecedented crisis over the integrity of its territory. As a result, Chinese scholars could not avoid turning their attention to research on the "Four Barbarians" (or China's "border areas") to refute Japanese scholars' discussions of the relationship between Manchuria, Mongolia, Xinjiang, Tibet, and China with evidence from historical, geographical, and ethnographic research. As Gu Jiegang stated in his "Letter Concerning the Yu Gong Scholarly Society's Plans for Research on Border Areas":

> We face enslavement, and our state may be lost at any moment, and thus we unite under the banner of nationalism. Moreover, because our enemies are swallowing up our lands, and our border regions are taking the brunt of these attacks, we are turning our efforts toward research on the history and geography of China's border regions. Manchuria, Mongolia, Xinjiang, Tibet, Southeast Asia (Nanyang), and Central Asia—people are working on all of these areas.[34]

In 1932, Hua Qiyun published *China's Border Regions* (*Zhongguode bianjiang*), the first such study of the modern era; in 1933, Fu Sinian and his colleagues published *Outline of the History of Northeast China* (*Huabei shi gang*); in 1934, Gu Jiegang and his colleague, Tan Qixiang (1911–1992), founded a bimonthly magazine, *Yu Gong*. As Gu Jiegang said, in times of peace, there is no harm in scholars practicing "scholarship for the sake of scholarship," but in times when "the country is in decline and fear reigns," then they can only "pursue scholarship for practical ends."[35]

Against this political, intellectual, scholarly backdrop, Fu Sinian published "The Chinese Nation Is All-Encompassing" in the 181st volume of *Independent Critic (Duli pinglun)* on December 15, 1935. In this essay, Fu argued that China had been under "strong political control" since the time of the Yin and Zhou dynasties, and that during the Spring and Autumn period "ideas concerning a grand unification [of China] were deep in people's hearts." It was these conditions, he argued, that made the unification of the Qin and Han possible. "Our Chinese nation (*Zhonghua minzu*) speaks one language, writes one script, and carries out the same set of ethics based on the same culture. We are one great family."[36]

The "Local" and "Diversity": Trends in Chinese Scholarly Research on the Chinese Nation and Chinese Culture before the Marco Polo Bridge Incident

Let us turn our attention to new developments that occurred in Chinese scholarship before the Marco Polo Bridge Incident of 1937.

Academia Sinica (Zhongyang yanjiuyuan, literally the "central research institute"), was established in 1928. According to Ding Wenjiang (1887–1936), who played an important role in establishing the institution, the founders of Academia Sinica and the Institute of History and Philology were motivated by a desire to seek out the foundations of Chinese identity.[37] Under Fu Sinian's leadership, therefore, the Institute of History and Philology was undoubtedly the scholarly force that represented the intellectual mainstream at that time. Despite the fact that Fu Sinian maintained a certain amount of Han nationalism, however, he still largely agreed with the view of history that included the "Four Barbarians" and assimilated them into China. For these reasons, then, when the Institute for History and Philology was established in 1928, he consciously advocated scholarly research in two areas: first, the history and languages of the peoples on the periphery of the Han, and, second, the study of the historical remnants and traces of a variety of national groups within China's borders.

The motivations behind these scholarly trends can be attributed in part to a desire to compete with and overcome European and Japanese Orientalist scholarship, and in part to a desire to gain a complete understanding and the peoples and regions that made up "China." Strictly speaking, these scholarly orientations could not yet really be called nationalist. Chinese scholars of this era consciously made efforts to use so-called scientific scholarly perspectives to seek out the local origins of Chinese culture, to rewrite Chinese history in terms of indigenous or autochthonous development (instead of foreign influence), to investigate the current situation faced by Chinese people at that time, and to survey the customs and habits of peripheral areas. In the 1920s and 1930s, however, a number of projects had in fact developed because of the impetus provided by Western and Japanese scholars. They include the trend toward gaining a new understanding of China's non-Han nationalities, efforts such as those promoted by Fu Sinian to master research materials on the economies, politics, and ways of life in China's peripheral areas, and work to understand the great variety of dialects and other languages that were not part of the standard National Language (*Guoyu*). These efforts were driven both by scholarly motivations to compete with the West and Japan and—unquestionably—also by political motivations surrounding efforts to resist discourses from the West and Japan concerning "China's" territorial domains and peoples.

In this era, then, scholarship and politics were inseparable.

1. Let us look at the field of historical studies. During these years, many of the topics covered by archaeology, anthropology, and historical studies were in dialogue with one another. Scholars attempted to explain the diverse elements of the formation of the ancient Chinese race and culture across history, as well as the historical origins of the various national groups within modern China. As I mentioned earlier, after the challenges put forward by the "debating antiquity" group led by Gu Jiegang, it was no longer possible to maintain an understanding of the Chinese nation or culture that was based on arguments that the Chinese nation emerged from one source or that Chinese territory had always been unified; as a

result, after discussions by a number of scholars, people gradually set aside ideas about the Western origins thesis as it related to the Chinese race or culture. The question remained, however: What cultural terrain eventually combined to form ancient China? Can all of these pieces of cultural terrain be considered "Chinese"? Some scholars put forth bold new analyses of historical documents. For example, Xu Zhongshu's "Conjectures, Based on Ancient Books, about the Yin and Zhou Nationalities" (1927), which was published in the very first issue of Tsinghua University's *Chinese Classical Review* (*Guoxue lun cong*), argued against the traditional notion that the Three Dynasties of Antiquity all came from the same cultural source, suggesting instead that the Yin and Zhou peoples were from different national groups. In the same year, Meng Wentong (1894–1968) published *The Subtleties of Ancient History* (*Gu shi zhen wei*), which argued that the peoples of ancient China could be divided into three national groups: the Jiang Han, which included contemporary Hubei and Hunan; the Hai Dai, which included modern Shandong; and the He Luo, which refers to the area centered around modern Henan Province. Not long after Meng's book, Fu Sinian published "The Hypothesis of the Yi in the East and the Xia in the West" (*Yi Xia dong xi shuo*), an essay that argued that ancient China was formed by the gradual melding of the Yi people in the eastern areas and the Xia in the western regions. His conclusion states clearly that his goal was to explain "the overall pattern [in ancient China] in which east and west had stood opposite from one another during the process by which tribal states transformed into kingdoms (and later an empire)."[38]

This idea was not limited to histories of ancient times; it also ran through the entire history of national groups in historical writings. It was during the 1930s, in fact, that the greatest number of monographs devoted to the history of the Chinese nation or *minzu* appeared. In 1930, Mou Fenglin's "Preface to a History of the Chinese Nation" was published in two parts in number 3 and 4 of the journal *History* (*Shixue zazhi*), and over the next few years a series of books with the exact same title, *History of the Chinese Nation* (*Zhongguo minzu shi*), were published by different authors: one each by Wang Tongling and Lü Simian in 1934, and another by Song Wenbing in 1935. Regardless of the differences and similarities between these national histories, for the most part they all defended the idea of the local origins and diversity of the "Chinese nation," working to describe the histories of the various national groups within China's borders as a process by which many different rivers converged and flowed together out into the sea. For example, the earliest *History of the Chinese Nation,* written by Wang Tongling, divided the yellow race into different groups according to the directions in which they moved geographically. He divided them into three southern groups (the Miao, the Han, and the Tibetans) and three northern groups (the Manchus, Mongolians, and the Hui [that is, Muslim groups, mainly Uighurs]). According to the contemporary historian Ma Rong, "Other than the addition of the Miao people," Wang's "division of the Chinese nation into the 'Three Southern Groups' and 'Three Northern Groups' basically coincides with the framework of 'Five Nations under One Republic' that people spoke of in the early years of the Republic of China."[39] For the most part, other histories of the Chinese nation made the same arguments, never departing from the basic categorization of the five nations or six nations that made up China. The script behind these histories of the Chinese nation was to call for incorporating the "Four Barbarians" into China so that China could truly become a great country of Five Nations under One Republic.

2. Let us take another look at the field of archaeology. Since the founding of this field, archaeology in China has been assigned the heavy burden of seeking out the sources of Chinese civilization and defining the boundaries of the Chinese nation. For example, while he was studying archaeology at Harvard University, Li Chi, who is known as the "father of Chinese archaeology," had a strong interest in describing the origins of the Chinese people. In his doctoral dissertation, "The Formation of the Chinese People" (Harvard, 1923), Li classified the Chinese people as six core groups: the descendants of the Yellow Emperor (that is, the Han); the Tungusic peoples; peoples who speak Tibeto-Burman languages; the Hmong-Khmer peoples; the Shan group; and three subgroups made up of the Xiongnu, Mongolians, and the Zhuru group. He argued that the source of the modern Chinese race could be traced to two areas: first, the area that was occupied by the Tungusic people after they invaded the territory of the descendants of the Yellow Emperor; and second, the area of the last three groups (the Xiongnu, Mongolians, and Zhuru) that had been

subsequently invaded and occupied by the descendants of the Yellow Emperor. The overlap of these two areas led to the formation of modern "Chinese people" (*Zhongguo ren*).[40] Even if it is true that, as some scholars have argued, Li Chi's views were "the response of a twentieth-century Chinese intellectual to the Chinese national movement and the international situation in both the ideological and intellectual sense,"[41] it is also fair to say that the intellectual motivations behind Li Chi's research in the 1920s were still focused on refuting the Western origins thesis. At this time, the use of physical anthropology and studies of language to seek the roots of the "Chinese nation" had not yet acquired a particularly nationalist significance.[42]

But even if archaeology were not seeking out a national perspective, the national perspective was seeking out archaeology. As Zhang Guangzhi has pointed out, the main characteristic of Chinese archaeology before the 1950s was its nationalism.[43] Looking back at the archaeology of this formative period we see that there were always certain questions to be resolved (mainly arguments about the local origins of Chinese culture and about the amalgamation of many peoples into one Chinese nation) that served as the basis for understanding archaeological materials that had been unearthed. This was true for discussions of the prehistoric Stone Age or the excavation of the ruins of Yin. When He Bingsong published "A New Myth of the Origin of the Chinese Nation" (*Zhonghua minzu qiyuan zhi xin shenhua*, 1929), which argued against the Western origins thesis, he placed his hopes on new archaeological findings. The writings described above all show that many people were looking to the work of archaeologists to see how they might use materials buried beneath the earth to refute Western and Japanese archaeology and to demonstrate that, first, the Chinese race and Chinese culture had independent origins; second, that the Chinese race and Chinese culture were indeed able to incorporate diverse elements; and, third, that the various national groups within China could be written about in terms of one history and one country.

This general mood served as the backdrop to the discovery made in 1929 of the cranium of "Peking Man" in Zhoukoudian, near Beijing. This discovery was an important symbol, as was the discovery of Longshan culture at the Chengziya archaeological site near modern Jinan, the capital of Shandong Province. The publication of the first report on archaeological finds at Anyang (in modern Henan Province) not only served to a certain degree as the declaration of the establishment of Chinese archaeology but also established an autochthonous or independent genealogy of the Chinese race and of Chinese culture. Alongside the writings of Xu Zhongshu (1927), Meng Wentong (1933), Fu Sinian (1933), and others discussed above, these archaeological findings worked together to offer theories and ways to frame the location of early Chinese culture as the place of mutual interactions between Chinese and foreign groups, thereby offering a larger historical context for understanding early China.

It is fair to say that Chinese archaeology, which has just been established as a field, was faced with questions that were not about archaeology but in fact were about history, or even nationalist history. The series of archaeological discoveries at Zhoukoudian, Yangshao, Longshan, and Anyang provided a context for a Chinese race and culture and irrefutable evidence to demolish arguments about the Western origins thesis. It was for these reasons that, in an essay on the Chengziya archaeological site, therefore, Fu Sinian would declare that that most important events in Chinese history were "entirely Han" Chinese, and that questions about the origin of ancient Chinese civilization and the Chinese race "were greater in significance, greater in number, and of greater importance for establishing a framework for the knowledge that makes up Chinese historiography."[44]

3. Finally, let us look at the field of anthropology.[45] At Academia Sinica in 1930, Ling Chunsheng, Shang Chengzu, and others undertook a survey of the Nanai (or Hezhe) people in the lower reaches of the Songhua (or Sungari) River, and published a report titled *The Hezhe People of the Lower Songhua River*. In 1933, Ling Chunsheng and Rui Yifu undertook a survey that they used as the basis for their "Report on a Survey of the Miao in Western Hunan." These surveys were followed by others: a survey of the She people in Lishui in Zhejiang Province conducted by Ling Chunsheng and Rui Yifu in 1934; a survey of the Yi people in Yunnan conducted by Ling Chunsheng, Rui Yifu, Tao Yunda, and others in 1935; and another survey by Ling Chunsheng and Rui Yifu in 1936–1937 of the Kawa people of Western Yunnan, the Lahu people, the Jingpo (Kachu) people, and the Baiyi people. It is clear that the scholarly mainstream was more and more interested in the national question and was moving toward

including ethnic groups on the periphery in the larger history of China. In April 1934, then, the ethnology research group that had been part of the Institute of Social Sciences (Shehui kexue yanjiusuo) at Academia Sinica was moved into the Institute of History and Philology, becoming the fourth group within that institute. As a result, ethnographic work and survey research became a part of the mainstream of historical studies, archaeology, and anthropology. At the Institute of Language and History at Sun Yat-sen University, in 1930, Pang Xinmin accompanied a collection team from the university on an expedition to the Bei River, after which he wrote "Notes on the Bei River and Yao Mountains." The same year, Jiang Zhefu, who also conducted a survey of the Bei River with Pang, published essays on the Yao people of their region and their rituals. In 1931, Pang Xinmin traveled to the Yao Mountains in Guangxi, publishing "Notes on a Trip to the Yao Mountains in Guangdong." In addition to these works, in the 1930s Shi Luguo and Yang Chengzhi conducted a survey of the Lolo people in Yunnan. In Yang Chengzhi's book from 1932, *Studies on Nationalities of the Southwest* (*Xinan minzu yanjiu*), their work focused on customs and cultures of people in the border regions.

It is worth pointing out that these "anthropologically" flavored surveys also revealed other intentions. Just as in the fields of history and archaeology, they sought to demonstrate a Chinese scholarly sensibility that was in dialogue with foreign scholarship and to realize in their various surveys of ethnic groups the goal of "including the Four Barbarians in China."

As for demonstrating a Chinese scholarly sensibility, the earliest example of this kind of work can be seen in a speech given by Yang Chengzhi of Sun Yat-sen University in 1929. Yang argued that the Yellow Emperor and Chi You were the ancestors of the Miao and Han national groups, and pointed out that those nationalities that had gradually spread out toward the border regions and mountains had received too little attention from Chinese scholars—so little, in fact, that foreigners had begun to see these groups as "non-Chinese." Although foreigners had written many books about these nationalities, none had been written in China, a fact that Yang thought was a "national humiliation."[46] The next year, Ling Chunsheng wrote in a preface to *The Hezhe People of the Lower Songhua*

River that "modern Chinese scholars who research the history of nation-alities (*minzu shi*) have been duped by Western Sinologists for some time and believe without a doubt that Tungusic peoples of today are the Eastern Hu of ancient times."⁴⁷ He pointed out that progress in historical studies had already demolished the idea of a single origin to the Chinese nation and included a variety of then contemporary ethnic groups as part of the origins of Chinese culture and the Chinese race; one such example, he argued, was the inclusion of the Yi (or Shang) culture as one source of Chinese civilization. Ling's work, which has been called "a ground-breaking document in China's scientific study of nationalities,"⁴⁸ was produced in the context of a number of dialogues with foreign scholar-ship. Ling's discussion of the history of the Hezhe people conformed to Fu Sinian's thesis concerning "the Yi in the East and the Xia in the West" and to Fu's *Outline of the History of Northeast China,* arguing that in prehistoric times the northeastern areas of China had connections to central China; this argument worked to refute theories put forward by Yano Jin'ichi (1872–1970) and Torii Ryūzō (1870–1953).⁴⁹ Research on southwestern China sounded much like these discussions of north-eastern China. Fang Guoyu, for example, published an article in 1936 in the newspaper *Social Welfare* (*Yi shi bao*) titled "The Bo People and Bai zi," which attacked arguments made by Western scholars such as the French Sinologist Paul Pelliot that the Thai people were from the kingdom of Nanzhao and argued that Nanzhao was not founded by Thai peoples. The significance of this article, then, was to show that Yunnan Province was still a part of China.⁵⁰

We already see this tendency to "bring the Four Barbarians into China" in Ling Chunsheng's *The Hezhe People of the Lower Songhua River.* As one scholar has noted, the book's "use of ancient Chinese texts and doc-uments to tease out the history of the Heishui Mohe people during the Sui and Tang dynasties and the many changes that took place through the Liao, Jin, Ming, and Qing dynasties is clearly tinted by 'nationalist' views, as many later scholars have pointed out. The book brings the Hezhe people into the genealogy of the Chinese nation and defines this people according to those terms."⁵¹ In his "Report on a Survey of the Miao in Western Hunan," which was based on fieldwork from 1933, Ling Chun-sheng was responding to Torii Ryūzō's surveys of the Miao, and his discussions of their origins, distribution, names, and historical changes all hinted at his views about the shared origins of the Miao and Han peoples.[52] Ling's assistant, a Miao named Shi Qigui, went even further. His "Report on Field Surveys of the Miao of Western Hunan" used evidence from history, geography, crafts and production techniques, song, and language to fill in the gaps in work done by Ling Chunsheng and others. His arguments about similarities between the Miao and Han in terms of language, ethnic origins, names, and customs lent additional support to the argument that the Miao and Han had shared origins.[53] To a certain degree, these conclusions drawn by Han and Miao scholars served to bring the Miao peoples of the southwest into the whole of the Chinese nation. Tao Yunda's essay, "On the Distribution and Dispersal of Names of the Mexie People," which was based on fieldwork Tao conducted among the Mexie people of Yunnan, argued that, in the area around Lijiang:

> From the beginning of the Tang dynasty through the end of the Song dynasty, it was the tribal peoples of Yunnan who were the real holders of political power. Official positions created by Han people existed in name only, while business was conducted as if the area were a vassal state [and not fully a part of the empire]. When the founders of the Yuan dynasty subdued Yunnan, the clans' power was gradually wiped out. The Yuan did the most to open up and develop Yunnan. Without their tremendous energy, it is open to question whether Yunnan would be a part of China today.

To phrase Tao's conclusions another way, it was from the Yuan dynasty on that the power of local clans was swept away, which led to the inclusion of these border peoples into China.[54] Here we see anthropologists demonstrating their independent sensibility as Chinese scholars as they criticize ideas put forward by Western and Japanese scholars. At the same time, we also see them demonstrate a national perspective that "brings the Four Barbarians into China" and proves the existence of "the great family of the Chinese nation."

It may be the case that although the field of archaeology made great achievements with regard to projects such as Peking Man, Longshan culture, and the ruins at Anyang, these projects still only contributed to understanding the core regions of Yin and Zhou culture. It is also the case, however, that many historians, archaeologists, and anthropologists made even stronger efforts in the border regions outside of China proper to look for cultural remnants and relics that would demonstrate that this "China" of today may have previously been divided into different cultural systems that influenced one another and eventually merged with one another. In his afterword to *Newly Discovered Divination Texts* (*Xin huo buci xieben hou*), Fu Sinian made an interesting comment when discussing the ancient peoples of Jing and Chu. According to Fu, the early peoples of the ancient southern state of Chu

> were originally divided into many ethnic groups, depending on where they lived and their degree of civilization. The early descendants of the ancestors of the peoples of Jing and Chu may have [as a result of wars] become slaves [of the victors], with many remaining as slaves, and a few fleeing to distant places. The eventual prosperity of the state of Chu can probably be credited to the descendants of the ancestors of Jing and Chu who were there at the time, and not the work of those descendants of the ancestors of the peoples of Jing and Chu who had fled their captors [from the central plains]. This is much the same as the way that both incursions by the Jurchens into China were the result of the revival of local national groups, and were not led by Jurchens who had returned from China.[55]

Li Chi also made an equally interesting comment: he argued that scholars of ancient China should "demolish the view that Chinese culture is sealed within the Great Wall and use our eyes and legs to go north of the Great Wall to find materials on the history of ancient China, because an even older 'old home' of ours is there."[56] Li paid even greater attention to the links between the Chinese culture and race and the peripheral regions. In an essay titled "The Work and Challenges of Rebuilding the History of Ancient China," he argued that Chinese culture was not a world unto itself, and that its origins could be found "from the Black Sea, through the grasslands of Central Asia, to Dzungaria in Xinjiang, to the Gobi Desert in Mongolia, all the way to Manchuria."[57] Another young scholar, Liang Siyong, who had just returned from America to join Li Chi's archaeology team (and who was encouraged by his famous father, Liang Qichao), worked both to refute Western scholars' arguments about the non-Chinese origins of the Chinese race and culture and to refute Japanese scholars' arguments that "China" was limited only to the territory of the central plains region. He turned his sights to northeastern China,[58] which not only had been the place where Torii Ryūzō and others had repeatedly undertaken archaeological expeditions but also was the region (that is, Manchuria and Mongolia) that Japan had continuously attempted to say was a territory outside of "China."

We see, then, two important tasks undertaken by Chinese scholarship of the 1920s and 1930s: First, to maintain the local, autochthonous origins of the Chinese race and culture when, competing with Western and Japanese scholarship, they faced the question of who gets to explain China. Second, they addressed the question of how to explain China by gradually developing ways to "include the Four Barbarians within China."

"When the Chinese Nation Faced Its Greatest Crisis": The Changing Mood of Chinese Scholarship during the Japanese Invasions

Previously I mentioned the Mukden Incident of 1931, the establishment of the Manchurian puppet state in 1932, the founding of the Republic of Eastern Turkestan in 1933, and the "North China autonomy movement" of 1935. Prior to the Marco Polo Bridge Incident of 1937, a tremendous sense of emergency had already taken hold in the Chinese scholarly world. If we look closely, it is not hard to see complex changes in the outlook of Chinese scholars of that era. As described by the phrase "national salvation crushing enlightenment" (*jiuwang yadao qimeng*), when faced with the emergency presented by the enemy, Chinese scholars always chose "national salvation," and it was against this backdrop of national salvation that a variety of writings about China's borders and nationalities came into print.[59]

It may help to begin by observing the changes in Liu Yizheng's (1880–1956) thinking through the prefaces that he wrote in honor of the founding of three scholarly journals. Liu Yizheng was a leading scholar who strongly advocated for what he called local perspectives on Chinese culture. The outlines of his thinking, therefore, are a good barometer for the transformation of scholarly ideas and sentiments that took place at that time. In 1921, Liu and some of his friends founded the *Journal of Historical and Geographical Society* (*Shi di xuebao*). In his preface to the inaugural issue, Liu emphasized that the Chinese scholarly world should expand its range of knowledge; he put special emphasis on the need to compete with foreign scholarship. He argued that scholars absolutely could not "look up at the sky from the bottom of a well" and should not blindly follow foreign scholars when it came to issues concerning Chinese history and geography. Otherwise, he argued, "We will be unable both to compete with our contemporaries and to hold on to the knowledge gained by our predecessors."[60] In another foreword, which Liu wrote for the first issue of *History and Geography* (*Shixue yu dixue*) in 1926, he again argued for placing equal emphasis on history and geography, arguing that traditional Chinese learning had suffered from the eight-legged essay and the examination system, from poor instructional materials in schools, and from commercialized publishing, all of which caused Chinese scholars to be overly cautious about foreign learning. This foreword stressed the importance of historical and geographical knowledge while maintaining the local identity of Chinese scholarship as a perspective that could compete with and balance out foreign Orientalist scholarship. In September 1932, however, after the Mukden Incident, in an essay for the inaugural issue of the bimonthly journal *Airs of the States* (*Guo feng banyuekan*), although he maintained a cultured and scholarly outlook, readers easily see the deep influence of the "national salvation movement" and a larger sense of crisis. Liu Yizheng used the word *wuhu* (alas!), an interjection that, in classical Chinese, expresses sadness or pain. He worried that China was about to suffer the same fate as the Song and Ming dynasties, or perhaps a fate even worse than that of the Song and the Ming. Liu raised a cry of warning not to "surrender our cultural relics and follow the barbarians," and called for scholarship to "put the nation above the individual" in this extraordinary time.[61]

"In the spirit tower is no plan to elude divine arrows."[62] Scholars in southeast China felt this way, as did scholars who formed the mainstream

of Chinese scholarship. Many scholars of history and literature transformed in the face of a massive national emergency. One of the central
figures in Chinese scholarship of that time, Gu Jiegang, did not originally believe that "the eighteen provinces where the Han people live
have been as unified as they are now since ancient times." "To do so," he
argued, "would be to apply the perspective that arose after the Qin and
Han dynasties to understand [Chinese] domains from before the Qin
and Han." He repeatedly stressed that arguments about "continuous
unity" were "absurd understandings of history."[63] Just a few years later,
however, he took a new view of the story of Chinese history, going from
an argument that China did not have a continuous unity to an emphasis
on the legitimacy of China's borders. After the publication of *Yu Gong
Bimonthly* began in 1936, Gu Jiegang, Shi Nianhai, and others published *A History of the Transformation of China's Territories* (*Zhongguo
jiangyu yange shi*); Gu argued in the first chapter, "In ancient times, the
Han people lived in the central plains, while foreign peoples lay in wait
all around them. The ancients spilled their heart's blood, spent all their
energy, and worked tirelessly to reach the present situation [that is,
modern China]." In his discussion of "glorious ancient times" (*huang
gu*) he argued, "As for the drawing of borders, it seems that in ancient
times were already traces to be found. From the time of *The Tribute of
Yu* on, there were what were called the Nine Provinces, the Twelve Provinces, and the Greater Nine Provinces (*Da jiu zhou*). Each was prominent in its own time and could represent the ancients' ideals concerning
the system of borders." It is clear that these ideas are quite different from
the image put forward by the leaders of "debating antiquity" scholarship
in the 1920s. Gu Jiegang uses the term *huang gu* (glorious ancient times),
which subtly links to arguments about "glorious Han emperors of antiquity" (*huang Han*) made by Zhang Taiyan and others and implies a certain Han nationalism. Gu Jiegang also emphasized "the difficulty with
which ancient people expanded their territory," thus including arguments made by Liang Qichao and others about "Five Nations under One
Republic."[64] Gu seems to have abandoned the arguments from his "debating antiquity" perspective that the ancient Chinese did not descend
from a single lineage and that the territory of China was not historically
unitary. By this point, he had turned toward "bringing the Four Barbarians

into China" and was working to show that there was one "China" and one "Chinese people."

Owing to space limitations, we cannot discuss all of the details of the transformation of the Chinese intellectual sphere. One aspect deserves attention, however. From 1930 on, public opinion in China was sensitive to Japan's interest in Manchuria. In addition to scholarly works such as "Looking at the Dawn of East Asia from the Standpoint of Archaeology" (1931) by Hamada Kōsaku (1881–1938) and "Researches on the Ancient Peoples of China" (1931) by Ogawa Takuji (1870–1941), many other writings from Japan about Manchuria drew the interest of Chinese scholars. In the political realm, discussions about the establishment of a separate Manchurian state or Mongolian independence, as well as works such as "The Japanese Colonization of Manchuria and Mongolia" (1932) by Sō Mitsuhiko, provoked even greater outrage. This mood had a strong effect on the world of scholarship, as in the following episode involving Gu Jiegang, the most important modern-style historian of the first half of the twentieth century and promoter of the "debating antiquity" (*gu shi bian*) movement. Gu, who upheld the use of scientific methods in the study of ancient China and took a skeptical approach toward ancient documents and origin myths in Chinese history, certainly would not have agreed with the idea that the history of ancient "China" was homogenous and unified. In 1933, however, the Japanese met with the nobility of Inner Mongolia and encouraged the Mongolians to split from China in favor of independence. At this time, Tan Muyu, a female scholar Gu Jiegang had always admired, personally went to Mongolia to survey the situation, after which she delivered a series of lectures at Yenching University in December of 1933 on the theme "Experiences at the Bailingmiao Conference and Impressions of Inner Mongolia," exposing Japan's role in the movement for Inner Mongolia's independence. Gu Jiegang's diary makes note of the lecture over many days, and says that, after hearing her speak, Gu "began to take an interest in researching questions of borders and territory." It's very clear that Ms. Tan's research and lectures had an influence on the transformation in Gu Jiegang's thinking, and may have led him to work with Tan Qixiang the next year to found the famous scholarly magazine, *Yu Gong Bimonthly*, a publication that argued for the historical continuity and unity of ancient China and modern China.[65]

"The Chinese People Are One": From a 1939
Debate in *Social Welfare* to Chiang Kai-shek's
Theory of the Chinese People in *China's Destiny*

In 1937, violence finally broke out during the Marco Polo Bridge Incident, which was quickly followed by the capture of Beiping (Beijing). The Japanese armies continued southward in their invasion, routing the Chinese forces repeatedly. The capital eventually had to be moved south away from Nanjing, and the provinces of Sichuan, Yunnan, Guizhou, and Guangxi became the last base of power for the government of the Republic of China. Research institutes, colleges, and scholars also moved to the southeast. Places that had once been the margin of China became the center, and borderlands that had not been the focus of attention became an important topic of discussion for scholars.

One symbolic event is found in an inaugural essay that Gu Jiegang wrote in December 1938 for the "Borderlands Weekly" (*Bianjiang zhoukan*) supplement, which he had created for the newspaper *Social Welfare* (*Yi shi bao*). He exhorted readers to remember "the history of the nation and the history of the borderlands" as a way to "resist invasion from wildly ambitious countries."[66] Shortly after this essay, on January 1, 1939, Gu Jiegang published another essay in the year's first edition of *Social Welfare*, which he titled "We Need to Dispense with the Phrase 'China Proper'" (*"Zhongguo benbu" yiming ji ying fangqi*). Gu argued that the phrase "China proper" "was fabricated by the Japanese to distort history and provide justification to seize our country's territory." In February he published another piece titled "The Chinese Nation Is One" (*Zhonghua minzu shi yige*), which stated categorically that "all Chinese people are part of the Chinese nation" and declared solemnly that from that day forward no national group—the Han, Manchu, Mongolian, Uighur, Tibetan, or Miao—should be seen as outside the Chinese nation. This essay, which appeared on February 13, drew a strong response from the intellectual sphere. It not only was reprinted in many other newspapers but also received replies in print from scholars such as Zhang Weihua, Bai Shouyi (1909–2000), and Ma Yi.[67] Even in a time of national crisis, Fu Sinian, who was not on the best terms Gu Jiegang, wrote to Gu to plead with him not to speak so casually about "volatile words like the nation and territory" and not to publish the "Borderlands Weekly" supplement in *Social Welfare*. Fu Sinian did, however, praise Gu Jiegang's argument that "the Chinese nation is one." He wrote that Gu Jiegang's "original approach was excellent, and was the only possible position to take now in relation to the national question." In a letter to Zhu Jiahua and Hang Liwu, Fu Sinian bitterly criticized some ethnologists for following the tenets of imperialist science: "In places where assimilation is occurring, this group of scholars arrives and uses these ideas to attack assimilation and push for breaking up the nation (*guozu*)."[68]

According to Gu Jiegang, Fu Sinian objected to "Borderlands Weekly" because he believed that it "published too many writings that analyzed the various nationalities that were part of the Chinese nation, which might cause catastrophic divisions within the nation." In fact, Gu Jiegang had written "The Chinese Nation Is One" to allay the concerns of Fu Sinian and other scholars.[69] Those "ethnologists" Fu Sinian mentioned largely referred to Wu Wenzao and Fei Xiaotong. After receiving their academic training abroad, Wu Wenzao and Fei Xiaotong returned to China. It is said that they drew the opprobrium of Fu Sinian, Gu Jiegang, and others because they were still working to distinguish between different national or ethnic groups during the Second Sino-Japanese War and even accepted the definition of "China proper" as the traditionally recognized eighteen provinces of China within the Great Wall.

Looking back today with a less partisan perspective, it would seem that the ideas of anthropologists and ethnologists like Wu Wenzao and Fei Xiaotong were simply the work of specialized ethnologists who accepted Western definitions of national groups (*minzu*) and wanted to undertake the classification of different national groups in China on the basis of such characteristics as body constitution, language, and culture. These ethnologists' understanding of the nation and the state were clearly different from how the historians described in this chapter understood the same questions. For example, in his response to Gu Jiegang's essays, Fei Xiaotong argued that the nation and the state were not one and the same. Fei argued that the state, as established in the political sense, largely worked to guarantee equality for all people, but state identity could not wipe out the differences between different national groups that existed on the basis of characteristics such as body constitution, language, and culture. Within one China, then, differences could still exist between Manchu, Han, Mongolian, Uighur, Tibetan, and Miao groups.[70] It probably did not occur to Fei Xiaotong, however, that historians would see the classification of different nationalities as "promoting the breakup of the nation." He probably also did not understand mainstream thinking in the scholarly world about the state, the nation, and its territory during the Second Sino-Japanese War. After a couple of rounds in this debate, then, Fei Xiaotong fell silent. As Fei remembered many years later:

> Later I understood that Mr. Gu [Jiegang] was filled with patriotic concern and deeply enraged that Japanese imperialism had managed to establish [an independent] "Manchuria" (*Manchukuo*) and was promoting efforts to break Mongolia away from China. For these reasons, he strongly opposed actions that used ideas about "national groups" to break apart China. I completely supported his political position. Nonetheless, I did not agree with his argument that acknowledging that the Manchus and Mongolians were [distinct] national groups amounted to binding oneself hand and foot or to giving the enemy a reason to act, or that this question had become a factor in the way imperialist forces had split apart our country. Moreover, he believed that if one did not recognize these different national groups, then one could avoid inviting the wolf into the house. [I believed that] the excuse [for imperialism] was not the cause, and setting aside what had been used as an excuse would not prevent the same people from taking violent action. These politically charged debates were of no benefit at the time, however, so I did not continue to debate the matter in print.[71]

Fei Xiaotong's silence captures the way that, during the Second Sino-Japanese War, the Chinese scholarly world had already reached a consensus to set aside "Five Nations under One Republic" (*Wu zu gonghe*) in favor of "the Chinese nation" (*Zhonghua minzu*). We also see that the debates in scholarly circles and pressure from public opinion influenced political parties and the government. From this time on, we see not only the Republican government establishing a variety of committees on southwest China but also both the Nationalist and Communist Parties beginning to offer ideas and opinions related to the Miao and Yi peoples of the southwest. Even the Committee on Historical and Geographical Education (Shi di jiaoyu weiyuanhui) and the Committee on Border Education (Bianjiang jiaoyu weiyuanhui) in the Republican government's Ministry of Education took a role in ensuring that educational materials had a "national perspective" and a clear "historical narrative." These ideas won unanimous praise from the political and scholarly worlds. Fu Sinian called for "bringing together the Three People's Principles, Chinese history and geography, the history and geography of border regions, and the relationship between China and neighboring states into a clear and simple text that would be translated into the languages of various groups," including Tibeto-Burman languages, the Shan language, the Miao and Yao languages, Vietnamese, and Puxian Min.[72] Gu Jiegang and Ma Yi also advocated rewriting history textbooks and educational materials to "make a new historical context" and "critique the fragmentation and destruction of scholarship that has occurred since the late Qing due to imperialist pollution."[73]

Coda: "Large and Small Branches of the Same Bloodline": Establishing Greater China

At the time "when the Chinese nation faced its greatest crisis," mainstream scholarship returned completely to Liang Qichao's use of culture to define the nation and set the limits of the national question. These ideas can be summarized as follows: First, the Chinese nation (*Zhonghua minzu*) includes the Han and was formed over time through the amalgamation of different national groups. Second, national groups such as the Han, Manchu, Mongolian, Uighur, and Miao are all part of the Chinese nation. Third, "nation" is not "race"; the primary meaning of nation is defined in terms of culture, not bloodlines or physical constitution. Fourth, China is a nation-state called *Zhonghua,* and in times of emergency it must support its people uniting because they all "grew from the same roots." During these years, Chiang Kai-shek's *China's Destiny,* published in 1942, became the most important voice on these matters. This document, which Chiang drafted himself and was edited by Tao Xisheng (1899–1988), begins with a chapter titled "Growth and Development of the Chinese

Nation," in which Chiang called the various ethnic groups within China's borders "large and small branches of the same bloodline." Chiang was keen to point out that China's history could be traced back three thousand years, and that its territories included the Yellow River, the Yangtze River, the Amur River (Ch. Heilongjiang), and the Pearl River, and that the peoples within China included the Khitan, Jurchen, Mongolian, and Manchu, and they had all been assimilated into the Chinese nation, "blended into one body, without the slightest trace of any difference between them." He also said: "According to its historical development, our Chinese nation was formed by the blending of numerous clans."[74]

For people who were in the scholarly world at that time, which was filled with deep feelings about the nation and strong consciousness of the importance of the state, Chiang's words undoubtedly worked to put the strategy of "bringing the Four Barbarians into China" into practice. Although there may have been some noises of disagreement in the background, these ideas became the key in which all songs were sung in this era of crisis.[75]

❧ 4 ❧

HISTORY

Chinese Culture from a Long-Term Perspective

Why Discuss the Plurality of Chinese Culture?

A few years ago, when I was taking part in a scholarly forum, I argued that Chinese cultural tradition is plural, not singular. At the time, I merely wanted to show a sense of caution about the fact that, as China expanded, trends would rise that would push people toward returning to tradition, promoting national learning (*guoxue*), and singing the praises of patriotism. The doubt that I had at that time was that the national learning that people were discussing might narrow into the study of the Han nation, or that tradition would serve to narrow Han Chinese culture into one form of Confucian learning or another. Might this trend in reviving Chinese culture result in a dangerous and extreme new direction? If this were to happen, it could very easily combine with social fashions that have emerged in China, such as wearing traditional Han clothing, sacrificing to the Flame Emperor and Nüwa, venerating Confucius, and reading the classics in a way that would operate under the discourse of cultural self-awareness to turn respect for traditional culture and an emphasis on identity into a way to promote cultural nationalism and even statism. For these reasons, on many different occasions I have argued that the plural nature of Chinese culture is also the complexity, tolerance, and openness of Chinese culture.

As time passed, I continued to hold this view. In this chapter, however, I am more interested in discussing why the Chinese cultural tradition is plural, and will do so from the historical perspective that takes into account the processes of how, over thousands of years, Chinese culture grew layer by layer and gradually solidified. By reviewing the roughly hundred years that have elapsed since the late Qing and early Republican periods, during which time China faced many moments of continuity and discontinuity with the past, I demonstrate the plurality of the Chinese cultural tradition and show why today it is necessary to maintain an open attitude and accept various aspects of foreign cultures as new layers of Chinese culture.

Exactly What Is "China's" Culture?

Let us begin with this question: What counts as China's culture?

Over the past few years I have criticized on many occasions some of the methods that are used for describing and narrating Chinese culture, because books and articles that study Chinese culture often use an overview (or macro) model, looking from the top down to provide a vague introduction to so-called Chinese culture. In my view, it is important to be clear about what is meant by "Chinese culture." Even the word "Chinese" is important, because "culture" is something that all nations have. If you could explain clearly that this culture is something that China has (or is prominent there), and other countries do not have this (or it is not prominent there), or you can describe what the Chinese world has (or is prominent there), and what other nations do not have (or it is not prominent there), only then have you arrived at the relatively "typical" version of Chinese culture; you cannot include those atypical things in your definition of Chinese culture.[1]

What, then, are those aspects of culture that quintessentially belong to "China"? Here I focus my discussion on Han Chinese culture, because it must be conceded that since ancient times Han culture has served as the mainstream and core of Chinese culture. I see five key facets of Han Chinese culture.

First: the use of Chinese characters (*Han zi*) to read and write, as well as the ways of thinking that are derived from Chinese characters. Ancient legends tell of the creation of Chinese characters by Cang Jie, whose invention was said to be so remarkable that it caused grain to fall from the sky and the ghosts to howl in the night. Although this story comes from myth, it also shows the significance of Chinese characters in the formation of Chinese culture. Chinese characters, which are originally based on ideographs, have indeed had a massive influence on Han Chinese people's modes of thought and expression, and continue to be used down to the present day (while, for the most part, other cultures no longer use forms of writing that could be traced back to ideographs).[2] This influence has not been limited to Chinese culture but has also made its presence felt among neighboring areas that are known as the cultural sphere of the Chinese script (*Hanzi wenhuaquan*).

Second: the structure of family, clan, and state in ancient China. This traditional rural order, beliefs about family morality, and state order all served as the basis for Confucian teachings, including the entire set of political arrangements related to the state, society, and the individual (which were different from the culture that developed out of the Greek and Roman system of city-states),[3] as well as ideas derived from these political arrangements that were related to self-cultivation and governance of the state.[4] All of the preceding ideas and structures shaped the traditions of daily life and political life in ancient China.[5]

Third: the belief system of "three teachings in one." In traditional China, "Buddhism was used to cultivate the mind, Taoism was used to extend life, and Confucianism was used to govern the world."[6] Confucianism, Taoism, and Buddhism existed side by side, supplementing one another, and no single religion could lay claim to status as the absolute or sole religion. For these reasons, too, no religion could supersede the secular power and authority of the emperor, and thus religions accommodated one another while remaining under a dominant political power. Because of the absolute authority of the emperor, China did not have religions that attempted to claim a sphere of their own that was separate from imperial power.[7] As a result, Buddhism and Taoism, and later on Catholicism, Protestantism, and Islam, all had to submit at some point to mainstream ideology and morality and allow for changes in the essence of their religious beliefs and their positions in society,[8] assisting society within the limits proscribed by imperial power. Of course, these arrangements led many believers to take a perspective on religion that was not particularly clear or fixed in one place, resulting in practical admixtures of different religious beliefs. Although religion did not have the absolute power that could be granted by faith, there were very few wars between religions in China—a phenomenon that was quite rare in other regions and countries around the world.[9]

Fourth: understandings of and interpretations of ideas about "the unity of Heaven and man" (*Tian ren he yi*) in the universe, the study of Yin and Yang and the Five Elements, as well as the knowledge, ideas, and technologies that were developed on the basis of these scholarly practices.[10] The origins of this type of scholarship is found early in history,[11] and its influence on later eras reached Chinese medicine, feng shui, building and construction,[12] and even politics and aesthetics.[13]

And, finally: the unique idea that formed in ancient China of All-under-Heaven, which was influenced by the cosmology of "round Heaven and square Earth," as well as the way of looking at the world that developed out of this idea of All-under-Heaven. From this imagination of All-under-Heaven, ancient China saw the development of an international order based on the tribute system.

If we take these five aspects of Chinese culture and hold them up in comparison to Christian civilization, or with the Islamic world, or even with the regions of East Asia and South Asia (which also follow Buddhism and use Confucian principles), then we see that these five characteristics can only be considered "China's" "culture." I continue to hope, therefore, that people will not use sprawling concepts cast in empty, universal language to arrive at abstract and overly broad definitions of Chinese culture. (Some examples of this tendency include emphasizing the Doctrine of the Mean, placing stress on ethics, or a strong emphasis on the family, and so on.) It is more important to point out that these cultural origins are complex and simply cannot be contained under the rubrics of Confucianism, neo-Confucianism, the Five Classics, or classical learning, just as they cannot be covered thoroughly by current practices of so-called national learning.

What, Then, Is "China"?
The Long History of China's Formation

The question not been resolved, however, because "China" is a concept that still must be defined. Although the cultural phenomena that I sketched out above can be found throughout several thousand years of Chinese history and always occupied the position of the mainstream, they still are only part of Han national culture. If we recognize that "China" is not just Han national culture, then the "Chinese" cultural traditions described above still cannot be equated simply with Chinese culture.

More and more historical evidence shows that, since ancient times, each dynasty (or China) had either close or distant relationships of exchange with cultures outside the dynasty (or foreign cultures). Even in the period of early antiquity, which previously had been considered to be relatively closed off from outside influences, there was a substantial overlap between the land of what is now China and surrounding cultures, peoples, religions, and material goods. It is not necessarily the case that the bloodlines of each of the Three Dynasties of Antiquity were as pure as they were described in ancient histories and stories, which spoke of "the progeny of the Yellow Emperor."[14] For example, can we really say that the Shang dynasty was made up of Han people (*Hanzu*) or Huaxia people (*Huaxia zu*)? Fu Sinian did not believe it to be the case. He argued instead that the people of the Yin dynasty were "foreigners," and that the dynasty established by the Yin and Shang was an amalgamation resulting from a conflict between Eastern Barbarians (*Dong Yi*) and the Xixia, and even was the product of "barbarians defeating the Xia."[15] Fu Sinian also reminded us that the regions of Qi and Lu, which had been thought to be the historical headwaters of Chinese culture, were in fact a center of foreign territory.[16] Other scholars have argued that the sources of Yin and Shang culture "had relatively strong connections to what later became known as Tungusic culture."[17]

Even if these arguments are just conjecture, the overlap between cultures at that time was quite common. Important evidence comes from the Yin-dynasty ruins at Anyang in Henan Province, a site that has been the subject of extensive research. Li Chi argued in 1932 in an essay on the Yin ruins that although it had previously been believed that a direct line of succession linked the Xia, Shang, and Zhou dynasties, and that the Yin ruins were purely a part of ancient Chinese culture, it was actually quite diverse. Scapulimancy, plastromancy, sericulture, tattooing, black pottery, and jade *cong* came from the east, while bronze making, hollow-head adzes, and spears came from Central Asia and West Asia. Rice, elephants, buffalo, and tin came from South Asia.[18] Even if the rites and music of Hua-Xia (that is, Chinese) had reached a point of relative maturity by the Zhou dynasty, foreigners from all areas continued to come to China; peoples such as the Yue people, who were said to cut their hair and tattoo their bodies, and the people of Chu, who were said to believe in witches and ghosts and partake in strange rites, gradually came within the cultural sphere of the Zhou dynasty.[19] Although "rites and music" (*li yue*) became an important symbol of the cultural community of the Zhou dynasty, the peoples of regions under control of the Zhou dynasty—in Zhao, Wei, and Han in the north, the Qi and Lu in the east, the Jing and Chu in the south, the Rong and Qin in the west, and Zheng and Wei in the central plains—all developed their own individual cultures.[20] It was under the restraints provided by the system of enfeoffment and feudal lords that they developed together into a complex, diverse, and loosely bounded Zhou civilization. In my opinion, those versions of "Zhou-dynasty culture" that are completely unified, with clear political order, and clear borders are more often than not the product of later people's reminiscences and imaginations, much like those who argue that the rites of the Zhou dynasty were created by the Duke of Zhou himself. In fact, what we can generally call the core of Zhou-dynasty culture was largely the product of two overlapping traditions: the tradition of rites and music and the shamanic tradition.

From today's perspective, before the Warring States period (and Confucius), people's ideas about so-called culture and tradition were not self-conscious, but, rather, unrestrained. It seems that the harmonious relations of these earliest times had room for many differences in physical features among people. It is for precisely this reason that the era in which some lamented that "the rites had fallen into disorder and music had been ruined" also became an era of cultural enlightenment, one whose arrival resulted in the rise of distinctions between various schools of thinkers, leading to a situation where "the various schools held to several ways, and could not come back to the same point, nor agree together."[21] Thinkers such as Confucius, Mozi, and Laozi, and the Confucian, Mohist, and Taoist orientations that emerged from them, along with the knowledge, faiths, and customs that were in conflict, were all the product of this era of diversity and division. As Ying-shih Yü has argued, it was this time when "the system of the Tao was about to be torn apart all under the sky"[22] that proved to be the "central era" of Chinese thought, one that provided endless resources for the intellectual thought and cultures of subsequent eras.[23]

For these reasons, the "Middle Kingdom" (*Zhongguo*) that was inherited and expanded by the unified dynasties of the Qin and Han was originally a mixed space that intermingled a wide variety of races, ideas, cultures, and regions.[24] The national identity, state ideology, and cultural orientation of Han "China," however, first took shape out of these mixed elements during the period of unification under the Qin and Han. The intellectual openness of the *Lü Commentary to the Spring and Autumn Annals* and the *Huainanzi*, which were credited with including aspects of "Hundred Schools" thought and ideas, and the intellectual ordering that was undertaken by the *Luxuriant Dew of the Spring and Autumn Annals* (*Chunqiu fan lu*) and the *Virtuous Discussions Held in the White Tiger Hall* (*Bai hu tong*), which were credited with dismissing the "ways of kings and hegemons" advocated by the Hundred Schools, all contributed to the formation of a "Chinese" cultural world. In them, we see "Chinese" cultural identity begin to emerge. This emergence was also spurred by pressure from the "Xiongnu," the "western regions" (*Xi yu*), and the "southern and eastern barbarians."[25]

We should recognize that because under the Qin dynasty "all weights and measures were standardized, the gauge of wheeled vehicles was made uniform, and the writing system was standardized,"[26] and the Han dynasty "dismissed the hundred schools and embraced only Confucian ways"[27] that the "China" that was centered around the core regions of the Nine Provinces began to appear, and a Han nationality that took the "Hua-Xia" as its core began to form. At the same time, a "Hua-Xia" (Chinese) culture began to take shape, one that took the idea of All-under-Heaven as its central ideology, that subscribed to ideas about Yin and Yang and the Five Elements, that engaged in politics based on a mixture of political ideas (especially Confucian and Legalist), that was accustomed to writing in Chinese characters, and that possessed its own religious and ethical order. As Sima Qian described it in the "Basic Annals of the First Emperor of Qin" of the *Records of the Grand Historian*, the "Middle Kingdom" of that time "extended east to the sea and to Chaoxian [Korea], west to Lintao and Qiangzhong, and south to Beihu. In the north fortresses were established along the Yellow River and then over the Yin Mountains to Liaodong."[28] It is also as Sima Qian remarked in the "Biographies of the Money Makers" (*Huo zhi lie zhuan*): "the Han rose to power and prominence." This self-description of China provides evidence of how Chinese people in ancient times defined the Middle Kingdom. By the time of Sima Qian, China extended west to Guanzhong, Bashu, and Tianshui; to the south, Panyu (in Guangdong) and Dan'er; to the north, the Longmen and Jieshi, the Liaodong Peninsula, the Yan region, and Zhuozhou; to the east, Mount Tai, the Bohai Sea, Jiangsu, and Zhejiang. These places already made up the "domains" of the "Middle Kingdom" and showed its initial formation.[29]

The Former and Latter Han dynasties, which stretched across over four centuries, seem to have established the cultural world of "China." Despite this, however, contacts between China and the cultures on this periphery did not come to an end. In fact, from the time of the Qin and Han dynasties to the Wei-Jin period, and then again down to the Sui and Tang dynasties, convergence and contact became even more prominent. This was especially true especially during the Sui and Tang period, an important time when foreign cultures recast Chinese culture. Allow me to provide a very rough outline of this history.

First, in terms of nationalities, during the Qin and Han periods, China had a great number of contacts and interactions with the thirty-six states of the western frontiers, with the Xiongnu in the north, and with the Baiyue in the south. The period of the Northern and Southern dynasties saw extensive contacts with the Xianbei and the Xiang. Intermixing between these racial groups was a common occurrence.[30] It was so common that, by the Western Jin dynasty, Jiang Tong, a Han man of letters, wrote "Discourse on Moving the Rong" to warn people against such intermingling.[31] In fact, this intermixing happened not only among the Hu and

Han peoples to the north but also in the south. Tan Qixiang once pointed out that, in both the north and the south, the peoples of the middle ages were the result of a mixture of many bloodlines of different nationalities. Han people in modern-day Hunan, for example, descend in part from the "Southern barbarians" (*Nan man*) of the middle ages.[32] The Sui and Tang dynasties witnessed the rise of the Jurchens, the Turfans, and the Huihe, as well as migrations by people from Persia and India, and the common presence of the Sogdians and Shatuo people. China, then, had already become a cultural community where Han and non-Han were mingled together. Foreigners did not necessarily see themselves as foreign, while the Han people did not necessarily see themselves as being absolutely superior to others.[33] Even the eldest son of the Emperor Taizong of Tang (r. 626–649) was particularly fond of "foreign styles" (*Hu feng*), with a passion for the Jurchens' language and customs.[34] In the core regions of China, many foreigners also rose to the highest ranks. Two examples can briefly illustrate this phenomenon. First, the members of the Gautama family from India served for several generations as high-level officials in the Tang dynasty who were engaged in technological questions.[35] Second, the rulers of the Sassanian dynasty in Persia, as well as their elites and religious figures, we able to become subjects of the Tang and even residents of the capital, Chang'an.[36] Many people of foreign nationalities or from other countries were blended into China, not only becoming Chinese people (*Zhongguo ren*) but also becoming people of the metropolitan capital.[37] It is because the bloodlines of people from distant places were blended with the Han nation that scholars such as Chen Yinke would argue that the prosperity of the height of the Tang dynasty came from "bringing in wild and vigorous blood from north of the into the decadent body of the central plains. The old diseases were driven out and new possibilities arose and unfolded, resulting in an unprecedented era."[38]

Second, in terms of the flow goods and objects, we learn from works such as Edward H. Schafer's *The Golden Peaches of Samarkand* (which is translated in Chinese under the title *Foreign Civilizations of the Tang Dynasty*) and Berthold Laufer's renowned *Sino-Iranica*[39] that, in the middle ages, all variety of goods made their way to China, including not just curios, medicines, perfumes, grapes, Amboyna wood, lotuses, and the like, but also *baixi* (the "hundred entertainments," which included music, dancing, acrobatics, and so on), foreign dances, clothing, peppers and spices, and so on. All told, these good created an atmosphere in which, according to Yuan Zhen (779–831), "Foreign music, foreign soldiers, and foreign clothes have been everywhere for fifty years."[40] This point requires no further elaboration.

Third, in terms of religion, we have Buddhism from India and the western frontier, local religions that arose within China, and Zoroastrianism, Nestorianism, and Manichaeism, which came from lands even further away; all of these were incorporated into China. Whether on the western frontier, in Dunhuang, or in Chang'an, various religions came into conflict with one another and also blended with one another. To what extent did various cultures blend in with one another or come into conflict with one another? Here we might look to one example, *The Record of the Dharma-Jewel through the Generations (Lidai fabao ji)*, a historical document on Chan Buddhism that was completed somewhere around Chengdu in the middle of the eighth century. The book records stories about the conflicts between Buddhism, Manichaeism, and Nestorianism, and shows that in Jibin (modern-day Xinjiang) conflicts arose between religions originating from South Asia, West Asia, and even Europe, and that these stories of conflict had not only made their way to the interior regions of China but had also stimulated the development of religious beliefs there.[41] What is more important, however, is that the many religions that made their way to China caused a crisis in traditional Confucian thought, and new ideas and culture gradually emerged from this sense of crisis and from attempts to resist foreign religions.[42]

In recent years, then, more and more scholars have spoken out against earlier historical accounts that described China as closed, inward-looking, and conservative. They have also weighed in against the idea that early modern China was forced to "respond" to Western "stimulus," arguing instead for an account that emphasizes China's long-standing openness across history. The year 2000 saw the publication of two notable books: first, the American scholar Valerie Hansen's *The Open Empire,* which argued through an examination of China in the Middle Ages that premodern China was a vibrant, vital, outward-oriented empire.[43] Second, in *The Sextants of Being,* a book on early modern China, the American scholar Joanna Waley-Cohen also discussed the early global orientation in China, refuting arguments about a closed, inward-looking China with historical evidence from politics, religion, and trade.[44]

The Mixed, Multilayered State of Chinese Culture: The Song-Dynasty Transition

I have previously written about the emergence of a "China sensibility" in the Song dynasty and argued that the open attitudes toward race, culture, and religion that originally were found in ancient China (all of which overlapped with one another) underwent an important transformation during the Song dynasty. Han Chinese culture, which had been overlaid with many aspects of foreign cultures in the Middle Ages, was reconstructed, reordered, and stabilized once again, forming the Chinese cultural tradition that carries influence down to the present day. This tradition, of course, is both old and new.[45]

I noted earlier that, in the middle of the eighth century, non-Han national groups such as Turkic peoples, Persians, Sogdians, Huihe, Turfan, and Shatuo peoples arrived in great numbers because of wars in other places. Down through the middle of the tenth century (the Five Dynasties and Ten Kingdoms period), many different foreign groups made their way into central China. These migrations resulted in both ethnic and religious problems and presented a substantial threat to the Han civilization of central China. Although the Song began as a unified state, the non-Han political powers to the north, which included the Liao (Khitan), the Xia (Tangut), the Jin (Jurchen) and, later on, Mongolia, all posed a serious threat to Han political power. As the Japanese scholar Nishijima Sadao said:

> Although a unified state appeared during the Song dynasty, the Sixteen Prefectures of Yan and Yun (which includes modern-day Beijing) were occupied by the Khitans, the Xixia established a state in the northwest and fought with the Song, and both the Khitans and Xixia had parity with the Song in referring to their respective "emperors" (*Huangdi*). Moreover, the Song court made annual payments

to the Liao (Khitan) and was constantly at a state of war with the
Xixia. This state of international relations in East Asia, then, was
quite different from the situation of the Tang dynasty, which ruled
All-under-Heaven and bestowed the status tributary states on the
countries that surrounded it. From this [that is, the Song] period onward, then, East Asia began to reject the idea that Chinese dynasties
were at the center of the international order.[46]

When the self-centered ideology of All-under-Heaven suffered a set-
back, a self-centered nationalism arose. This development revealed a
sharp contrast between the real world and the world of ideas: as the status
and power of the nation and state were diminished, the self-consciousness
of the nation and state grew ever stronger.[47]

This situation led to one of the great transformations in the history of
Chinese culture: the rise of all-out efforts to protect and, eventually, to
promote forcibly the spread of Han culture. During this era, the high level
of suspicion toward the cultures of other national groups played a role in
the formation of ideas about the "proper way of handling state affairs"
(*guo shi*), or the overall intellectual and cultural consensus. As "China"
was surrounded by "foreign" countries, it asserted its possession of its
own space and delineated finite borders, thereby gradually forming, in
cultural terms, a "country" or "state" (*guojia*). Han culture, coming under
pressure from foreign cultures, no longer resembled the Tang dynasty
or the dynasties that came before it, and no longer could freely open its
territories and absorb great numbers of foreign peoples. Instead, China
worked to establish its own unique traditions and clear territorial
boundaries.[48]

These intellectual trends, which were focused on restoring the power
of Han-ethnic dynasties and defending Han Chinese cultural traditions,
arose during the middle of the Tang dynasty. Beginning with Han Yu
(768–824), a trend that we might call "glorifying the throne and casting
out barbarians" in the fields of politics and culture appeared among groups
of educated elites who were beset by a deep sense of emergency. Chen
Yinke has discussed five major areas of significance in Han Yu's work:
the establishment of a Confucian orthodoxy (*daotong*); the sweeping aside
of ornate and trivial writing styles; the rejection of Buddhist and Taoist

practices in politics and social customs; the improvement of writing styles to aid the dissemination of ideas; and the promotion of new men of talent who would disseminate his ideas. In terms of cultural history, Han Yu worked to reestablish the authority of Han-ethnic culture and to reject the infiltration of the cultures of other national groups.[49] This cultural orientation spread until, during the Song dynasty, we see the court of the early Song reestablishing court rituals, scholars of classical learning using the *Spring and Autumn Annals* to call for glorifying the throne and casting out barbarians, and historians reflecting on the rise and fall of the Tang dynasty and the social problems that arose in the Five Dynasties period. We then see a discussion about Confucian orthodoxy (*daotong*) that begins with the essay "On the Central Kingdom" (*Zhongguo lun*) by Shi Jie (1005–1045) and includes the work of Ouyang Xiu (1007–1072), Zhang Heng (1025–1099), and Sima Guang (1019–1086). At the same time, we also see how, in addition to facing a new international order, Song-dynasty gentry elites also faced a domestic crisis of legitimacy. The cause of this crisis was simple: because this new dynasty was not an aristocratic authority with a natural hold on power, new justifications had to be provided to show why the Zhao family of the Song dynasty was a legitimate power and why the emperor was a sacred and authoritative figure. The presence of these issues explains why, from the very founding of the Song dynasty, it was important to conduct the sacrifices to Heaven, make sacrifices to the Earth Lord at Fenyin, ensure the appearance of messages from Heaven (*Tian shu*), go back to the Three Dynasties of Antiquity to establish appropriate rites and music, establish new policies, and guarantee that the court ruled All-under-Heaven together with the gentry elites.

People in ancient China always saw the Three Dynasties of Antiquity as the highest ideal that could be achieved. As a result, it was not only Song emperors such as Huizong and Zhenzong who were enthusiastic about the revival of ancient cultural traditions but also officials and gentry elites (whether conservative or radical, such as Wang Anshi and Zhu Xi) who also strongly advocated "unifying morality and customs" (*yi daode tong fengsu*). These ideals also influenced ordinary elite groups and exercised a deep influence over efforts to reestablish the cultural boundaries and intellectual guideposts of this empire.

Establishing a New Tradition for Han Chinese Culture:
The Song-Dynasty Transformation and Beyond

Against this backdrop, the Song dynasty worked at both the level of the state (that is, the court) and (local) gentry to reestablish gradually a new cultural unity based on Han traditions and Confucian ethics. As I discussed in detail in the second volume of *An Intellectual History of China,* the state employed institutions, while the gentry employed moral education. These actions worked together to establish certain Confucian principles as the bedrock of ethics and morality. A system for ordering life that was based on these principles won support and was gradually spread out to all different regions. Filiality (*xiao,* also "filial piety"), which served as the basis for the family and clan system, and loyalty (*zhong*), which served as a fundamental concept for ordering the state, became overriding ethical values. Even religions that had foreign origins (including Buddhism and certain local practices) had to recognize at all times the presence of imperial power. The system of rites that originated in ancient Confucian ritual ceremonies was extended into the lives of the common people in all parts of the realm, becoming a new part of social customs. Some ways of living and habits that had been rejected by authoritative "culture" came to be recognized as wrong. For example, excessive drinking, love of beauty and sex, aggressive accumulation of wealth, and other excessive expressions of personality—"wine, women, avarice, and ill temper" (*jiu se cai qi*)—came to be seem more and more and shameful behavior. To explain this process in modern terms, we would say that in Han-ethnic China, the unity of ethics and morality was gradually established, and a universally recognized cultural world began to form, establishing the foundations of daily life for people in China.[50]

The remaking and cementing of "Chinese" culture as the culture of Han China during the Song dynasty in fact meant the re-creation, reestablishment, and normalization of those "Chinese" cultural characteristics that I described above. As proponents in the international scholarly arena of the idea of the "Tang-Song transformation" have pointed out, enormous changes took place between the Tang and Song periods, with Song-dynasty China becoming quite different from the Han and

Tang periods that had preceded it. Once there was a so-called Other (*tazhe*), China began to have a sense of what was "non-Other," which came to be seen as "Chinese" culture and "Han" traditions. There is no question that this culture would later become the mainstream of Han Chinese culture. Even so, this was not a complete or unchanging Chinese culture. For "China," however, this history was quite strange, as the Song dynasty re-created a culture based on the Han nation and reestablished an ethical system based on Confucian thought, thereby forming a consciousness of a Han "China."

It is especially worth pointing out that even though the Song dynasty re-created Han Chinese culture and formed new traditions, two other major transformations also occurred in the history of China. In Chinese history, the entry of Mongolians and the Manchu Qing into the core regions of Han Chinese culture and the subsequent rule of China by non-Han peoples again brought new foreign bloodlines and brought more of foreign cultures to China. These two dynasties also expanded China's territory beyond its original boundaries. As a result, in all three of these periods, it became much more difficult to define the limits of so-called Chinese culture.

During the thirteenth and fourteenth centuries, following the years of Khitan and Jurchen rule in the northern areas of China proper, Mongolian culture made its way (along with the change in political power) throughout Han China. The cultures of these non-Han peoples had a deep influence on the cultural world of China, but even today we have not completed sufficient research on this century or more of "foreignization" and "Mongolization."[51] The founding emperor of the Ming dynasty, Zhu Yuanzhang, would later say that "When the Yuan occupied Hua-Xia [that is, China], they did not follow the rituals of Hua-Xia. Therefore, in the ninety-three years that they ruled, the customs of Hua [that is, China] died out, and human affairs fell into decadence."[52] Although Zhu was exaggerating, it is true that China foreign customs—dismissed as "rituals without hierarchy" and strange fashions in clothing and hair—were deeply influential.[53] It is said that the Han Chinese from the northern areas of China proper—even the gentry elites—were not particularly attuned to distinctions between Han and non-Han.[54] As a result, later scholars would lament that "the corruption of All-under-Heaven increased by the day, and neither men of learning nor senior officials recognized what was happening."[55] Some bemoaned the way "the traditions remaining from the Song had been wiped out."[56]

Foreign cultures, then, layered onto and accumulated within Han culture. Mongolian hairstyles and fashions, "the dances and music of the Hu," and "Hu surnames and Hu personal names" all enjoyed popularity in Han China for nearly a century, so much so that "people's customs had changed for so long that they thought nothing strange of them."[57] When the peoples of the plains, who rode horses and carried swords, performed rituals that made no distinctions of hierarchy and enjoyed a lavish lifestyle when they took up residence in cities, they also posed a threat to Han cultural traditions. Likewise, with the intermarriage of Mongolians, Hui, and Han, both marriage and funerary traditions came to influence family life among the Han. After a century of Mongol rule, the Song dynasty's efforts to establish a unified morality and set of customs seemed to have been set back a great deal, because a deep intermingling of foreign culture and Han culture had already taken place. What had been come to be seen by Han cultural traditions as the most important markers of culture (clothing, customs, and language) and the most important aspects of cultural order (the divisions between the scholarly elite, the peasantry, craftspeople, and merchants, as well as the rural clan system) all developed serious problems. For these reasons, when the Han regained power at the beginning of the Ming dynasty, a movement for "de-Mongolization" took place under the new political regime. This movement discouraged wearing foreign clothing and using foreign surnames, and promoted the remaking of Confucian ritual, the restoration of Confucian social order, and a return of the cultural center to the original fifteen provinces of China proper. It seems that the early Ming worked to reestablish a Han version of All-under-Heaven, and the people of Ming believed that the cultural shifts of the early Ming were "the making of a new era, washing away a century of degraded customs. . . . They were able to return to the grandeur of the Three Dynasties of Antiquity and achieve what the Han, Tang, and Song dynasties could not."[58] Here it appears that the cultural world of the Middle Kingdom was once again stabilized and reestablished; once again, the boundaries of tradition Han culture were reaffirmed.[59]

It is important, however, to note another turn in this history, which once again broke the movement toward the reestablishment of a Han Chinese cultural tradition. As I noted in the Introduction, from the Manchu conquest of 1644 onward, China gradually became a multiethnic empire that included the Manchu, Han, Mongolian, Uighur, Tibetan, Miao, and other groups, and a variety of foreign cultural elements, including religious faith, modes of living, and intellectual outlooks were all gathered into the cultural system of the Great Qing. All the way down until the establishment of the Republic of China in 1911, and to the establishment of the People's Republic of China in 1949, there was no way to change this situation, and people accepted the call made by the last Qing emperor's edict of abdication to "combine all of the territories of the Manchus, Han, Mongolian, Hui, and Tibetans to form a great Republic of China." The state inherited the lands and territories of the Great Qing empire. This culture of "China," then, clearly had broken through what I previously discussed as the Han Chinese culture and its five characteristics.

Does the "plural" nature of Chinese culture, then, allow for the inclusion of Manchu, Mongolian, Hui / Uighur, Tibetan, and Miao culture? Currently, the fevered interest in China for national learning and traditional culture is running up against precisely this problem: in the face of a plural culture, national learning opts for a singular one.

On "China" as a Unique (Multi-)Nation-State

Right now many people in China advocate this national learning. Some say that national learning is the Five Classics of Confucian learning; others say that national learning is what Hu Shi called the "study of the national past" (*guo gu zhi xue*); and still others say that because modern China includes a variety of national groups and has inherited the massive territories of the Qing dynasty and the Republic of China, then we should have a "greater national learning" (*da guoxue*). To discuss this issue, I need to turn once again to what "China" means, because we have to ask: As a special kind of (multi-)nation-state, can China also exist as a complete historical world or cultural world?

My view is as follows. I oppose narrow nationalism and statism, and, in my historical research, I work to go beyond ossified borders of the nation and state. I must also point out, however, that the state (*guojia*) (or dynasty [*wangchao*]) still has considerable power to shape culture. This relationship between the state and culture is a notable characteristic of all countries in northeast Asia: in China, Japan, and Korea, political forces are much more powerful than they are in Europe, and the territorial boundaries of the state are much more stable than what is found in Europe. The national states of Europe only took shape in the early modern period, while the area of the central regions of China has been clearly known since the Qin and Han dynasties, even if the exact borders have been changing constantly. The same is true for the cultural spaces of the Japan, Korea, Vietnam, and the Ryukyus. As I noted before, in East Asia no single religion extended beyond the borders of individual states and superseded the power of the emperor, conditions were lacking for free travel and exchange between different states, and there was no transnational community of intellectuals in East Asia. In East Asia the boundaries between greater and lesser, inner and outer, and us and them were quite clear, and the role of the state (or dynasty) was huge, to the point that it functioned to set boundaries between cultures and create identities. This situation was quite different from what was found in Europe, where people came and went between different countries, ruling families intermarried, and knowledge circulated back and forth. Europeans not only shared the Greek and Roman cultural traditions but also shared a world of faith, unified by the great power of religion, under which the pope enjoyed greater power than the secular power of the king. For these reasons, although I laud efforts to view China, Korea, Japan, Vietnam, and the region of the East China Sea and South China Sea as a "mutually linked and entangled history,"[60] and to study the area as a single region, I am also concerned that scholars who are interested in "rescuing history from the nation" have overlooked the role of the state, the dynasty, and the emperor in the periodization of history and molding of culture. Likewise, we cannot blindly apply new theories while ignoring the fact that China is a nation-state (or multinational empire) with deep origins, one that is not only a stable historical space but also a stable cultural world.

As I noted earlier, as a cultural world, "China" or the Middle Kingdom did not become static once it had formed, but gradually spread outward in all directions from its center in the regions of the Yellow River and the middle and lower reaches of the Yangtze River. "Chinese culture" is not a single culture but is a community that formed as its core, Han culture, melded with many other cultures. We need to look at the problem in two ways, however. First, during the formation of the cultural worlds of the Qin and Han dynasties, the Song dynasty, and the Ming dynasty, these areas gradually formed the center and boundaries of Han Chinese culture. This was particularly the case during the Song and Ming dynasties, which gave rise to a very clear sense of (Han) "China" and an awareness of "foreign lands" (*waiguo,* that is, regions on the periphery), as well as the clear distinction of differences between Chinese (*Hua*) and foreign or "Barbarian" (*Yi*). Through the combined efforts of the Song and Ming courts and the gentry elites, these areas became relatively stable and solid, making the central regions of China (the so-called traditional eighteen provinces of China) protect this culture and gradually spread outward toward its periphery, forming a relatively distinct cultural world. Here we see that Han Chinese culture is the most important core of this culture. The Xiongnu, Xianbei, Turkic peoples, Mongolians, and Manchus, as well as the Japanese, Koreans, and Annamese were all influenced by this Han culture, and all Chinese dynasties, including the Liao, Jin, Yuan, and Qing treated Han culture as a legitimate and rational civilization through which to promote themselves and to establish their own political power.

I want to emphasize, however, that we need not insist on understanding everything within the frame of "Han assimilation" or "Sinicization." Chen Yuan, for example, argued in *The Sinicization of Peoples from the Western Frontier in the Yuan Dynasty (Yuan xiyu ren Huahua kao)* that after the Mongols took control of China, many different foreign national groups from the west and the north were assimilated into Han culture. Likewise, the Chinese American scholar Ping-ti Ho maintained that the Manchus would not have been able to rule China were it not for their eventual Sinicization. It is important to understand the backstory and the sentiments behind these ideas. Chen Yuan, a hard-core Han Chinese nationalist, wrote works during the during the national emergency of the Second

Sino-Japanese War that were filled with nationalist pride, such as *The Subtleties of Hu Sanxing's Commentary on the Comprehensive Mirror to Aid in Government* (*Tongjian Hu zhu biao wei*) and *Investigations in New Folk Religions in Hebei during the Early Southern Song* (*Nan Song chu Hebei xin daojiao kao*). As for Ping-ti Ho, as a Chinese person in America he always emphasized the power of his culture, and his debate with Evelyn Rawski about Sinicization clearly shows his feelings as a Han Chinese person.[61]

Why is it so important today to emphasize this aspect of the question? It is important because different aspects of culture are constantly overlapping. When we look at history, although you can say that there were strong tendencies toward Sinicization during the Yuan among the peoples who came from the western frontiers, and that the Manchus also were strongly assimilated into the Han during the Qing, it also the case that Han traditions underwent changes during Mongol rule, just as the Manchu Qing wrought tremendous changes on Han China. Put in terms of fashionable theories of modernity, I suspect that the development of urban enterprises, entertainments, and lifestyles may have developed most quickly during these periods of so-called foreign rule: that is, during the Mongol Yuan dynasty and the Manchu Qing. Why is this the case? Because Han Confucian culture is founded on the order of rural society. Han Confucianism criticizes and resists the city's modes of living, order of daily life, and value orientations. The rapid development of cities during the Yuan may be the result of the fact that, for a period of time, Confucian ethics lost some of their power as a controlling force. The Mongol rulers did not fully apply Confucian values to govern life under their rule. For example, the flowering of drama and theater in the Yuan was closely related to urban growth and changes in the gentry elites' values. Those members of the elite who could not be officials went to live in the city and set aside their aspirations to "govern the state and bring peace to All-under-Heaven," and some became "idle people wandering about" (*youmin*), people of the market, protégés of the powerful, and libertines.[62] These people spurred an interest in writing for, performing for, and appreciating the theater. Likewise, to a certain degree the Qing also temporarily reduced the role of Confucian ethics as a controlling force in the *Lebenswelt* (even if, on the surface, the Qing emperors upheld Confucian thinking). In the debate between Ping-ti Ho and Evelyn Rawski about Sinicization, both sides have made important points, but we should avoid going too far in either direction.

My view is shaped in part by the many accounts I have read of Koreans' tribute embassies to Beijing and other travels to China. Many accounts written by Koreans confirm that, because the Manchus ruled the state, it was the case that, although the upper levels of society and the Han gentry elites held on to their traditional values, during the Qing period great leaps of development took place in what we now call capitalism and modernity. For example, the process of urban commercialization was so strong that even high officials such as Grand Secretaries could go to the Temple of Abundant Blessings (Longfu si) to do business. Korean emissaries noticed that Han customs had gradually lost their pride of place, as they saw many things that were out of character with northern China, such as the inter-mingling of men and women, no separation of masters and servants, decadent lifestyles, a panoply of urban entertainments, clanging funeral music, and people flocking to worship Guan Yu and the Buddha while paying little heed to Confucian temples. All of these experiences led Korean embassies to believe that Han cultural traditions were on the wane after the Manchu Qing had gained power.

It seems to be the case, then, that the assimilation of foreign groups by the Han can also be seen as the dilution of the power of Confucian morality and ethics as a result of foreign rule. Should we call these events the foreignization of the Han? Or the assimilation of foreigners? Does the Chinese culture that we see today come only from traditional, Confucian Han culture, or do we include other new and "foreign" cultural elements?

Continuity and Discontinuity: Chinese Culture and the Western Challenge since the Late Qing

Tradition continuously stretches on and influences life today. The classics also continue to be reinterpreted and to this day serve as a source of our spirit. China is different from Europe in that, because of the spread of theology in the Middle Ages, there was a clear moment of discontinuity in European history; it was only because of this discontinuity that a renaissance could take place through a rediscovery and reordering of the classics. Early modern Europe was originally established on the cultural traditions of ancient Greece and Rome and on the Christian faith, and, when each nation-state was established, it broke away, solidified, and took shape.

In the same period, however, China expanded outward from a central state to its peripheries; in terms of culture, it developed from one system into a combination of many. Within this culture, the traditions and classical texts of Han China from ancient times persisted across thousands of years. They were not truncated or broken for several reasons. First, the authority of the sages and the classical texts were established very early on and were always integrated with politics, which guaranteed the transmission of this culture and its ideas. Second, these texts and traditions borrowed the power of the political authorities and the examination system to ensure that they were preserved by educated people. Mainstream educated people took part in examinations on knowledge about these texts and traditions in order to reach the upper levels of society and to ensure their role and their position once they were there. Third, both official and private education, in places such as private academies and village schools, were always important, and this support combined with the support of political authorities. For these reasons, we were still on the thread of our traditions, history, and culture that extended for thousands of years—at least until the end of the Qing and the beginning of the Republic of China.

However, aside from the ongoing encounters with the cultures of other national groups, it was the movement of Western learning toward the East that began in the fifteenth century and, more important, the gunboats of the nineteenth century that changed traditional China's political and cultural orientation. Especially after the end of the first Sino-Japanese War in 1895, China began to speed up its turn to the West, and the worry and anxiety surrounding the pursuit of "wealth and power" became a continuous source of radicalism. The 1911 revolution, the May Fourth Movement, the Second Sino-Japanese War, the founding of the People's Republic of China, and the Cultural Revolution gradually changed cultural traditions handed down across the millennia, so much so that we often now understand the Western saying "the past is a foreign country," and it seems that traditional culture is far away from us. Nowadays most people would agree with the assessment offered by Zhang Zhidong (1837–1909), who argued that the entry of early modern Western culture into China resulted in "tremendous changes never before seen" and a "rupture" between China and tradition.

Here I will point out five important aspects of this rupture, with an example for each.

1. Although China continues to use the Chinese writing system, the characters, vocabulary, and grammar of modern Chinese have all undergone major changes. Modern Mandarin Chinese shows considerable influence of the spoken language used during the Mongol Yuan and Manchu Qing dynasties, but more important, the advocacy of written vernacular (*baihua wen*) during the May Fourth Movement caused traditional oral language to become part of the written language, which then was jumbled up with many, many new words from modern terminology or terms from Western languages. Whether in newspapers, documents, or spoken language, we often see old terms that took on new meanings, such as *jingji* (economics), *ziyou* (liberty or freedom), and *minzhu* (democracy), just as we see words that previously had never been part of the written language, such as "ideology" (*yishi xingtai*), "computer network" (*diannao wangluo*), various "-isms" (*moumou zhuyi*), and "layoff" (*xia gang*). If language is a means of understanding and transmitting meaning, then the world that is understood and expressed through modern Chinese is already quite different from that of tradition.[63]

2. Although some traditional family and clan organizations continue to be maintained in modern China—especially in the countryside—and Chinese people to this day place importance on the home, family, and following elders' wishes, the relationship between the family, society, and the state have changed. With many modern cities, modern transportation, modern information, and modern lifestyles, the social basis of traditional culture has already been broken apart in China. In the past, the spaces people lived in were courtyard houses, gardens, and farmhouses, and relations between people were determined by family, clan, and intermarried family groups. The relationships within and between families that were formed by these bloodlines were important and reliable: as it is said, "blood is thicker than water." The ethical order that was founded on

"separation between men and women, and clear authority between elder and younger" allowed the family, the clan, and the larger state to coexist peacefully. In *From the Soil: The Foundations of Chinese Society,* Fei Xiaotong argued that the fundamental social unit in China was different from the West: our pattern is not like "distinct bundles of straw" in the West, but rather "like the circles that appear on the surface of a lake when a rock is thrown into it."[64] Modern cities, transportation, and media have changed everything, however, and modern law requires equality between men and women and free marriage and divorce between one man and one woman. The close relationships and interdependency found in neighborhoods, villages, and clans disappeared in the face of calls for greater democracy and the process of urbanization. As a result, Confucian ethics and state ideology that had been established in this traditional society also lost much of their basis.

3. Since the late Qing period, Confucian thinkers have been challenged by Western democratic ideas and have gradually lost their hold on politics and political ideology. Likewise, Buddhism and Taoism have been challenged by Western scientific thought and have been the targets of campaigns to wipe out so-called superstition. As a result, they have retreated from the true world of faith, just as many other religions no longer retain their essential meaning and significance. Even though Confucianism, Buddhism, Taoism, and other legal religions such as Islam and Christianity can coexist peacefully under the control of other political powers, this kind of ostensible unity of religions is not at all like ideas held during the Tang dynasty that advocated the mutual exchange of ideas, knowledge, and faith. Instead, it is the isolation of religion as a result of a high degree of political control.

4. Ideas, knowledge, and technologies concerning the relationship between humans and nature, Yin and Yang, and the Five Elements have been weakened in the face of challenges from modern Western science. As a result, they have separated gradually into different fields and relinquished their role in understanding both politics and the natural world. They have only retained their importance in areas where science remains inadequate, such as in medicine (Chinese medicine), geography (feng shui), and food and drink. Modern Chinese people no longer uphold ideas about the Yin and Yang and the Five Elements, and they even

do not follow traditional ideas about time such as the four seasons and the twenty-four divisions (*jie qi*) of the traditional calendar. China also no longer marks years on the calendar according to the dynasty or the emperor's reign, opting instead for the Western calendar. According to traditional beliefs, "If heaven does not change, the Tao does not change." In this view, adopting a different calendar system would change everything, much like changing the calendar to mark the beginning of a new emperor's reign.

5. Ever since the Peace of Westphalia (1648), the international order and the set of treaty relationships established in modern Europe has worked as part of the larger movement of the West into the East both to wipe out Chinese ideas of All-under-Heaven and the tribute system and to redefine the relationship between China and all the various countries of the world.[65] Even if China still holds on to some sense of itself as a kingdom at the center of All-under-Heaven, as Xu Zhuoyun (1930–) has argued, "It is because of this idea of China as the center of the world that, for thousands of years, China could not adjust to the idea of equal co-existence with other states. Right down to the early modern period, Chinese people seemed to be unable to get past this idea."[66] The world will change, however, and in this globalized era, the ancient Chinese worldview that was based on the cosmology of "round Heaven and square Earth" and the international order based on the tribute system lost its validity some time ago.

Conclusion: Rediscovering the Plurality of Chinese Culture across History

We can certainly understand the feelings that lie behind the recent surge of interest in traditional culture and national learning. I believe that three aspects of these developments are quite important: First among these is the desire to return to a different starting point, to escape the grip that Western culture has had on our ideas, our institutions, and our faiths since the early modern period and to return to the resources of traditional culture to seek a foundation for rebuilding modern Chinese values. The second is the search for identity. This means working, in an era when faith is all but absent, to reestablish cohesion among "Chinese" citizens in their views on history, culture, values, and, especially, the state. The third is a new scholarly direction: an effort to extract China from a century of influence by Western scholarly institutions and find a new direction, whether in terms of the division of fields of knowledge, jargon used to express ideas, or in institutions that support research. On the surface, these ideas and feelings that lie behind the interest in traditional culture and national learning seem perfectly fine, but the problem lies in the fact that tradition is not fixed in place, and "China" is not singular.

First, culture forms across history, and history is always adding and subtracting from culture. By "addition," I refer to the borrowing of traditional resources to undertake creative interpretations of elements of foreign culture that are continuously encountered. This addition took place, for example, in the way educated people in China in the middle ages "matched meanings" (*ge yi*) of Indian Buddhism with local ideas, transforming foreign ideas into a part of Chinese thought. By "subtraction," I refer to the selective forgetting of aspects of native culture. Examples of this subtraction include the ways that, in ancient China, some customs that did not adhere to the moral order were remade, or, in modern China, the way that science was used to conduct campaigns against so-called superstition. For these reasons, we cannot say that a fixed, unchanging tradition exists.

Second, I also want to remind people that the history of ancient China demonstrates the plurality of Chinese culture; ancient China contained many different national groups and many different cultural elements. Even if the Qin and Han Empires gave rise to a core of Han culture, the repeated addition of foreign people and foreign cultural elements created new complexity and richness. By the time of the Song dynasty, the state and the gentry elites, facing the international environment and external pressures, took actions that gave rise to a cohesion of Han Chinse culture, which, in turn, began to give prominence to the divisions of inner and outer and self and other in the Chinese cultural world. During the Mongol Yuan dynasty, however, China once again mingled with foreign peoples, and the layering of cultures resulted in a new and hybrid culture. After a period of "de-Mongolization" in the early Ming dynasty, Han Chinese culture may have solidified again, but the establishment of the

Great Qing Empire brought another expansion of territories and peoples and new layers of culture. Because ancient China was a cultural community in which all streams flowed into one, and China now is also a (multi) national state, we must therefore recognize the plurality of Chinese culture.

Finally, in the late Qing and early Republican period, China underwent tremendous changes never before seen in two thousand years, events that marked a moment of discontinuity in Chinese culture. Of course, in the present we do need to reacquaint ourselves and discover new aspects of tradition, but we also need to understand that, since tradition is continuously changing, the ways that modern values can reassemble traditional culture is a major problem. As others have said in the past, "Tradition is the living resources of the dead; traditionalism is the shackles of the living." An inflexible, "fundamentalist" approach to preserving an imagined tradition is simply a way to refuse any and all progress.

I can sense at a very deep level that the growing anxiety in China, which makes extremely strong demands to "develop and spread" (*hongyang*) Chinese tradition, Chinese perspectives, and Chinese values, can be traced back to the way that, from the late Qing and early Republic onward, people have had stronger and stronger feelings about the need to pursue "wealth and power," to highlight memories of the glorious dynasties of the past. All of these sentiments are the reason why, for more than a hundred years, China has traded one article of fashionable clothing for another. Mao Zedong said, "Ten thousand years is too long; we must seize the day." This is an important image, because it carries a deep sense that "backwardness must be combated" and poverty and weakness must "have its hold on the world broken." As China "rises," then, it becomes essential in the eyes of many to show the world that our vast country has not only taken its place among the so-called great nations of the world but also should have a commanding position, specifically in terms of culture. What concerns me is exactly this "tradition fever" (*chuantong re*) and "national learning fever" (*guoxue re*) in China. I believe we absolutely cannot allow these strong sentiments to turn tradition fever and national learning fever into scholarly practices or forces that mobilize nationalism or statism.

5

PERIPHERIES

How China, Korea, and Japan Have Understood One Another since the Sixteenth and Seventeenth Centuries

Three Stages in China's Understanding of the World

Before launching into a discussion of how China and the states on its periphery understood one another, I should explain how, from ancient times to the present, Chinese people understood the relationship between the world and the self. Generally speaking, this understanding passed through three stages.[1]

The first stage was quite long, basically stretching across the whole of traditional China, from the Spring and Autumn and Warring States periods all the down through the Ming and Qing dynasties. As Han civilization and traditions enjoyed great power across East Asia, with no competition from other strong cultural forces, China lived in an era in which it seemed it had no mirror to look into. This era gave rise to the notion of All-under-Heaven, in which China was the center, and the so-called Four Barbarians were on the periphery. This era also gave rise to the notion of the tribute system. Across the centuries, even though

China's actual knowledge of the world went well beyond the limits of Han China, and foreign relations with the states on China's periphery were not conducted only in terms of the simple relations between the central state and tributary states,[2] China nonetheless was still accustomed to imagining itself as a huge "Middle Kingdom" at the center of All-under-Heaven.

The second stage was one in which China had only one mirror. I view the period that began in the late Ming to the present, when Westerners arrived in Japan, China, Korea, and Southeast Asia, as the opening of a process of globalization that extends down to the present day. I should say that, since the late Ming, and especially after the Ming-Qing period, when faced with challenges from the West and comparisons to the West, Chinese people began to seek a new understanding of the world and of China—these were, of course, monumental steps forward. This new understanding, however, was based on a system of reference that treated the West as "Other." From arguments in the late Ming that Western learning had emerged from Chinese sources (*Xi xue Zhong yuan*), to debates in the late Qing about treating "Chinese learning as the foundation, and Western learning for practical applications" (*Zhong ti Xi yong*) and vice versa, to the debates about science and life following the May Fourth period, and even down to the "culture fever" of the 1980s—all of these cultural moments involved searching for the self in one mirror.[3]

The third stage, what I call the era of "rediscovering oneself through many mirrors," should begin now. Although the West is extremely important mirror, everyone knows that one mirror is not enough, and we will ask: Does this one mirror give an accurate reflection? Is this the only mirror that we can use to see ourselves? Do we need one angle or many angles, in other words, do we need mirrors other than the West? In the past, China rarely made a conscious effort to see itself from the perspectives of its neighbors in Korea, Japan, Vietnam, India, or Mongolia. In fact, the comparison of China and the West can only provide a crude measure for understanding ourselves. China can begin truly to understand what "the world" and "China" really are only through comparisons with countries with which we seem to have fewer differences and with which we may have shared some traditions, even if now we have different, independent cultures.

For these reasons, I am particularly interested in northeast Asian countries such as China, Japan, and Korea. As a historian, however, I also want to point out in this chapter that although these countries of Northeast Asia may be close to one another geographically and have many aspects of their traditions that overlap and share the same historical sources, from the sixteenth and seventeenth centuries down to the present day, the relationships between them have been filled with biased ideas, enmity, and distrust. Little seems to have changed today. What I discuss, then, is in the past but continues to influence the history of our present moment.

Drifting Together, Drifting Apart: China, Japan, and Korea since the Seventeenth Century

The relationship between these three countries is a large topic, and I cannot go into great detail here. In this chapter, I stick to materials from the seventeenth century and later—roughly equivalent to the Qing dynasty in China, the latter Joseon dynasty in Korea, and the Edo period in Japan—to discuss how these three countries, all of which are now seen as part of the "Northeast Asia" region, saw one another, including the mutual enmity between them. During the Ming and Qing periods, Japan, Korea, and China moved from being all part of "one family" to finding one another unrecognizable. This process reflects at a deep level the collapse of "Northeast Asia" as an identity that originally was formed on the basis of Han- and Tang-dynasty culture. The gradual process of estrangement and slide into mutual disregard were the result of a major internal fragmentation of what appeared to be one civilization within Northeast Asia.

We can see clearly this major change in East Asian cultural identity that occurred across the Ming and the Qing through records of mutual exchanges and observations made by Koreans, Japanese, and Chinese people. The numerous *Records of Embassies to Beijing* (*Yan xing lu*) published in Korea, letters and documents concerning diplomatic visits from Korea to Japan, as well as "brush-talk" (*bi tan*) documents and other records from Nagasaki, have all been the subject of growing attention in recent years. These materials offer a glimpse into the disintegration and fracturing of the "Eastern" world.[4] In the era when the Great Qing Empire was flourishing to its fullest, the Korean emissaries sent to China witnessed an imperial scene that was no longer "Chinese." At the same time, the Japanese who conducted brush talks and inquiries with Chinese sailors and merchants cast a cold eye on their neighbors, who were growing ever more unfamiliar. From these documents we see a mutual disdain and guardedness between Japanese and Chinese people that, though subtle, was based on their respective national chauvinisms. In the eyes of Korean and Japanese from this era, one China had become two: on the one hand, there was a historical and cultural China, rooted in the China of the Han and Tang dynasties that existed in their memory and imagination. On the other hand, there was the China that actually existed before their eyes, the practical and political China that was represented by the Qing Empire. In that era, although they may have held deep respect for the historical and cultural China that they remembered, they had begun to despise the practical and political China. We can also see Korea and Japan measuring each other up to see who was the real representative of cultural orthodoxy in the region.[5]

From "Tributes to Heaven" to "Missions to Beijing": How the Joseon Dynasty Saw China after the Ming

From the middle of the seventeenth century onward, as Qing-dynasty China continued to believe in a two-thousand-year-old worldview that took itself as the center of the world, Korean people arrived at a very different view of China. Although the Ming dynasty had been wiped out, over a long period of time the Koreans showed a real nostalgia for the Great Ming and a sense of dissatisfaction with the Qing Empire, referring to the Qing Empire as "barbarians" and calling the Qing emperor the "barbarian Emperor" (*Hu huang*). During the Qianlong period of the Qing dynasty, a Korean emissary to Beijing named Kim Chong-hu wrote in a letter to Hong Dae-young (1731–1783), who had been an emissary to the Qing court, that "After the Ming, there is no China. I do not blame them [the Chinese] for not yearning for the Ming, but I do blame them for not yearning for China." In their eyes, China (*Zhonghua* or *Zhongguo*) originally referred to a civilization, and thus if Chinese civilization was not to be found in the Qing state, then they "would rather be among the lowly of the Eastern Barbarians than to be counted among the nobility of these people."[6] Koreans of this era had long since stopped thinking of the Qing Empire as "China."

For these reasons, it was difficult for them to understand why Han Chinese would submit to the Great Qing Empire's rule. During the Qianlong reign, Kim Chong-hu told Han Chinese literati quite bluntly that Korea had deeply held memories of the Great Ming, which had sent troops to attack Japan and provided them with an indispensable lifeline in their battle against Japan. However, for the Manchu Qing state, which had attacked Korea and coerced it into signing unfavorable treaties, they harbored a deep hatred. He said:

> During the Wanli reign (1572–1620), the [Japanese] bandits streamed into Korea . . . and the Wanli Emperor dispatched the armies of All-under-Heaven and expended the treasure of All-under-Heaven and put down the invasion in seven years. Two hundred years hence, the happiness and well-being of the people are all the gifts of the Wanli Emperor. The onslaught of the [Qing] bandits in the final years [of the Ming] may have been caused in part because of this [defense of Korea]. Thus our country believes it may have been the cause of the fall [of the Ming], and our lamentations for the dynasty continue to this day.[7]

In their heart of hearts, the Koreans felt that when they came to the Qing Empire, they were no longer coming to pay tribute to the Son of Heaven, but were simply coming to Beijing on business. They were no longer, in cultural terms, pilgrims, but rather were, in political terms, obedient servants. For these reasons, the records written by these emissaries largely came to be referred to as *Missions to Beijing* and not *Tributes to Heaven*. More than a century after the fall of the Great Ming, memories of the dynasty remained clear as ever in Korea, all the way down to the times of the Qianlong emperor (r. 1735–1796) and Jiaqing emperor (r. 1796–1820).

I found it significant that the Koreans were very proud of the way they insisted on continuing to wear clothing in the Ming style and looked down on the new styles of clothing adopted by the Qing Empire. When they wore their clothing in the Ming style, they saw themselves as culturally superior to the Qing. According to their descriptions, the customs of the Qing Empire were already in decline and were no longer a part of *Hua-Xia* (cultural China) because Confucian rituals in China could not match the purity of those found in Korea. This destruction of ritual orthodoxy and disintegration of Confucian learning gave even more reason for Koreans not to identify with the Qing in terms of culture. Those Korean emissaries who had from the beginning seen the Manchu Qing as barbarians because of their customs and scholarship had even less regard for the Qing state.

Beginning in the seventeenth century and across another three hundred years, the Koreans discovered that the Manchu emperors had misgivings and a sense of anxiety toward Han cultural traditions. These misgivings led them, on the one hand, to promote Confucian learning as a way to silence Han gentry elites, while using high-handed methods of the literary inquisition (*wenzi yu*) to intimidate educated people. The Koreans attributed this cultural transformation to changes in the race of the rulers of the state, believing that these changes occurred because the emperor was "barbarian" (Hu) and not Han and, therefore, the bloodline of Chinese culture was no longer purely Chinese and had fallen into utter decline. Some believed, in fact, the words written by one Korean emissary: "Now, in All-under-Heaven, the institutions of China (*Zhonghua*) are preserved only in our country."[8]

Who Is China? The View from Japan in the Edo Period

From the seventeenth century onward, even though political and cultural exchanges diminished with an isolationist Japan, a brisk trade continued with the port city of Nagasaki. In books such as *Changing Situations between China and Foreigners* (*Ka'i hentai*), *Daily Record of the Office of Chinese Interpreters* (*Tō tsūji kaisho nichiroku*), and *Overview of Maritime Relations* (*Tsūkō ichiran*), we see numerous records of questionings of Chinese travelers to Nagasaki. The Japanese officials who oversaw these inquiries were not just interested in whether ships arriving in Japan were carrying works by Catholic missionaries, which were considered heretical. Many of their questions sought information about political and military issues in China. One book, for example, quotes an official named Hayashi, who said, "The northern barbarians [that is, the Manchus] seized China forty years ago, but none of these events have been recorded in official histories, so we have no way to distinguish between what is true and what is false." They inquired, therefore, about whether China was at peace, whether there were any talented men outside of the imperial court, where key defenses against Japan were located, and where important places from ancient and contemporary times were located, and so on. From these questions, we can see what the Japanese were thinking.[9] At the same time Korean emissaries made numerous goodwill visits to Japan, and the Japanese were keen to find out information about China from the Koreans, who once again were making tribute visits to China. For example, in the twelfth year of the Shunzhi reign (1655), not long after the Qing had taken power, people in Japan were at a loss to understand the changes under way in China. When a goodwill mission (*Tongsinsa*) from Korea came to Nagasaki in the tenth month of that year, Hayashi Hōto, the son of Hayashi Gahō (1618–1688), had a long list of questions ready for the visitors. According to records made by Jo Hyeong (1606–1679), a diplomat and ambassador to Japan, Hayashi Hōto's questions included: "What has happened with the military of the Great Ming? Have the fifteen provinces [of China proper] fallen into the hands of the Qing? Are they continuing to use the calendar based on the reign of the Shunzhi emperor? Has the family line of the Ming emperors been maintained? Are Zheng Zhilong and Wu Sangui alive or dead? Did Li Zicheng of Shaanxi and Zhang Xianzhong of Sichuan escape with their lives?" In this case, the Korean ambassador gave a cautious answer, saying only that "the territories [of China] are far away, and they did not know such details," but the embassies sent by Korea (as well as the Japanese residence at Busan) always served as an important source of information about China for the Japanese.[10]

Additionally, when Chinese trading ships traveling to Nagasaki were blown off course into other areas of Japanese waters, they often engaged in written conversations with Japanese literati who were sent out to intervene. These conversations left behind precious written materials that offer a glimpse into the subtle and complicated relations between Chinese people and Japanese people.

When people from foreign lands arrive for the first time, they will often be the object of local peoples' curiosity and, for this reason, the first impression is often important. Like the Koreans, Japanese people were also taken aback by the clothing worn by Qing officials, because they were quite different from official Chinese imperial clothing described in the historical record. The Japanese asked detailed questions and spent a great deal of effort to record what they saw, and even made illustrations not only to show their strangeness but to express their low opinion of the Qing state. According to Shinoba Seizaburō, the rise of the Qing state led Japanese people of the time to recall the Yuan dynasty, which, in turn, led them to be hostile toward the Manchu Qing.[11] For these reasons, after providing a description of the colors of officials' clothes, the Japanese writer did not forget to add another comment: "The founding emperor of the Qing unified Tartary with China, and rules China wearing the clothing of foreigners from the north, which we see here."[12] Since the Qing no longer wore clothing that was in line with tradition, and since their own clothing could be traced to the proper sources of antiquity, then it was of course the case that ancient Chinese culture could be found in Japan—and not China. It was not only the color of clothing in China, but also music, customs, and history that had all lost their relation to tradition. According to one Honda Shimei, "In your country [that is, Qing-dynasty China], you shave the hair on the top of your heads and wear clothes that are different from ancient times. How can this accord with the rites set out by the Duke of Zhou?"[13] Some Japanese people even went so far as to question the legitimacy of the Manchu Qing Empire because of this decline in cultural traditions.[14]

Japanese people at this time believed that the China of the Han and Tang dynasties had vanished, and the arrangement of positions between the Middle Kingdom and the Four Barbarians had been turned inside out. Although they acknowledged that China was a major country and that Japan was a smaller one, they believed that Japan should be referred to as the "Middle Kingdom," because only a cultural centers "whose waters and soil are superior to all others and whose personages are the most brilliant in the world" could be called the Middle Kingdom.[15] When they saw Han Chinese, then, they were keen to argue:

> In ancient times, Empress Jingū conquered the Samhan [three early kingdoms of Korea], and her brilliance illuminated the world. From that time until now, the line of imperial succession has continued without interruption, earning the trust of the people for many generations. How could this not be an ideal form of rulership? Indeed, it is the glory of our land.[16]

In contrast, they argued, China lost its former glory. As one Japanese scholar put it, "Nowadays the elegant clothing and styles of emperors in former times have been swept away, and everyone has fallen into wearing the stinking queue. The customs of this country are not worth discussion."[17] During these years, then, many in Japan felt a mixture of caution and loathing toward China.

The Qing Empire: Stuck in the Vision of All-under-Heaven from the Han and Tang Dynasties

It is true that, from as far back as the time of the Wanli reign of the Ming dynasty (1572–1620)—when Matteo Ricci had arrived in China—that Chinese people had begun to reach a new understanding of the world. After seeing Ricci's map, Li Zhizao acknowledged his own sense of shock upon discovering this new knowledge about the world: "The lands of the world are so vast, and are yet but a grain of millet when compared to the heavens, and my home province and town are just the tip of this grain of millet."[18] Later Qu Shisu would also say in his *Comments on the Chronicle of Foreign Lands* (*Zhifang wai ji xiao yan*), "According to this map, China occupies one-tenth of Asia, and Asia occupies one-fifth of All-under-Heaven. Therefore, outside of the Spiritual Country of the Red Region [*chi xian shen zhou*, that is, China], there must be another nine Spiritual Countries of the Red Region that are just as large." He recognized that, when China took saw itself as a great country, it was a little bit like a frog at the bottom of a well. At this time, the traditional Chinese view of All-under-Heaven began to break apart and collapse, and people came to accept this new version of the world. For these reasons, those strange images and tales of foreign lands that came from the *Classic of Mountains and Seas* or *Record of the Ten Continents* came to be displaced by accurate knowledge brought by Westerners. By the time of the Qing dynasty, even major official publications, such as the authoritative *Bibliography of the Emperor's Four Treasuries* (*Siki quanshu zong mu*), which was completed during the Qianlong reign (1735–1796), classified books such as *Classic of Mountains and Seas, Record of the Ten Continents*, and *Classic of Divine Wonders* (*Shen yi jing*) as fiction, not geography. This decision shows an important change in official understandings of geography and the idea of All-under-Heaven. It also shows how people of that time accepted the results of evidential investigation (*kao suo*) and seeking facts (*ze shi*), which is also to say that in the century that passed between the time that Ricci arrived in China and the Qianlong reign, views handed down from ancient China about foreign lands (and, by extension, about China itself) had already moved from an imagined All-under-Heaven to a sense of the real "Myriad States" (*wanguo*).[19]

Let us return, then, to the problem of East Asia. People in China were also cautious and uneasy about the rise of their neighboring countries to the east and about possible confrontations with them. After protracted efforts to control piracy in the mid-Ming and the intervention in the Imjin War (1592–1598), an official named Zhou Kongjiao wrote that Toyotomi Hideyoshi's invasion of Korea and attempt to stand up as a rival to the Ming Empire demonstrated that "although the dynasty had not had an enemy in two hundred years, it now has enemies from this day forward." Seeing the threat from Japan, he called on the Ming empire to prepare itself, "lest a surprise turn of events results in a catastrophe that brings despair."[20] The great majority of Chinese people, however, felt no such sense of urgency; this was even more true for the rulers of the Qing. China at this time remained mired in the idea that it was the center of All-under-Heaven, the central state in the tribute system. If we look at paintings such as *The Myriad States Pay Tribute to the Emperor* (*Wanguo lai chao tu*), we can see how learned elites and the court still thought they were like the China of the Han and Tang dynasties, receiving ambassadors from different countries who had come to pay obeisance.[21] It was because of this outlook that the Qing court maintained its blind optimism and self-regard and why the Qianlong emperor treated the Macartney Embassy from England with such disdain.

But this was only one narrow point of view. It is very clear that, from the middle of the seventeenth century onward, the West was beginning to move into the East, and the three countries of East Asia were beginning to part ways. Even if the Qing Empire was waiting for "the myriad states to pay tribute" and put on the airs of a great country toward Japan and Korea, in terms of culture, neither Japan nor Korea identified with the Qing Empire anymore, and they certainly did not recognize the Qing's ability to represent "Chinese culture." By the end of the nineteenth century, these cultural fault lines and mutual hostilities would become even clearer with the unfolding of the Meiji reforms in Japan, Japan's annexation of the Ryukyu Islands, and the colonization of Taiwan and Korea following the First Sino-Japanese War.

Parting Ways: Did an East Asian Identity Still Exist after the Seventeenth Century?

When we see how groups observed one another, we also come to see those blind spots that are so difficult to discover on one's own; even more so, we see their differing outlooks and perspectives. Historical records written in Sino-Korean (or *hanmun*) show us Koreans' opinions of the Ming and Qing dynasties and let us see the substantial break in Koreans' views about their political allegiance to China, their duties as a tributary state to China, and their cultural identity in relationship to China. At the same time, Japanese materials also show Japan's desire to establish an independent international order, as well as the rise of particularism and ethnocentrism, as thinkers from Yamaga Sokō (1622–1685) down to Motoori Norinaga (1730–1801) all contributed to a line of thought that held that Japan was a "central state."[22] For these reasons, from the times of the Imjin War and the fall of the Ming (1644) onward, Japan had largely abandoned its posture of cultural identification with the Chinese Empire. How, then, did this transformation in East Asian countries' views toward the Chinese

Empire affect the international situation at the time, as well as the history and ideas of subsequent decades? This is a question that we still need to discuss today.

In recent years, many scholars in Japan, Korea, and China have taken a liking to talking about the problem of "Asia" or "East Asia." Sometimes these discussions seem to operate with the unspoken assumption that "Asia" or "East Asia" is a cultural region that corresponds to "Europe" or "the West." But if we say that this East Asian world really exists, then we are only talking about events that took place before the seventeenth century. If, as I have argued, all of this began to change with the seventeenth century, then it is the case that by the end of the seventeenth century the countries of East Asia no longer enjoyed mutual trust, close political relations, or a shared identity. What existed in the Han and Tang dynasties may have been an East Asian cultural community, but this has already broken apart, and what people now look to as a new East Asian cultural community is far from being established.

For these reasons, I believe that if we wish to promote mutual trust and cooperation between "China" and its "periphery," then we must first examine this period of history and search for a new basis for cultural identity.

✺ 6 ✺

PRACTICAL QUESTIONS

Will Cultural Differences between China
and the West Lead to Conflict?

Beginning with Huntington

Will conflicts arise between different cultures? The American scholar Samuel P. Huntington put this question forward in the 1990s in *The Clash of Civilizations and the Remaking of World Order*.[1] According to Huntington, by the 1990s the ideology of the Cold War had gradually receded, while conflicts between different civilizations were coming to the forefront. He predicted that Confucian and Islamic civilizations would join forces against Western civilization.

Is this conflict happening now? Regardless of whether Huntington's predictions were on or off the mark, his predictions sparked worldwide debate about civilizations, conflict, history, and the future. Nowadays in China we are discussing the topic of "world peace and Chinese culture," a theme that clearly is formulated in response to Huntington's thesis. I am more than willing to believe that people who discuss "world peace and Chinese culture" have good intentions and hope not only that conflicts will not arise between various cultures but also that

Chinese culture can play a special role in creating world peace, much in the way that the ancients hoped their states would, in the famous words of the literatus Zhang Zai (1020–1077), "create peace for ten thousand generations."

As a historian, however, I cannot help but see many unanswered questions here. For example: What is Chinese culture? What aspects of Chinese culture can lead to clashes between civilizations or promote world peace? Will emphasizing the significance of Chinese culture lead to new, not-so-peaceful scenarios?

Once again, then, we must return to the question, "What is China's culture?"

All-under-Heaven: A Traditional Chinese View of "the World"

In Chapter 4 I discussed the importance of answering the question, "What is Chinese culture?" In this discussion, "Chinese" (*Zhongguo*) is an important word, because all peoples have culture: once you can explain those aspects of a culture that exist in China (or are particularly prominent) and those aspects that do not exist among other peoples (or are not very prominent), then you have arrived at typical aspects of Chinese culture; other, nontypical elements cannot be thrown in and counted as part of Chinese culture.

What, then, is typical of "China's" culture? Allow me to repeat some of what was said in Chapter 4: if we consider Han culture to be the mainstream, then we can refer to five basic aspects of Han Chinese culture. First among these is the use of Chinese characters to write and the modes of thinking that come from them. The second aspect is the home, family, and state found in ancient China, as well as the ideas they gave rise to: Confucian political and ethical ideas about the state, society, and the family. The third aspect is the "unification of three teachings" of Confucianism, Buddhism, and Taoism. No single religion in China surpasses all others or can make the claim to absolute or singular authority; as they are all dominated by political authorities, they tolerate one another. The fourth aspect is the "unity between Heaven and Man" (*Tian ren he yi*);

the philosophies of Yin and Yang and the Five Elements, as well as the knowledge, ideas, and technologies that emerged from them. The fifth aspect is the unique idea of All-under-Heaven, which developed under the influence of the "round Heaven, square Earth" cosmology, as well as the international order, based on the tribute system, which developed out of the idea of All-under-Heaven. If we compare these five aspects with Christian civilization or Islamic civilization, or even with those regions in East Asia and South Asia that follow Buddhist beliefs and also make use of Confucian ethics, then we see that it is these five aspects that make up the "culture" of "(Han) China."[2]

If we want to isolate certain important aspects of history and cultural traditions when we discuss the outlook and possibilities for world peace, then the concept of All-under-Heaven in ancient China and the tribute system, as well as the way these ideas and orders extend into modern China's hopes and visions for a new world order, are most worthy of our attention and discussion.[3] In recent years, some scholars in China have felt that, as China begins its "rise" after several centuries of a world order led by the West, an "All-under-Heaven order" (*Tianxia zhixu*) or "All-under-Heaven-ism" (*Tianxia zhuyi*) that is rooted in traditional China should be treated as an important new resource for replacing the world order that has held sway since the early modern period. Some works by Western scholars, including *On China,* by former Secretary of State Henry Kissinger, and *When China Rules the World,* by Martin Jacques, follow a similar line of thought, mentioning repeatedly that in the past China had its own Chinese world order. They argue that China will use the traditional tribute system to imagine and establish an East Asian order and even a world order.[4] Likewise, when I was interviewed by a journalist in South Korea in November 2012, my interviewer asked repeatedly whether China's rise would lead to a revival of the tribute system.[5]

It is necessary to discuss, therefore, whether these cultural traditions, which understand the world in ways that are vastly different from the West, can bring peace to the world. Do we not also see the potential for conflict? What can reduce or resolve conflicts between cultures?

The Traditional Chinese Ideal of Grand Unification
and Culturalist Strategies

It need not be the case that, because we are Chinese people, we have to heap praise on Chinese culture and feel that every aspect of the culture is good, or even the basis for building the human culture for the future. It is my belief that while there is a hierarchy among civilizations, there are no questions of good or bad when it comes to culture.[6] As a scholar of history, I am interested in the historical analysis of Chinese culture.

The concept of All-under-Heaven and the tribute system developed in ancient China on the basis of the "round Heaven, square Earth" cosmology. "All-under-Heaven" is actually a self-centered cultural imaginary. On the one hand, it was this cultural vision that, by placing itself (China) at the center of the world, produced "distinctions between Chinese and barbarian" (*Hua Yi zhi fen*). On the other hand, these distinctions between Chinese and barbarian were not really based on racial distinctions expressed in statements such as, "If he is not my kin, he is sure to have a different mind."[7] Instead, they were established on differences in culture, between the uncultured and the culturally developed. It was these two sides of the concept of All-under-Heaven that would produce two ideas for how to manage the distinctions between "inner" (*nei*) and "outer" (*wai*). These two ideas are grand unification (*da yitong*) and culturalism (*wenhua zhuyi*).

It is certainly the case that, after a long series of conflicts, the Han Chinese and the peoples on their borders, the core regions, and the peripheries gradually formed into a sprawling empire rule by a central political power. Throughout this historical process, the vision that held that "under the whole Heaven, every spot is the sovereign's ground" and "to the borders of the land, every individual is the sovereign's minister" spurred on the desire for a unified and complete state. As a notion handed down from ancient China that All-under-Heaven can be "settled by unification" (regardless of which unification does the settling), "grand unification" has been a political ideal, some might even say a dream, throughout Chinese history. Both strong and weak states sought to realize the dream of a grand unification, as is seen in the way the Qin state dealt with the Xiongnu,

the way the Sui and the Tang dealt with the Goguryeo and the Turkic
peoples, the way the Song dealt with the Liao and Jin, or in the way the
Qing state dealt with the "Four Barbarians" (*si Yi*). This is particularly
important because today China's territories come from the Qing dynasty;
the means by which the Qing state established the territories of today's
China always make one recall the Ten Great Campaigns of the eighteenth
century. It was this pursuit of grand unification—and the use of military
force in the conquest of the Four Barbarians—that resulted in a great empire that stretched from "Sakhalin Island in the east to Shule in Xinjiang
and the Pamir Mountains in the west, to the Stanovoy Range in the north,
to Mount Ya (Yashan) in Guangdong in the south."[8] Here there was much
blood and fire; the history of opening new territories is not particularly
peaceful. To insist that China always "cherished men from afar" is to de-
ceive oneself and others,[9] and it is hardly always the truth to say that
"China is a country that has loved peace since ancient times."[10]

History also shows us another side of these questions. Although China
has always been accustomed to applying the methods used to manage its
internal order to the management of external orders,[11] ancient China was
more interested in "spreading light in the Four Directions" and less interested in invasion and colonization because China tends to emphasize
cultural differences over racial or ethnic differences. It is probably
because of this self-satisfied sense that "our dynasty lacks nothing" that
the tribute system in ancient times usually emphasized *bestowing* gifts
over receiving them, requiring only respect, glorification, and recognition
of the supreme dynasty's Heavenly Emperor—this attitude was quite different from the rapacious colonial strategies of early modern states such
as England, France, Spain, and Portugal. Another important aspect of
this question to consider is that ancient China was relatively isolated in
terms of its geography and its knowledge of the outside world. As a result, people in traditional China usually imagined all foreigners as barbaric, poor, and backward; foreign lands were not worth crossing the
seas and mountains to set up territories that had to be controlled from
afar.[12] A passage from the *Instructions by the Ancestor of the August
Ming* (*Huang Ming zu xun*) expresses this attitude well: "The barbarians of the four directions are cut off from the world by mountains and
seas, isolated in their respective corners. If we controlled their territory,

we could not extract tribute from it; if we ruled the people there, we could not extract labor service from them. If they overstep their bounds and attempt to trouble us, they will suffer. Likewise, if they cause us no trouble, and we still take up arms against them, then we will suffer."[13]

Modern China can no longer serve as an "empire" and should not take an imperialist attitude, but China in the Qin and Han times onward certainly was an empire. Even if this empire was forced in the early modern period to transform into a "nation-state," the history, ideas, and imaginations of empire continue to exercise influence, even down to the present day. In *Dwelling in This Middle Kingdom,* I argued that, while the idea of a limited state was contained within the notion of the empire without borders, this limited state also continued to imagine an empire without borders. China as a modern nation-state is precisely that which evolved out of the traditional centralized empire, yet the modern nation-state continues to hold within it remnants of the ideology of centralized empire, and thus the two are entangled throughout history.[14] Obviously, China has a strong desire to protect its "national territory" (*Guo tu*); losing the imperial capital is the worst outcome, and signing unfavorable treaties under duress is the greatest shame. In particular, because China was bullied by both East Asian and Western countries in the early modern period, none of its rulers can accept the ignominy of losing sovereignty or giving up territory. We also see, however, that in their complacency the dynasties that ruled China did not necessarily have much interest in the territories of others.[15] Even though China often worried about threats to the core regions, it usually intended to "pacify" and "assuage" the areas on its periphery.[16] At times China would also try to use the peoples on its periphery as buffers against outside threats, but China often was not interested in actual "foreign" territory and remained within its limited domains.[17]

Over a long period of time, the peripheries of "China," or the so-called All-under-Heaven of traditional China, by and large referred only to the eastern part of Central Asia. For this reason, other than the aspirations to bring revolution to every part of the world that were expressed during the "Cultural Revolution," China's idea of itself as a ruler of All-under-Heaven (*Tianxia ba zhu*) meant at most that it was a "suzerain" (*gong zhu*) state of the Asia region. Of course, when the "imperial" mentality of this

(Chinese) regional suzerain meets with the "imperial" behavior of (Western) global hegemons, then conflicts may in fact arise if we add in threats rooted in political ideology.[18] If political ideologies are not involved, however, and there is no direct involvement in Chinese territory or interests, then compromise will often carry the day.[19]

Religion as a Factor in Cultural Conflict: The Decline of Absolutism and Claims to Uniqueness in Chinese Religion

Here we can also turn to the question of religion. Religion is a core problem in Huntington's discussion of the clash of civilizations; he argues that "religion is a central defining characteristic of civilizations."[20] Scholarship on religion has also become a natural point of focus for contemporary cultural studies. It is often said that the ability or inability of civilization formed by so-called world religions, such as Christianity (including Catholicism, Protestantism, and Eastern Orthodox) and Islam, to coexist has a decisive influence on the global order.[21] For these reasons, historical research on these fields often has a very practical dimension, because their subjects relate directly to the field of international relations and also speak to concerns about whether religion can actually promote peace in the world today.

I will take a brief look at the perspectives, lines of thought, and conclusions drawn by recent scholarly works on various religions. Many scholars are addressing one problem: Across history, is conflict between world religions unavoidable? Are they unable to coexist? If conflicts are unavoidable, what draws them toward violence? If they can exist side by side, what factors lead followers of these religions to tolerate one another? In other words, what differences in perspectives, spirituality, and values between these religions cannot be overcome? What compromises can be reached between each religion's faith in its "one and only" God and "absolute" truth?

If we look back to traditional China, despite the fact that we see the attempt to wipe out Buddhism by the imperial court,[22] rivalries between Buddhism and Taoism,[23] and attacks on foreign religion,[24] by and large there were no major wars between religions. Instead, the "unification of the three teachings" (*san jiao he yi*) of Confucianism, Buddhism, and

Taoism has been the main course taken in both the history of religion and the history of politics. It has been said that the Xiaozong emperor (r. 1189–1194) of the Song dynasty, the Yongle emperor (r. 1402–1424) of the Ming dynasty, and the Yongzheng emperor (r. 1722–1735) of the Qing dynasty all spoke in favor of the unification of the three teachings, under which, it is often said, Confucianism was used for worldly affairs, Buddhism was used for the heart and mind, and Taoism was used to cultivate the body. Why did this happen?

We cannot simply conclude that these developments can be attributed to openness or tolerance between Confucianism and Taoism. Why, instead of this tolerance, do they not claim to be absolute? I would offer a simple explanation. First, religion in China has never acquired a status that allowed it to supersede or compete with secular political powers. No similarities are to be seen in China with those places where religion has held absolute spiritual and political power, as has occurred in the divine authority attributed to the pope in Europe and the unity of religious and political power in West Asia. Such phenomena were not possible after the disappearance of medieval Taoist traditions that organized the faithful into groupings that imitated military organizations and managed groups of households and people; it has not been possible since arguments that had been made from the time of the Eastern Jin dynasty through the Tang dynasty that monks do not bow to political power were rejected by the imperial court, establishing the requirement that monks pay respect to the ruler and bow to their parents. From the point that Confucians came to accept Buddhists' and Taoists' interpretations of the afterlife and the supernatural, Confucianism, Buddhism, and Taoism effectively all came under the control of secular political power.[25] Second, the great power of the emperor in ancient China ensured that all religious groups and organizations fell under official control of some sort.[26] The Buddhist Controller (Seng tong) and Taoist Controller (Dao tong) were appointed by government officials, permits for individuals to join monasteries were issued by the government, and the distribution of monasteries and temples were controlled by local governments. Religions organizations not only did not have the tight organization of churches, they also did not have a single unified leader like a pope. More important, they did not have their own military, so both religious organizations and the state could live in peace with one another.[27] Third, the worlds of belief to which Confucianism, Buddhism, and Taoism attended were different from one another, with a separate emphasis for each—hence the saying "Confucianism is used for worldly affairs, Buddhism is used for the heart and mind, and Taoism is used to cultivate the body." No single religion could claim an absolute or complete interpretation of the truth or establish a monopoly on thought, knowledge, or the world of faith. This was especially true among elites, where such beliefs became a kind of culture represented in the form of religion.[28] This role developed into a special characteristic of traditional Chinese culture.

For the reasons I have described, "religion" in traditional China transformed into "culture" and thereby lacked a single or absolute sense of spiritual truth. At the same time, elite society made a habit of separating mundane, secular life from the more transcendent aspects of religion, and elites became accustomed to achieving those transcendent aspects of religion within secular life.[29] Could these practices from Chinese culture provide perspectives and resources for other world religions on how to peacefully coexist with one another? A few years back, an attempt was made to bring together the various religions of the world and to find the "highest degree of compatibility" within each religion. In the end, however, they were only able to argue for a shared ethic based found in the "Declaration toward a Global Ethic" or in the Confucian teaching, "Do not do to others what you would not have others do to you." Is it not possible now, then, that we could find the spirit of peaceful coexistence from within the history of Confucianism, Taoism, and Buddhism in China?

China in Conflict: Predicaments of the "Modern," the "Nation-State," and "Culture"

From 1895 on, faced with the multiple challenges presented by Western politics, science, and culture, China was dragged step-by-step into the world. Whether in terms of culture, politics, or the world of faith, China faced numerous, complex struggles. In the three major questions of the modern, the nation-state, and culture, China has faced a series of dilemmas and predicaments.

The first dilemma is the meaning of "modern." On the one hand, "modern" means the laws, democratic institutions, science, and technology of modern Western nation-states, which are seen as the source of wealth and power. They are, in this view, the necessary and ideal path that must be taken; China should, according to this view, work to become "modern" and find its route to the "future." On the other hand, the modern is understood as the path by which the Western powers spread out across the world and by which "the strong eat the weak."[30] From this point of view, the modern is what led China to weakness and poverty, and, therefore, China should find another path toward a new version of the modern.[31]

The second dilemma is the "nation-state" (*guojia*). Many have accepted in concept the notion that the modern West take the "nation" as the basis of the "state" and believe that establishing a modern nation-state will enable China to pursue "modern civilization" in the same way as the West. At the same time, many are sympathetic to the idea that has held out in history that China is a state that is formed on the basis of culture, and feel that it is important to defend the idea of a great multinational state that has existed since the Han and Tang dynasties and was exemplified in the Qing-dynasty ideal of "spreading virtue in the four directions" across vast territories.[32] People who share this point of view still support "bringing the Four Barbarians into China."[33]

The third dilemma is "culture." On the one hand, China tends to see itself as the place that "gathers together all that is good"[34] of Eastern culture, such that it can stand on equal footing with the West, and thus many in China have become accustomed to speaking of "Chinese and Western culture" or "Eastern and Western Culture" as if they had the same meaning. On the other hand, China is also eager to show that its culture is *the* representative of Eastern culture, competing with Japan (the West of the East), India, and Iran, and other Eastern cultures for this status.

The question of culture has been the greatest source of complexity, contradiction, and conflict for Chinese thought since the late nineteenth century. These contradictions and conflicts all arise from the fact that China was an empire with a long history and powerful traditions. Even though this empire was challenged in the early modern period, it never went through a period of complete colonization and thus never lost its sense of cultural agency. For these reasons, to this day scholars are always working to find a unique perspective on the matter, whether in terms of historical narratives or theoretical expressions, that will resolve this dilemma.

It seems to me, however, that in modern people's world of ideas, it is important to maintain rational divisions. The political, the historical, the cultural, the popular, and the official (or state) all need rational boundaries. Take, for example, the question of "culture": if you concede that (universal, modern) civilization and (particular) cultures are always in conflict with one another, and that you can use reason to distinguish between civilization and culture, then you might not be inclined to engage in a simple and forceful rejection of globalization and modernity, which together are also a kind of "civilization." You would not think that this "civilization" is a barbarian onslaught, or that this new "civilizing" of our culture means that our culture will be broken apart by globalization and modernity. Simply put, globalization or modernization means for everyone to use one rhythm, one principle, one common understanding to associate and communicate with one another. If this association and communication does not have a shared rhythm, principle, and common understanding, then it will be like playing soccer on a basketball court, with no referees in sight—a complete mess.[35] Since the world has become smaller, and everyone lives on one planet, then we need to have generally recognized principles, an ethics that is followed by all, and a common understanding that is accepted by the majority of people. These principles, ethics, and common understanding are the "civilization" that is brought by globalization. The problem now lies in how to preserve and maintain with care many different cultures as they operate under the principles of modern civilization. Of course, this is a difficult question, one that cannot be resolved in a few words.

Conclusion: Cultural Traditions Are but One Resource—They Must Be Selected Rationally and Subjected to Modern Interpretation

Chinese intellectuals have a deep-seated faith in All-under-Heaven and a "Celestial dynasty" mentality. Many intellectuals, spurred by the so-called rise of China and troubled by the Western-led (and especially

American-led) world order have begun to trumpet the idea of All-under-Heaven-ism, the All-under-Heaven system, or "Neo-All-under-Heaven-ism" (*Xin Tianxia zhuyi*).[36] Some scholars argue that, at a philosophical level, the Confucian world is a world without borders, without notions of inner (*nei*) and outer (*wai*) and no distinctions between us and them. It is a world, these scholars argue, in which all people are treated equally; this All-under-Heaven order, therefore, should replace the current world order. Some people even go so far as to argue that, as calls for world governance grow louder, "China, whose national strength grows with each passing day, should reconstruct Confucian orthodoxy and take up once again the Confucian view of the world that 'All-under-Heaven is one family.' This set of ideas is better suited to maintaining fairness and peace in a world that is both interlinked and riven by conflict."[37] When they look back in history, these scholars suddenly discover that across all of history, China was the only "civilization that had brought the era of Warring States (*Zhan guo shidai*) to a close and established a culture of All-under-Heaven." "Her cultural traditions," one scholar argues, "may serve as the spiritual source for efforts to establish a culture of All-under-Heaven in the present."[38]

We can certainly sympathize with these sentiments. But because they want to rebuild All-under-Heaven, which is the self-centered outlook of a traditional empire, if this slapdash version of a new global thought is not stripped of its core of nationalism (which sees China as the "center of All-under-Heaven") and the attitude of arrogant self-regard, then it can very easily become a new form of chauvinism that claims to have universal relevance through its gestures toward the "equality of the multitude of states" and "all in the four seas are one family." No matter how ideas about All-under-Heaven are updated for new fashions, for the simple reason that they come from the history and traditions of ancient China, they cannot avoid bringing with them a certain associations with ideas about the "celestial dynasty." Although the idea that all people are "one family" seems warm and friendly, as soon as memories of China serving as the center return, then there is also a need for a head of the household who is at the center and controls everything. For these reasons, it is unavoidable to end up applying the All-under-Heaven order of traditional China to replace the vision for international order that emerged in the early modern period.[39]

If we take an evenhanded look at the idea of All-under-Heaven from a scholarly perspective and discuss Confucian ideals in a way that takes into account the historical background, then this would not be a problem. The problem lies in the fact that, these days, some Chinese scholars' discussions of All-under-Heaven attempt to understand what took place during imperial history as a universal order for the modern world.[40] Even more troublesome is that current discussions have gone beyond the realm of academic scholarship and attempted to reach the level of practical governance, which means that behind them lies all kinds of complex motivations and issues. Simply put:

First, excitement and even exuberance over the so-called rise of China has prompted these discussions. This exuberance has led what originally was a rational strategy by which China would "keep a low profile and bide its time" (*tao guang yang hui*) to fall apart,[41] and has also weakened the principles of order found in arguments for formal equality among the multitude of states; even the "five principles of peaceful coexistence,"[42] which took shape after 1949, are also pushed to the side. When people speak of a new order of All-under-Heaven, therefore, they show what one scholar has called a concern for power politics: "We will manage resources that are far greater than what we had before, undertaking economic management and political leadership. We want to exercise leadership over this world."[43]

Second, the emotional factors behind this narrative often come from China's long history of fierce struggle to resist humiliation and oppression. This fierce resistance is both the main storyline used in writing the history of early modern China and a key influence on China's attitude toward the rest of the world. For these reasons, as China becomes more powerful, it is easy for people to begin to agree with some scholars who argue that, after a century of the West plundering, oppressing, and plotting against China, *they* are now facing a crisis. China, however, has grown strong, and China can save the West. As a result, some argue that "future eras will see a political unification of humanity carried out by Chinese people and the establishment of a world government."[44]

Third, aside from the history of the Han and Tang Empires, the most important historical evidence for these narratives comes from the Mongol Yuan and Manchu Qing dynasties (especially the latter). They believe that these two "Chinese Empires" (*Zhonghua diguo*) not only "had no pagans"—meaning that, unlike Christian states, they tolerated all religions—but also "had no clear geographical borders and no cultural borders."[45] These historical empires "with no 'outside'" are then imagined as the future world of the "great unity" (*da tong*). These scholars further argue for the prescience of Qing-dynasty scholars of the Gongyang School, who, they contend, put forward ideas (buttressed by their classical scholarship) about a "world of peace" in which "all far and near, great and small are one" that provided the basis by which to establish the legitimacy of a (multi)national state under the banner of "Five Nations Under One Republic" in the Republic of China. Based on these arguments, they conclude that contemporary China has gone beyond the nation-state model that is based on early modern Europe and can point to its own practical legitimacy and historical rationality.

Fourth, at times the political bases of these discussions are supported by political ideology. We see an example of this when a scholar who also holds an official government position argues that the state should not only be "an entity established by law" but also "a cultural and civilizational entity" and concludes that the system of nation-states can be surpassed not only through the reconstruction of a cultural "China" but also through the revival of an ever-expanding All-under-Heaven (or what some call a "civilizational empire") that is rooted in the political and philosophical traditions of the Confucian classics.[46]

It is for precisely these reasons that ancient scholars' ways of remembering and imagining the Three Dynasties of Antiquity (the Xia, Shang, and Zhou), along with the Gongyang School's historiography of the "three eras" of history,[47] have all been newly rediscovered and elaborated upon by scholars in China, who have used them to support various political narratives and to construct new versions of world order.

I have noticed that quite a few scholars have enthusiastically discussed "China's moment in world history" and argued that "with the renaissance of Chinese civilization, humanity will begin to enter the 'Chinese moment in world history.' . . . China will fundamentally remake the world." According to this argument, promoting the concept of All-under-Heaven will be an important step in this work to change the world.[48] In all fairness, in an era of openness, some of this All-under-Heaven-ism and "Celestial dynasty mentality" could transform into a globalism that accepts universal values and universal truths and maintains a consensus within a framework of unity in diversity. These ideas would allow for the acceptance of the institutions, cultures, and ideas provided by other nations and countries while preserving one's own cultures and traditions. However, in times of impoverishment and weakness, when a crisis mentality reigns, or in times of ascendancy, when an attitude of arrogance and self-satisfaction holds sway, these ideas might also follow in the footsteps of nationalisms that look down on the "Four Barbarians" or hold one's own in higher regard than all others. As a result, these ideas might lead to ambitions to gain hegemony over All-under-Heaven with the wealth and military power gained through modernization. These ambitions, in turn, can become barriers that use culture to divide inner and outer—and you and me.

For these reasons, new questions arise: When promoting the revival of Chinese culture, is it possible to consider Chinese culture as a so-called resource that, according to the needs of modern civilization, can be subjected to reasonably selective and creative interpretation? Put another way, under conditions in which China is open to global culture, is it possible to align globalization and Chineseness, as well as universal values and Chineseness? If it is possible to strike that balance, then it is also likely that we can seek from that balance new inspiration for and ways of thinking about peace. If not, then the difficulty lies in the fact that when All-under-Heaven is brought to life, when imagined versions of the tribute system are taken to be real, and memories of the Celestial Empire are unearthed, then it is likely that Chinese culture and national sentiment will turn into nationalism or (or statism) that resists both global modern civilization and regional cooperation. Such a turn of events would truly lead to a clash of civilizations.

AFTERWORD

This little book became a reality because of the encouragement of Professor Tsuji Kōgo in Tokyo, Chan Koonchung in Beijing, and many other friends. The Japanese version, *Chūgoku saikō: Sono ryōiki, minzoku, bunka* (Rethinking China: Its territories, peoples, and cultures), was published in February 2014 by Iwanami Shoten. On the recommendation of Chan Koonchung, I published the Chinese version with the Hong Kong branch of Oxford University Press. Compared with the Japanese version, the Chinese version has been substantially revised and expanded, especially Chapter 3.

What I hope to share with readers in this book is how a Chinese scholar understands "China," "Chinese history," and "Chinese culture." I also hope readers will understand how a Chinese scholar might take a rational approach to analyzing some of the realities about China and its neighbors. I recognize that it can be difficult for scholars not to take positions colored by their national perspectives or feelings about their cultures, but for a scholar to be called a scholar, he or she must go beyond these perspectives and feelings and have the ability to work from historical knowledge and through rational thought.

The Introduction and Chapter 6 originally took shape as a number of different talks and papers; a portion of these chapters was published in *Here in "China" I Dwell* (*Zhai zi Zhongguo*, 2011). To make the arguments in the book more systematic and straightforward, however, I revised these chapters extensively and added new material. I also worked to make all of the chapters respond to their respective arguments.

The Introduction is a revised version of a lecture I delivered on November 11, 2012, for the Distinguished Lecture Series of the Korea Academic Research Council. The original title of the lecture was "History, Culture, and Politics: The Historical Formation of 'China' and Dilemmas of Identity."

Chapter 1 was revised from lectures written for my class on traditional China taught at Tsinghua University and Fudan University; I also gave a version of the lecture at the Department of Comparative Literature at the University of Michigan. A version of the text was originally published in *Lectures on Ancient Chinese Culture* (*Gudai Zhongguo wenhua jiangyi*) by Sanmin shuju (Taipei) in 2005.

Chapter 2 was originally prepared for a colloquium organized by the newspaper *Southern Metropolis Daily* (*Nanfang dushi bao*) of Shenzhen, which was later published in *Southern Weekend* (*Nanfang zhoumo*). The chapter has been extensively revised and expanded.

Chapter 3 was completed after I had submitted the Japanese version of this book to Iwanami Shoten and has not been previously published.

Chapter 4 was also prepared for the Korea Academic Research Council. The original title was "Multilayered, Solidified, Discontinuous: A Historical View of Chinese Culture."

Chapter 5 brings together materials prepared for lectures delivered at the Northeast Asian History Foundation in Korea (2007) and a "Forum on the Future of Asia" held in Bangkok, Thailand (2013).

Chapter 6 was prepared as a lecture for a "Cross-Straits Humanities Dialogue" held in Beijing and co-organized by the Chinese Culture Promotion Society and the Pacific Cultural Foundation. It has not been previously published and was substantially revised and expanded after that event.

Finally, I would like to express my gratitude to Professor Ying-shih Yü for providing the calligraphy for the cover of the Chinese version of the book. Since 2009 I have had the opportunity to spend half a month of each year at Princeton University as a visiting scholar. Over the past four years, nothing has brought me greater joy than to see Ying-shih Yü and Monica Shu-ping Chen and join them in the wide-ranging conversations from which I have learned so much. Since Professor Yu has retired, he may not go out often, but, as in the words of Laozi, "Without going out the door, one can know everything." Perhaps our many conversations together have been the "predestination" of which the ancients spoke.

NOTES

Translator's Introduction

1. See Ge Zhaoguang, *Here in "China" I Dwell: Reconstructing Historical Discourses of China for Our Time,* trans. Jesse Field and Qin Fang (Leiden: Brill, 2017), a translation of Ge's *Zhai zi Zhongguo: Chongjian youguan "Zhongguo" de lishi lunshu* (Beijing: Zhonghua shuju, 2011); and *An Intellectual History of China: Knowledge, Thought, and Belief before the Seventh Century BC,* trans. Michael S. Duke and Josephine Chiu-Duke (Leiden: Brill, 2014), a translation of a condensed version of the first volume of Ge's *Zhongguo sixiang shi* [An intellectual history of China], 3 vols. (Shanghai: Fudan daxue chubanshe, 1998). Articles that Ge has published in English include "A Stranger in a Neighbor's Home: Western Missionaries in Beijing, as Seen by Korean Envoys in the Mid-Qing Period," *Chinese Studies in History* 44, no. 4 (2011): 47–63; "Costume, Ceremonial, and the East Asian Order: What the Annamese King Wore When Congratulating the Emperor Qianlong in Jehol in 1790," *Frontiers of History in China* 7, no. 1 (2012): 136–151; and "A Dialogue on 'What Is China': Problems in Modernity, State, Culture," *Journal of Cultural Interaction in East Asia* 6 (2015): 79–90.

2. Li Zhiting, "Xuezhe ping 'Xin Qing shi': 'Xin diguozhuyi shixue' biaoben" [A scholar's assessment of the "new Qing history": A specimen of "neo-imperialist historiography"], Chinese Social Sciences Net, March 20, 2015, http://www.cssn.cn/zx/201504/t20150420_1592588.shtml. An English translation of an extract of the article was published by the China Media Project at the University of Hong Kong at http://cmp.hku.hk/2015/04/22/a-righteous-view-of-history/. See also "Why a Chinese Government Think Tank Attacked American Scholars," National Public Radio, May 21, 2015, http://www.npr.org/2015/05/21/408291285.

3. An oft-cited essay in Chinese on this question is "Shenme keyi cheng wei sixiang shide ziliao?" [What can serve as sources for intellectual history?], *Kaifang shidai* 2003, no. 4: 60–69. A portion of this essay is incorporated into Ge's *An Intellectual History of China,* 58–67. For further discussion, see Benjamin Elman, "The Failures of Contemporary Chinese Intellectual History," *Eighteenth-Century Studies* 43, no. 3 (2010): 371–391.

4. See, for example, Michelle Yeh, "International Theory and the Transnational Critic: China in the Age of Multiculturalism," in *Modern Chinese Literary and Cultural Studies in the Age of Theory: Reimagining a Field,* ed. Rey Chow (Durham, NC: Duke University Press, 2000), 251–280, as well as Rey Chow's introduction to the volume, esp. 1–7. For earlier discussions in the North American context, see *Modern China* 19, no. 1 (1993), which published a "symposium" on theory in literary studies, as well as *Modern China* 24, no. 2 (1998), a special issue on "theory and practice in modern Chinese history."

5. See Lydia Liu, *The Clash of Empires: The Invention of China in Modern World-Making* (Cambridge, MA: Harvard University Press, 2004), 75–81; and Arif Dirlik, "Born in Translation: 'China' in the Making of 'Zhongguo,'" *Boundary* 2, July 29, 2015, http://www.boundary2.org/2015/07/born-in-translation-china-in-the-making-of -zhongguo/.

6. See Liu, *The Clash of Empires*, 31–69.

Introduction

1. Ge Zhaoguang, *Zhai zi Zhongguo: Chong jian youguan "Zhongguo" de lishi lunshu* (Beijing: Zhonghua shuju, 2011). This work has appeared in English under the title *Here in "China" I Dwell: Reconstructing Historical Discourses of China for Our Time,* trans. Jesse Field and Qin Fang (Leiden: Brill, 2017). All subsequent citations will be to the English edition.

2. In a section titled "China in 1895" in the final chapter of volume 2 of *Zhongguo sixiang shi* [An intellectual history of China], I point out that the 1894 defeat in the first Sino-Japanese War and the 1895 signing of the Treaty of Shimonoseki constituted the single most important turning point in Chinese intellectual history and even Chinese history. See Ge Zhaoguang, *Zhongguo sixiang shi,* 3 vols. (Shanghai: Fudan daxue chubanshe, 1998), 2:531–550.

3. See the biography of the Qin Shi Huangdi, *Shi ji* [Records of the grand historian], 6:239. All subsequent citations from the twenty-four dynastic histories and the *Qing shi gao* [Draft history of the Qing] are from the standard punctuated editions from Zhonghua shuju. For the English, see "The Basic Annals of the First Emperor of Qin," in Sima Qian, *Records of the Grand Historian: Qin Dynasty,* trans. Burton Watson (Hong Kong: Renditions, 1993), 45. The *Doctrine of the Mean* summarizes this ideal in its lines, "Over the kingdom, carriages have all wheels of the same size; all writing is with the same characters; and for conduct there are the same rules." See "Zhong yong" [Doctrine of the mean], trans. James Legge, http://ctext.org/liji/zhong-yong/.

4. In 134 BCE, Dong Zhongshu advised Emperor Han of Wu (Han Wudi) to "follow Confucian ideas and no others." According to the biography of Dong in *History of the*

Han, Dong wrote that "Nowadays people study different versions of the Way and engage in different discourses, and the hundred schools of all different places are all
speaking of different ideas. For these reasons, the ruler has no way to maintain unity.
Your humble servant submits that all that is not within the Six Arts and the learning
of Confucius should be rejected and not allowed to develop" (*Han shu,* 2515). This recommendation, which came to be known as "rejecting the Hundred Schools and es-
teeming only Confucianism," was adopted to a marked degree by Emperor Han of Wu
and became part of the mainstream of Chinese thought. The latter remark is from Emperor Xuan of Han: "Emperor Xuan changed color and said: 'The Han dynasty has
its own institutes and laws, which are variously [taken from] the ways of the Lords Protector and the [ideal] Kings. How could I trust purely to moral instruction and use
[the kind of] government [exercised by] the Zhou [dynasty]?'" (*Han shu,* 277; translation modified from *The History of the Former Han Dynasty,* 3 vols., trans. Homer H.
Dubs [London: Kegan Paul, 1944], 2:301).

5. In the twenty-four dynastic histories, it is not until the *Song shi* (History of the Song)
    that we first see chapters such as "Biographies of Foreign States" (*Waiguo zhuan*) or
    "Biographies of Barbarians" (*Man Yi zhuan*), which make clear distinctions between
    "inner" and "outer" and possess a sensibility that is similar to that of the modern
    nation-state.

6. The Song dynasty was surrounded on all sides by powerful neighbors, as is discussed
    in a volume of essays on Song-era foreign relations, *China among Equals: The Middle
    Kingdom and Its Neighbors, 10th–14th Centuries,* ed. Morris Rossabi (Berkeley: Uni-
    versity of California Press, 1983). As these essays show, it was not until this era that
    China recognized that it lived among other powerful neighbors.

7. See Ge, *Here in "China" I Dwell,* 29–52.

8. The "Biographies of Japan" (*Wo guo zhuan*) in the *History of the Sui* records that
    letters of state from Japan at that time contained phrases like "the Son of Heaven
    from the Place Where Sun Rises sends greetings to the Son of Heaven from the Place
    Where the Sun Descends." See *Nihon shoki* [Chronicles of Japan] (Tokyo: Iwanami
    shoten, 1965), 189–191. Some Japanese scholars have also argued that, during the
    reign of Emperor Tenmu (673–686), the term *Tennō* (Ch. *Tianhuang,* Heavenly
    Emperor) was used in place of *Daiō* (Ch. *Da wang,* great king) to refer to the Japanese
    ruler as a way to demonstrate parity with China's emperor (who, as in the case of Tang
    Gaozong, was also referred to as Heavenly Emperor in 674), to secure a position higher
    than the King of Silla, who had also had titles conferred by the Chinese emperor, and
    to establish fully Japan's status as a state unto itself. See *Shōsetsu Nihonshi kenkyū*
    [A detailed study of Japanese history] (Tokyo: Yamakawa Shuppansha, 2012), 59.

9. Kawazoe Shōji points out that although these incursions did not result in extensive cap-
    ture of territory or colonization, they did have an important effect on the psychology
    of Japan; see *Mōko shūrai kenkyū shiron* [A historical treatise on studies of the Mongol
    invasions] (Tokyo: Yūzankaku, 1977), 26–28. As a result, after 1293, many documents
    and writings in Japan contain stories and visions of Mongol invasions. Naitō Konan
    once argued very strongly for the significance of the Mongol invasions in spurring the
    progress toward unification under Ashikaga Yoshimitsu (1358–1408); Naitō argued that
    "the Ōnin war (1467–1477) was a turning point for the independence of Japanese

culture." The reformist vision of Emperor Go-Uda (r. 1267–1324) and later members of the Southern Court were an important internal factor that pointed Japan toward cultural independence, while the Mongol rule of Japan and failed attempt to conquer Japan—which, in turn, led Japan to believe in its special role as the country of the gods (*Shinkoku*)—served as an important external factor toward cultural independence. See Lian Qingji, *Riben jindaide wenhua shixuejia: Neiteng Hunan* [Modern Japanese cultural historians: Naitō Konan] (Taipei: Xuesheng shuju, 2004).

10. In the Hongwu reign of the early Ming dynasty (1368–1398), the case of Hu Weiyong, who was executed in 1380, led to strained relations between the Ming dynasty and Japan. Of course, practical considerations took precedence over such grievances, and the Ming still allowed Japanese emissaries and scholars to visit China. By the time of the Jianwen (r. 1398–1402) and Yongle emperors (r. 1402–1424), Ashikaga Yoshimitsu (1358–1408) sent emissaries to communicate with the Ming, adopting a very humble posture of "submitting" (*cheng chen*) before the Ming court, but the Ming always kept a cool attitude toward them, conferring on Ashikaga only the title of "King of Japan" (*Riben guowang*); the Ming also, quite logically, referred to Japan, which had had hostile relations with the Yuan dynasty, as a "state that shall not be conquered" (*bu zheng zhi guo*). The *History of the Ming* records that "Fifteen states were designated as those that were not to be conquered, and Japan was among them. From this time forward, they did not pay tribute, and sea defenses were gradually reduced" (*Ming shi*, 8:344).

11. The year of the founding of the Joseon dynasty was also the eighth month of the twenty-fifth year of the Hongwu reign (1392). The Joseon sent emissaries to the Ming, and although the Ming Taizu emperor indicated that he accepted the change in political power in Korea, he also found reason to remind the rulers of Korea condescendingly that "in all affairs, you must be righteous and honest." See Wu Han, *Chaoxian Li chao shilu zhongde Zhongguo shiliao* [Materials related to Chinese history found in the veritable records of the Joseon dynasty] (Beijing: Zhonghua shuju, 1980), 1a, *juan* 1:111–113, 140.

12. Although titles of nobility were conferred on Annam during the Yuan dynasty, "When the king [of Annam] received the letter from the Son of Heaven, he stood with hands folded across his chest, not paying homage. When he met with ambassadors or ate with them, his seat was always placed in a position of superiority." See the "Annan zhuan" [Chronicles of Annam], in *Yuan shi* [History of the Yuan], 4644, 4637. It was not until the third year of the Hongwu reign that they accepted the titles bestowed on them by the Ming and begrudgingly became a part of the tribute system. They continued, however, to refer to their ruler as "The Emperor of Greater Yue" (*Da Yue huangdi*), which caused constant conflict with the Ming.

13. In 1516, a Portuguese explorer named Rafael Perestrello arrived in China by boat, raising the curtain on a long history of Western movement toward the East. In his *Zhongguo jin shi shi* [History of early modern China], Deng Hesheng named this day as the beginning of China's early modern history, stating, "From the Ming onward, sea traffic greatly expanded and European and American civilization flooded toward China. As a result, problems concerning international relations cropped up everywhere, and all actions could not but involve the many countries of the world."

14. Lynn Struve has pointed out that the effective control of the Ming was limited to the fifteen provinces of China proper, while Mongolia, Muslim-majority regions, Tibet, Manchuria, and parts of Mongolia were regularly ignored; it was not until the Qing dynasty that this fact changed. See Lynn Struve, "Introduction," in *The Qing Formation in World-Historical Time,* ed. Lynn Struve (Cambridge, MA: Harvard University East Asia Center, 2004), 2–3.

15. According to "Suzhou tu shuo" [Comment on a map of Suzhou], which is included in a 1544 copy of "Ganzhou zhen zhanshou tu lüe" [Maps of defenses of Ganzhou district] that is held in the Palace Museum in Taipei, "The Suzhou garrison is part of Jiuquan prefecture, and is an important defensive post on China's frontier . . . the lands outside of Jiayuguan are not our possessions." Quoted in *Menggu shan shui di tu* [Maps of the terrain of Mongolia], ed. Lin Meicun (Beijing: Wenwu chubanshe, 2011), 2.

16. Following the pacification of Xinjiang, in 1820 Gong Zizhen wrote an essay in favor of incorporating Xinjiang into the Qing state as a full-fledged province. In 1877, Zuo Zongtang also wrote a memorial to the emperor recommending that Xinjiang "be established as a province with prefectures and counties, thereby creating for Xinjiang a policy of lasting peace and enduring governance." In 1884, Xinjiang was finally made a province; as with the conversion of other peripheral territories into regular administrative regions (*gaitu guiliu*), the Qing government at last brought Xinjiang formally into its territory.

17. The first section of the chapter on geography in the *Draft History of the Qing* states that the Great Qing Empire "stretched from Sakhalin, which belonged to the Sanxing region, in the east, and from to Shule county in Xinjiang to the Pamir Mountains in the west and from Stanovoy mountain range in the north and to Mount Ya in Guangdong in the south." "All of these places paid obeisance to the central lands and were certainly a part of the dynasty" (*Qing shi gao,* 1891).

18. Zhang Taiyan produced a number of anti-Manchu writings, and Sun Yat-sen also gave consideration to calls to exclude Manchuria and Mongolia from China. Many scholars have researched these issues, so I will not go into detail here. See Chapter 3.

19. From 1895 on, China was brought fully into the histories of the world, of Asia, or of East Asia, and therefore one cannot avoid considering questions of identity, territory, and race, among others. In traditional times, these questions were not particularly prominent, but from 1895 onward, all of these questions rose to the surface. During and after the Second World War, China's many weaknesses, along with the movements for "national liberation," covered over the complexities of these questions. From the year 2000 onward, however, these questions became ever more difficult to avoid as a number of changes occurred in China's politics, culture, and economy, all of which were set against the international environment. This is the reason why we need to take up the question of "China" for discussion.

20. Ge, *Here in "China" I Dwell,* 23–25.

21. The following is only a simple overview. For a more detailed discussion, see ibid., 3–22.

22. Bai Shouyi, "Lishi shang zuguo guotu wentide chuli" [Resolving the historical problem of China's territoiries], in *Xue bu ji* [Steps in learning] (Beijing: Sanlian, 1978), 2. This article originally appeared in *Guangming ribao* [Guangming daily] on May 5, 1951.

23. The Japanese term *Shina* (Ch. *Zhina*) is often regarded in the Chinese context as a derogatory term, although its various historical meanings have been the subject of some debate.—Trans.

24. He argues that, as China has changed over the past eight hundred years, it is important to consider (1) internal developments within each region; (2) migrations between regions; (3) organization of government; and (4) the changes in elites' social and political activities. His research concentrated on the Tang-Song era through the Mid-Ming. Rather than focus on China as a whole, he focused on different regions, concentrating not on a single gentry elite (*shidaifu*) but rather a founding elite, professional elite, and local elite, placing particular emphasis on local elites. See Robert Hartwell, "Demographic, Political, and Social Transformation of China, 750–1150," *Harvard Journal of Asiatic Studies* 42, no. 2 (1982): 365–442.

25. William Skinner, "Regional Urbanization in Nineteenth-Century China," in *The City in Late Imperial China,* ed. G. William Skinner (Stanford, CA: Stanford University Press, 1977), 211–249.

26. See Ge, *Here in "China" I Dwell*, 150–171.

27. For example, Fukuzawa Yukichi's "Jūyonnenmae no Shina bunkatsuron" [The partition of China fourteen years ago] (1898), Nakajima Tan's "Shina bunkatsu no unmei" [China's destiny of partition] (1912), and Sakamaki Teiichirō's "Shina bunkatsuron" [The partition of China] (1917) all expressed similar views. Although Naitō Konan's famous essay "Shina ron" [On China] (1914) rejected these arguments, Naitō also argued that the idea of "Five Nations under One Republic" was an illusion.

28. Yano Jin'ichi, *Kindai Shina ron* [Theory of modern China] (Tokyo: Kōbundō Shobo, 1923), and *Dai Tōa shi no kōsō* [Imagining a history of greater East Asia] (Tokyo: Meguro shoten, 1944). See below for further discussion.

29. One of the earliest works in this vein was Yano Jin'ichi, *Dai Tōa shi no kōsō*. The Japanese government also commissioned the writing of a "history of greater East Asia" in 1942. More recently, many books concerned with "East Asia" have been published in Japan; one example is *Higashi Ajia shi nyūmon* [Introduction to East Asian History], ed. Nunome Chōfū and Yamada Nobuo (Kyoto: Hōritsu Bunkasha, 1995).

30. Mizoguchi Yūzō and the monograph series "Ajia kara kangaeru" [Reconsiderations from Asia] series published in the 1990s.

31. Tu Cheng-sheng is a Taiwan political figure and scholar. He has served as minister of education, director of the National Palace Musem in Taipei, and has taught at many universities in Taiwan.—Trans.

32. Tu Cheng-sheng [Du Zhengsheng], "Xin shixue zhi lu—jianlun Taiwan wushi nian laide shixue fazhan" [The path of new historiography—with a discussion of the development of historiography in Taiwan over the past fifty years], *Xin shixue* 13, no. 3 (2002): 39.

33. Richard von Glahn has pointed out that the latest scholarly trend is to treat the Qing Empire as a consciously multinational, colonial empire, as compared with the closed and isolated Ming dynasty, and thereby to determine the unique aspects of the Qing and to reject the idea of the Qing's "Sinification" into "Chinese culture." See his foreword in Struve, *The Qing Formation in World-Historical Time,* xi–xiii.

34. See Mark Elliott, *The Manchu Way: The Eight Banners and Ethnic Identity in Late Imperial China* (Stanford, CA: Stanford University Press, 2001); Pamela Kyle Crossley, *Orphan Warriors: Three Manchu Generations and the End of the Qing World* (Princeton, NJ: Princeton University Press, 1990); and *New Qing Imperial History: The Making of Inner Asian Empire at Qing Chengde,* ed. James Millward, Ruth W. Dunnell, Mark C. Elliott, and Philippe Forêt (New York: Routledge, 2004). For a very clear overview, see Wei Zhou'an [Joanna Waley-Cohen], "Xin Qing shi" [New Qing history], *Qing shi yanjiu* 2008, no. 1.

35. Problems arise immediately when this type of theory is applied wholesale to China. Under British colonialism, South Asia was forcibly divided into India, Pakistan, and Bangladesh, and even today it is unclear to which state places such as Kashmir belong. I suspect, then, that the experiences of India and such places makes it relatively easy for some scholars to accept postcolonial theories of the state. Drawing on their own feelings, experiences, and perspectives, they elucidate their ideas and reasoning concerning a postmodern historiography of the nation-state. They are correct to argue that attempts to reconstruct nations and states that had been torn apart did in fact draw from the model of the Western nation-state. This set of theories may not be applied to China, however, because China, with is long historical continuity, is not a new nation-state that was only reconstructed in the early modern period.

36. For further discussion of Hua-Xia, see Chapter 2.

37. See Prasenjit Duara, *Rescuing History from the Nation: Questioning Narratives of Modern China* (Chicago: University of Chicago Press, 1995). I accept that Duara's arguments have a grounding in theory and his personal experience, and that his desire to go beyond the historical framework of the nation-state is significant. But what are the results of this approach? Does it give us a better understanding of "China"?

38. During World War II, the Japanese Tōa Kenkyūjo (East Asia Research Institute) prepared a text called *Iminzoku no Shina Tōchishi* [A history of foreign nations ruling China], which sought to understand "from the national perspective" the history of the rule of China by the Northern Wei, the Liao, the Jin, the Yuan, and the Qing, as well as the rise and fall of these rulers. It concluded that the most important factor was the extent to which the spirit of the ruling nation could be relaxed—in other words, the Sinicization of the foreign dynasty. See the Chinese translation of this text: *Yi minzu tongzhi Zhongguo shi* (Beijing: Shangwu yinshuguan, 1964), 20.

39. See my discussion in Chapter 5.

40. *Fengjian* has also been translated as "feudalism," which may evoke too many associations with Western historical categories. For an extensive discussion, see Li Feng, "'Feudalism' and Western Zhou China: A Criticism," *Harvard Journal of Asiatic Studies* 63, no. 1 (2003): 115–144.—Trans.

41. These historical phenomena can all be compared with Japan and Korea, but the situation with China was clearly different. Religion (for example, Catholicism, Buddhism, and so on) occupied a position higher than what was seen in ancient China. Likewise, regional powers (whether feudal lords, kings, or military generals) had much more power in Europe and Japan than they had in ancient China, just as the

limitations that officials and powerful individuals could place on the king (or the emperor) was much greater.

42. See Benedict Anderson, *Imagined Communities: Reflections on the Origin and Spread of Nationalism,* rev. ed. (New York: Verso, 1991).

43. See Duara, *Rescuing History from the Nation.*

44. See Ge, *Here in "China" I Dwell,* 25.

45. Regarding this point, we can look at the many different versions of "China," large and small, that are found in *Zhongguo lishi ditu ji* [A collection of historical maps of China], edited by Tan Qixiang. We cannot, therefore, look back on China across history while using the modern political boundaries of China. It is not necessarily the case that Goguryeo was a "local power under the control of the Tang dynasty," just as it is not the case that Tubo [an ancient name for Tibet—Trans.] was not a part of "the territory of China (the Great Tang Empire)." Although the northeastern China of today and the Tibet of today falls within the domain of the control of the government of the People's Republic of China, they were not necessarily a part of the territory of ancient China. Moreover, we need not use a simple version of Chinese history to understand modern China, or feel that it is impossible to tolerate or understand Vietnamese independence, the separation of Outer Mongolia and Inner Mongolia, or that the Ryukyu Islands fell under Japanese control because, at some point in history, Annam fell under the rule of a Chinese court, Mongolia had been under the control of the Qing, or that the Ryukyu kingdom had offered tribute to a Chinese imperial court. Likewise, we need not be concerned about hurting the national sentiments (*minzu ganqing*) of the Korean people because parts of northeastern China that had once been under the control of the Goguryeo kingdom are now a part of China's territory.

46. This quotation is from the "Doctrine of the Mean" section of the *Li ji,* trans. James Legge, paragraph 29, http://ctext.org/liji/zhong-yong.—Trans.

47. At least since the beginning of the Song dynasty, China had formed into a cultural "community"; this community, however, was real, not imagined.

1. Worldviews

1. See Hong Weilian (also Hong Ye), "Kao Li Madoude shijie ditu" [An investigation into Matteo Ricci's map of the world], in his *Hong Ye lun xue ji* [Scholarly essays by Hong Ye] (Beijing: Zhonghua, 1981). For recent detailed research on this map, see Huang Shijian and Gong Yingyan, *Li Madou shijie ditu yanjiu* [A study of Matteo Ricci's map of the world] (Shanghai: Shanghai guji, 2004).

2. For discussions of "All-under-Heaven" in ancient China, see Xing Yitian, "Tianxia yi jia: Chuantong Zhongguo Tianxia guande xingcheng" [All-under-Heaven is one family: The formation of the idea of All-under-Heaven in traditional China], in his *Qin Han shi lungao* [Manuscripts on Qin and Han history] (Taipei: Dadong tushu gongsi, 1987), 1–41. See also Luo Zhitian, "Xian Qinde wufu zhi yu gudaide Tianxia Zhongguo guan" [The pre-Qin system of Five Zones and the idea of All-under-Heaven in ancient China], in his *Minzu zhuyi yu jindai Zhongguo sixiang* [Nationalism and early modern Chinese

thought] (Taipei: Dadong tushu gongsi, 1998), 1–34; and Ge Zhaoguang, "Tianxia, Zhongguo yu si Yi" [All-under-Heaven, China, and the Four Barbarians], in *Xueshu jilin* no. 16, ed. Wang Yuanhua (Shanghai: Yuandong, 1999), 44–71.

3. For a translation of the "Yu gong" or "Tribute of Yu," see Bernard Karlgren, *The Book of Documents* (Stockholm: Museum of Far Eastern Antiquities, 1950), 12–18.—Trans.

4. See *Shang shu* [Book of documents], in *Shisan jing zhushu* [The thirteen classics with commentaries and subcommentaries] (repr., Beijing: Zhonghua, 1979), 153. See also *Guoyu* [Discourses of the states] (Shanghai: Shanghai guji chubanshe, 1988), 4. Additionally, see Ge Zhaoguang, *An Intellectual History of China: Knowledge, Thought, and Belief before the Seventh Century BC*, trans. Michael S. Duke and Josephine Chiu-Duke (Leiden: Brill, 2014), 106–119.

5. Here the translation follows the summary and terminology used in Yü Ying-shih, "Han Foreign Relations," in *Cambridge History of China*, vol. 1, *The Ch'in and Han Empires*, ed. Denis Twitchett and Michael Loewe (Cambridge: Cambridge University Press, 1986), 379–381.—Trans.

6. *Zhou li zhu shu* [Rites of Zhou, annotated] (Beijing: Zhonghua shuju, 1979), *juan* 29:835. The *Zhou li*, a text believed to be of pre-Han origin, gives an extensive summary of what is said to be the governmental structure of the Zhou state. For a brief overview, see William G. Boltz, "Chou li," in *Early Chinese Texts: A Bibliographical Guide*, ed. Michael Lowe (Berkeley, CA: Society for the Study of Early China, 1993), 24–32.—Trans.

7. Yuan Ke, *Shan hai jing jiao zhu* [Classic of mountains and seas, annotated] (Chengdu: Bashu shushe, 1993), 257, 153, 416. The translations of place names are borrowed from *The Classic of Mountains and Seas*, trans. Anne Birrell (London: Penguin, 1999), 115, 71, 162.

8. Tao Yuanming, *Tao Yuanming ji* [Collection of works by Tao Yuanming], ed. Lu Qinli (Beijing: Zhonghua, 1979), *juan* 4:133. Translation borrowed from James Hightower, *The Poetry of T'ao Ch'ien* (Oxford: Clarendon Press, 1970), 229.

9. *Zhou bi suan jing* [A mathematical classic of Zhou gnomon], second *juan*, in *Suan jing shi shu* [Ten classics of mathematics], ed. Qian Baocong (Beijing: Zhonghua shuju, 1963), 2:54; *Lü shi Chunqiu* [Spring and Autumn Annals of Mr. Lü] (Shanghai: Shanghai guji, 1985), 726.

10. See Wu Hung, *The Wu Liang Shrine: The Ideology of Early Chinese Pictorial Art* (Stanford, CA: Stanford University Press, 1992), 245–247.

11. Zou Yan's phrasing comes from the *Shi ji* [Records of the grand historian], *juan* 74:2344.

12. Huang Huaixin et al., *Yi Zhou shu huijiao jizhu* [The remaining documents of Zhou, collated and annotated], *juan* 7:985.

13. *Mu Tianzi zhuan* [The tale of King Mu, son of Heaven], in *Congshu jicheng* [Comprehensive collection of collectanea] (Shanghai: Shangwu yinshuguan, 1937), vol. 3436.

14. "Dayuan liezhuan" [Annals of Dayuan], in *Shi ji*, 3157–3160; *Records of the Grand Historian: Han Dynasty II*, trans. Burton Watson, rev. ed. (New York: Columbia University Press, 1993), 231–252.

15. "Jiang Tong zhuan" [Biography of Jiang Tong], in *Jin shu* [History of the Jin dynasty], *juan* 56:1529–1534.

16. Kuwabara Jitsuzō, "Bukkyō no tōzen to rekishichirigakujō ni okeru bukkyō to no kōrō" [The eastward shift of Buddhism and the achievements of Buddhism in relation to historical geography], in *Kuwabara Jitsuzō zenshū* [Complete works of Kuwabara Jitsuzō], 6 vols. (Tokyo: Iwanami shoten, 1968), 1:293–334.

17. "Tian wen" [Astronomy], in *Yuan shi* [History of the Yuan dynasty], 999.

18. Gavin Menzies, *1421: The Year China Discovered America* (New York: William Morrow, 2003).

19. This text is from an inscription on a bronze mirror. See Lin Suqing, "Liang Han jing ming suo jian jiyu yanjiu" [A study of inscriptions of auspicious phrases observed on Han dynasty bronze mirrors], in *Han dai wenxue yu sixiang xueshu yantaohui lunwenji* [A collection of essays on a conference on Han-dynasty literature and thought], ed. Guoli zhengzhi daxue Zhongwen xi (Taipei: Wenshizhe chubanshe, 1991), 172.

20. This quotation comes from the *Zuo Commentary to the Spring and Autumn Annals*. Translation modified from James Legge, *The Ch'un Ts'ew, with the Tso Chuen*, in *The Chinese Classics*, 5 vols. (repr., Hong Kong: Hong Kong University Press, 1960), 5:355.—Trans.

21. See Lu Jiuyuan, *Lu Jiuyuan ji* [Collection of writings by Lu Jiuyuan] (Beijing: Zhonghua shuju, 1980), 273.

22. *Li ji zheng yi* [True meanings of the Book of Rites], in *Shisan jing zhushu*, 1338. Translation borrowed from James Legge's version of the *Book of Rites*, paragraph 36 (http://ctext.org/liji/wang-zhi).

23. See Ge Zhaoguang, "Zhou Kong heyi bu yan: Zhongguo Fojiao, Daojiao dui Rujiao zhishi shijiede kuochong yu tiaozhan" [Why the Duke of Zhou and Confucius did not speak: The ways in which Buddhism and Taoism expanded and challenged the Confucianist world of knowledge], in *Zhongguo shi xin lun: Sixiang shi fen ce* [New perspectives on Chinese history: Volume on intellectual history], ed. Chen Ruoshui (Taipei: Lianjing, 2012), 251–282.

24. See the Western Jin translation by Fa Li and Fa Ju, *Da lou tan jing* [Sutra of the great conflagration], in *Taishō shinshū daizōkyō* [Taishō Tripiṭaka], ed. Takakusu Junjiro and Watanabe Kaigyoku (Tokyo: Taishō Issaikyō Kankōkai, 1924–1932), *juan* 1:277; and *Fa yuan zhu lin* [A grove of pearls in the garden of the dharma], in *Taishō shinshū daizōkyō, juan* 53:280–281.

25. See Paul Pelliot, "La théorie des quatre Fils du Ciel," *T'oung Pao* 22, no. 2 (May 1923): 97–125. Pelliot pointed out that the *Shi'er you jing* did not seem to be included in recent editions but was found in the *Jin lü yi xiang* [Variant phenomena of Sutra and Vinaya] (completed in 516 CE) and in the forty-fourth *juan* of the *Fayuan zhulin* [Precious grove of the dharma garden] (completed between 668 and 671).

26. See the "Xuanzang zhuan" [Biography of Xuanzang] in the fourth *juan* of Daoxuan's *Xu gaoseng zhuan* [Supplement to the biographies of eminent monks], in *Taishō shinshū daizōkyō, juan* 50:454. Daoxuan also refers to "four rulers" in his *Shijia fangzhi*, but these refer only to the land of the Hu, the Turkic peoples, China (Zhendan), and India.

27. *Fozu tongji* [Chronicle of the Buddhas and Patriarchs], *juan* 31, in *Taishō shinshū daizōkyō, juan* 49:303.

28. There is another painting, now held in Japan, that was printed during the early Ming dynasty in Joseon-dynasty Korea. These maps have their origins in Yuan-dynasty

China, but the geographical knowledge they convey may also come from the *Consolidated Map of Territories Including Capitals of Past Dynasties* (*Hunyi jiang li lidai guodu zhi tu*), which came from Arab peoples. These maps show that Chinese people already possessed extensive knowledge of the world. The map of this "world" included Korea and Japan to the east, islands such as Luzon and Palawan to the southeast, Sumatra and Borneo to the southwest, the Arabian Peninsula and a cone-shaped depiction of the African continent to the west, and Lake Baikal to the north. In other words, it nearly covered much of the continents of Europe, Asia, and Africa. Miya Noriko, *Mongoru teikoku ga unda sekaizu* [The world map born of the Mongol Empire] (Tokyo: Nihon Kaizai Shinbunsha, 2007); prior to this, we also have Takahashi Tadashi's research on this map. See "*Hunyi jiang li lidai guodu zhi tu* zai kao" [A reexamination of *Consolidated Map of Territories Including Capitals of Past Dynasties*] and "*Hunyi jiang li lidai guodu zhi tu* xu kao" [Further examination of *Consolidated Map of Territories Including Capitals of Past Dynasties*], in *Ryūkoku shidan* [Journal of history of Ryukoku University] (Kyoto: Ryukoku University, 1966), nos. 56–57, and *Ryūkoku Daigaku ronshū* [Collected theses of Ryukoku University] (Kyoto: Ryukoku University, 1973), nos. 400–401.

29. Just before the arrival of Western missionaries, a man of letters named Ou Daren (1516–1595) was still writing harsh criticisms of the Buddhist worldview. "The Five Sacred Mountains [Taishan in the east, Huashan in the west, Hengshan (Hunan) in the south, Hengshan (Shanxi) in the north, and Songshan in the central plains] are the markers of All-under Heaven, while there are those who argue . . . that China is but one corner of Jambudvīpa. When I hear of them I laugh at nine out of ten, am shocked by one in three, wonder about one in ten, and believe not even one in a hundred." See *Ou Yubu ji: Wenji* [A collection of prose by Ou Daren] (Beijing: Shumu wenxian chubanshe, 2007), *juan* 7:659.

30. See Unno Kazutaka, *Minshin ni okeru Mateo Ricchi kei sekaizu: Omo to shite shinshiryō no kentō* [Chinese world maps of the Ming and Qing dynasties derived from the work of Matteo Ricci: An examination of new and neglected materials], in *Shinhatsugen Chūgoku kagakushi shiryō no kenkyū (ronkōhen)* [Research into newly discovered materials in the history of Chinese science], ed. Yamada Keiji (Kyōto: Kyōto Daigaku jinbunkagaku kenkyūsho, 1985), 512. See also Funakoshi Akio, "Kon'yo bankoku zenzu to sakoku Nihon" [*Kunyu wanguo quantu* and isolated Japan], *Tōhō Gakuhō* 41 (1970): 595–709. Zou Zhenhuan has pointed out that there were three sources for Ricci's maps, "including fifteenth- and sixteenth-century copperplate engravings and related materials; Chinese maps and gazetteers; and his own personal experiences and records. The Western sources he used largely came from the Flemish school, such as the world maps of Gerard Mercator, Abraham Ortelius, and Peter Plancius." See Zou Zhenhuan, *Yingxiang Zhongguo shehuide yibaizhong yizuo* [One hundred translations that influenced Chinese society] (Beijing: Zhongguo duiwai fanyi chuban gongsi, 1996), 4.

31. See the section on *si Yi* in *Huangchao wenxian tongkao* [Imperial compendium of documents] (Hangzhou: Zhejiang shuju, 1882), *juan* 298:4. See also *Siku quanshu zongmu* [Bibliography of the *Emperor's Four Treasuries*] (repr., Beijing: Zhonghua, 1981), 633.

32. For a discussion of the influence of Ricci's maps, see Chen Guansheng, "Li Madou dui Zhongguo dilixuede gongxian jiqi yingxiang" [Matteo Ricci's influence on and contribution to geography in China], *Yu Gong* 5, no. 3–4 (1936). For the social significance of Ricci's maps, see Lin Dongyang, "Li Madou shijie ditu jiqi dui Mingmo shiren shehuide yingxiang" [Matteo Ricci's maps of the world and their influence on late-Ming scholarly society], in *Jinian Li Madou lai Hua sibaizhounian Zhong-Xi wenhua jiaoliu guoji huiyi lunwenji* [Papers from a conference on East-West cultural exchange in honor of the four hundredth anniversary of Matteo Ricci's arrival in China], ed. Ji nian Li Madou lai Hua sibai zhounian Zhong-Xi wenhua jiaoliu guoji xueshu huiyi mishuchu (Taipei: Furen daxue chubanshe, 1983), 311–378.

33. Henri Bernard, *Li Madou pingzhuan* [Chinese translation of Père Matthieu Ricci et la société chinoise de son temps (1552–1610)], trans. Guan Zhenhu, 2 vols. (Beijiing: Shangwu yinshuguan, 1993), 2:559. Ricci also realized that many educated elites were unhappy with his work and would resist his ideas.

34. "Dong Yi liezhuan" [Biographies of the eastern barbarians], in *Sui shu* [History of the Sui], 1827.

35. See Alain Peyrefitte, *The Immobile Empire,* trans. Jon Rothschild (New York: Knopf, 1992), 223–231.

36. For a discussion of the complex shifts that took place during the early modern period in China's view of the world and self-consciousness as China, see Chapter 3 of this volume.

37. Joseph R. Levenson argued, "In large part the intellectual history of modern China has been the process of making a *guojia* [nation] of *Tianxia* [All-under-Heaven]." See Joseph R. Levenson, *Confucian China and Its Modern Fate: The Problem of Intellectual Continuity* (Berkeley: University of California Press, 1958), 103.

2. Borders

1. Du Fu, "Chun wang" [A spring scene], in Pu Qilong, *Du Fu xin jie* [Understanding Du Fu] (Beijing: Zhonghua, 1981), 363.

2. According to Gu Yanwu, "losing the state" was different from "losing All-under-Heaven." When a "different clan" "changed the name of the dynasty," this was merely "losing the state"; in other words, a change in dynasties was simply the change in political rulers. "Losing All-under-Heaven" meant an "end to benevolence and righteousness" (*ren yi chong se*)—if civilization itself were lost, and if people no longer maintained a sense of propriety, justice, honesty, and humility, then All-under-Heaven itself would fall to pieces. There are obvious differences here between a spatial understanding of the state and a political understanding of the government (or dynasty), on the one hand, and, on the other hand, a cultural understanding of community. Gu Yanwu believed that protecting the state (the government or dynasty) was the responsibility of politicians, but protecting civilization was the responsibility of all. See *Gu Yanwu quanji* [Complete works of Gu Yanwu], 22 vols. (Shanghai: Shanghai guji, 2011), 18:527.

3. "Diversity in unity" is an idea put forward by Fei Xiaotong. See Fei Xiaotong, "Zhonghua minzude duo yuan yiti de geju" [The Chinese people's pattern of diversity in unity], *Beijing daxue xuebao* 1989, no. 4: 1–19.

4. For a discussion of this debate, see Nan Liming, "Hanguo dui Zhongguode wenhua kangyi" [Korea's cultural resistance against China], and Qian Wenzhong, "Gaojuli shi Zhong-Han gongtong wenhua yichan" [Goguryeo is the shared cultural inheritance of China and Korea], *Yazhou zhoukan* (Hong Kong edition), July 25, 2004, 16–20.

5. See Ge Zhaoguang, *Here in "China" I Dwell: Reconstructing Historical Discourses of China for Our Time*, trans. Jesse Field and Qin Fang (Leiden: Brill, 2017), 150–171.

6. Yano Jin'ichi, "Shina mukokkyōron" [Treatise on a borderless China], in Yano Jin'ichi, *Kindai Shina ron* [Theory of modern China] (Tokyo: Kōbundō Shobō, 1923), 1. This book also has a chapter titled "Manmōzō ha Shina honrai no ryōdo ni soshiru ron" [Refutation of the idea that Manchuria, Mongolia, and Tibet are intrinsically Chinese territories], 92–112. See Goi Naohiro, "Dongyang shixue yu Makesi zhuyi" [Oriental studies and Marxism], in *Zhongguo gudai shi lungao* [Papers on the history of ancient China], trans. Jiang Zhenqing and Li Delong (Beijing: Beijing daxue chubanshe, 2001), 58. Goi has pointed out that Japan's occupation of China during the period leading up to World War II spurred the enthusiasm for Oriental studies, and Yano's ideas on these topics became more and more popular. Works such as the twenty-six volume *Sekai rekishi taikei* [A systematic overview of world history] (Tokyo: Heibonsha, 1933–1936) and the eighteen-volume *Iwanami kōza Tōyō shichō* [Iwanami lectures on Eastern thought] (Tokyo: Iwanami shoten, 1934–1936) are examples of this trend.

7. Yano Jin'ichi, *Daitōashi no kōsō*, 31. For a critique of this argument, see Fu Sinian, *Dongbei shigang* [Outline history of the northeast], in *Fu Sinian wenji* [Collected prose of Fu Sinian], vol. 1 (Shanghai: Shanghai guji, 2012). Fu Sinian argues that Yano deliberately misrepresented the issue, and that his argument "served as an excuse for Japan to invade the northeast"; his argument was clearly written in response to the foreign aggression that China suffered in the 1930s. See my discussion in Chapter 3 of this volume.

8. Bai Shouyi, "Lishi shang zuguo guotu wentide chuli," in Bai Shouyi, *Xuebu ji* [Steps in learning] (Beijing: Sanlian shudian, 1978), 2.

9. Is it necessarily the case that states made up of many different nations and regions are traditional empires, and not modern nation-states? Must they be governed under a system of federation and not a unified government? This is a question worth discussing in depth. Yu Fengchun has pointed out that "Early modern China, as a multi-national state, presents a theoretical challenge to the great powers of the United States, Europe, and Japan, which formed 'a state built on a single nation.' . . . Today, it is common sense to see argue that 'many nations can make up a modern nation-state,' but this idea was not accepted in the world of the first half of the twentieth century." See Yu Fengchun, *Zhongguo guomin guojia gouzhu yu guomin tonghe zhi licheng—yi 20 shiji shangbanye dongbei bianjing minzu guomin jiaoyu wei zhu* [The formation of the Chinese national state and the path toward unifying the citizenry: Civic education of nationalities on the borders of the northeast in the first half of the twentieth century] (Harbin: Heilongjiang jiaoyu chubanshe, 2006), 7.

10. Sun Zuomin, "Zhongguo gudai shi zhong youguan zuguo jiangyu he shaoshu minzude wenti" [Questions related to borders of the motherland and minority peoples in ancient Chinese history], *Wen hui pao*, November 4, 1961. See also Sun Zuomin, "Chuli lishi shang minzu guanxide jige zhongyao zhunze" [Important standards for understanding historical relations between nationalities], in *Zhongguo minzu guanxi shi lunwenji* [Essays on the history of relations of China's nationalities], 2 vols. (Beijing: Minzu chubanshe, 1982), 1:157.

11. Owen Lattimore, *Inner Asian Frontiers of China*, 2nd ed. (New York: American Geographical Society, 1951), 238–242.

12. Nicola Di Cosimo has shown that ancient China had varying borders; see his *Ancient China and Its Enemies: The Rise of Nomadic Power in East Asian History* (Cambridge: Cambridge University Press, 2002), 313–317. His discussion of different types of borders may not be entirely without problems. Borders between ancient China and its peripheries existed in terms of cultural differences between Chinese and foreigners and as ideas drawn out on maps; there were also divisions between administrative regions determined by military control; and there were borders negotiated between states, such as the mid-Tang-era borders negotiated between the Tang state and the Tubo.

13. See *Shao shi wenjian lu* [Things seen and heard by Master Shao] (Beijing: Zhonghua, 1983), *juan* 1:4. This sense of helplessness about the state's territory plagued the gentry elites for generations. For example, an inscription that accompanies a "Map of Lands" (*Dilu tu*), which was carved during the Southern Song in 1247, takes a similar tone. The author, Huang Chang, could not help but describe an incomplete All-under-Heaven: even if "the dynasty and the emperor had fought off every hardship to bring peace to the land," "the Son of Heaven's troops had been dispatched [to the north] many times," the land and troops of Youzhou and Ji [areas in northern China in and around contemporary Beijing] were held by the Khitan and could not be regained. Therefore, "when looking at the lands of the north and south, one can be saddened or enraged." Quoted in the appendix prepared by Qian Zheng and Yao Shiying on the "Dilu tu bei" for *Zhongguo gudai ditu ji (Zhanguo zhi Yuan)* [A collection of maps from ancient China: From the Warring States era to the Yuan] (Beijing: Wenwu chubanshe, 1990).

14. See *Chanyuan zhi meng xin lun* [A reassessment of the covenant of Chanyuan], ed. Zhang Zhixi et al. (Shanghai: Shanghai renmin chubanshe, 2007).

15. "Fan yi er" [Second entry on foreign barbarians], in *Song hui yao ji gao* [Draft collection of fragments of *Collected Documents of the Song Dynasty*], comp. Xu Song (1957; repr., Beijing: Zhonghua, 1997). ["One China with different interpretations" makes a slightly irreverent reference to the so-called 1992 consensus between Taiwan and the People's Republic of China, which agreed to the principle of "one China" with "different interpretations."—Trans.]

16. See Tao Jinsheng, *Song Liao guanxi shi yanjiu* [Researches on the history of relations between the Song and the Liao] (Beijing: Zhonghua, 2008), 84–85.

17. Even though the Tang dynasty and the Tubo had signed a treaty or covenant (*meng shu*) to indicate "Han territory" (*Han jie*), this document did not state that the other

side of the border belonged to Tubo, but rather said that the Tang and Tubo states were like "uncle and nephew." They definitely were not considered equal to one another, but more important is that the document laid out lines to separate areas of authority. See *Jiu Tang shu* [Old book of Tang], 5247.

18. For a discussion of these issues, see Wang Gungwu, "The Rhetoric of a Lesser Empire: Early Sung Relations with Its Neighbors," in *China among Equals: The Middle Kingdom and Its Neighbors,* ed. Morris Rossabi (Berkeley: University of California Press, 1983), 47–65.

19. See Ge, *Here in "China" I Dwell,* 29–52.

20. See Ge Zhaoguang, *Zhongguo sixiang shi* [An intellectual history of China], 3 vols. (Shanghai: Fudan daxue chubanshe, 1998), 2:253.

21. Because of this type of phenomenon, in recent years some scholars have argued that rather than use this idea of political space (which evolved out of later historical understandings) to narrate history, it is more effective to weaken the basic unit of this narrative. Thus we see a new fashion for postcolonial theories such as those related to "imagined communities" and "border-crossing histories." See Benedict Anderson, *Imagined Communities: Reflections on the Origin and Spread of Nationalism,* rev. ed. (New York: Verso, 1991).

22. See Ge, *Here in "China" I Dwell,* 29–52; see also Chapter 3 of this volume.

23. See Nishikawa Nagao, "Kokumin kokkaron kara mita 'sengo'" [The postwar era seen from the perspective of nation-statism], in Nishikawa Nagao, *Kokumin kokkaron no shatei* [The striking range of nation-statism] (Tokyo: Kashiwa shobō, 1998), 256–286.

24. For example, Eric Hobsbawm noted that the nation is "the product of particular, and inevitably localized or regional historical conjunctures," and therefore, in his discussion of China, points out that China may be an important exception to the general trend toward choosing a national vernacular over and above the prestigious languages of the elites. See Eric Hobsbawm, *Nations and Nationalism since 1780: Programme, Myth, Reality,* 2nd ed. (Cambridge: Cambridge University Press, 1990), 5, 56.

25. Recently Yoshimoto Michimasa, in an article titled "Chūgoku kodai ni okeru kaishisō no seiritsu" [The formation of the Chinese/barbarian dichotomy in ancient China], discussed ideas about differences "Chinese and barbarians" from the Western Zhou down to the Warring States period. Yoshimoto points out that prior to the middle of the Warring States period, there were three methods of dealing with foreigners: assimilation (*tonghua*), casting out (*yiqi*), and "loose reins" (that is, indirect rule, *jimi*). Tsuji Mashahiro, in an essay on "Kikushi Kōshōkoku to Chūgoku ōchō" [The Qu-Shi Gaochang kingdom and Chinese dynasties], took up the example of the Gaochang (or Karakhoja) Kingdom to discuss the various policies employed by China in the medieval period to handle neighboring states and peoples, including tribute, "loose reins," enfeoffment, and conquest. Tsuji also compares the fate of Gaochang with others states, such Goguryeo, Baekje, and Silla, noting that Chinese dynasties' perspectives on foreign policies often changed along with the international environment. See Fuma Susumu, ed., *Chūgoku Higashi Ajia gaikō kōryūshi no kenkyū* [Studies of the history of diplomatic exchanges between China and East Asia] (Kyoto: Kyōto Daigaku gakujutsu shuppanka, 2007).

26. Zhang Guangda, "Cong Anshi zhi luan dao Chanyuan zhi meng" [From the Wang Anshi rebellion to the Chanyuan covenant], in *Jidiao yu bianzou: Qi zhi ershi shijide Zhongguo* [Themes and variations: China from the seventh through the twentieth century], ed. Huang Kuanzhong (Taipei: Zhengzhi daxue lishi xi, 2008), 18.

27. We should not take "All-under-Heaven" to mean that there was no sense of "China" in ancient China. The Han dynasty referred to itself in terms of All-under-Heaven, but inscriptions on bronze mirrors from the Han frequently use the term *Zhongguo* (China or the Middle Kingdom), often in contrast with "Xiongnu." Japan also referred to itself as All-under-Heaven: as Sadao Nishijima has pointed out, Japan's version of All-under-Heaven referred only to territory under Japanese political control. For China, it appears that All-under-Heaven refers to a world with China at the center, whereas for Japan, All-under-Heaven refers to Japan itself. See Sadao Nishijima, *Nihon rekishi no kokusai kankyō* [The international environment of Japanese history] (Tokyo: Tōkyō Daigaku Shuppankai, 1985), 77–78.

28. See Gu Jiegang's essay from 1926, "Qin-Han tongyi youlai he Zhanguoren duiyu shijiede xiangxiang" [The origins of the Qin-Han unification and understandings of the world in the Warring States period], in *Gu Jiegang quanji* [Complete works of Gu Jiegang], 62 vols. (Beijing: Zhonghua, 2010), 6:33.

29. Diao Shuren, "Zhong-Chao bianjie yange shi yanjiu" [A study of changes in the China-Korea border], *Zhongguo bianjiang shi di yanjiu* 2001, no. 4. See also Yang Shaoquan and Sun Yumei, *Zhong-Chao bianjie shi* [History of the China-Korea border] (Changchun: Jilin wen shi chubanshe, 1993).

30. For a discussion of another side of this history, see Chapter 3 of this volume.

31. Regarding this discussion, see Chapter 3 of this volume. In fact, this question was addressed some time ago in a book coauthored by Gu Jiegang and Shi Nianhai, *Zhongguo bianjing yange shi* [A history of changes in China's borders] (Shanghai: Shangwu yinshuguan, 1938). However, it was written during the Second Sino-Japanese War, and is mostly interested in defending the legitimacy of China's territory as a multinational state. It therefore emphasizes the unity of "Chinese" territory since ancient times. Later, we have Ge Jianxiong's *Lishi shangde Zhongguo: Zhongguo jianyude bianqian* [China in history: Changes in Chinese territory] (Shanghai: Jinxiu wenzhang chubanshe, 2007), which works along similar lines to provide a good summary.

32. Nishijima Sadao has argued that the East Asian cultural sphere, which originally included Japan, was marked by four characteristics: Chinese characters, Confucianism, Buddhism, and a legal system with a shared structure. However, the rise of a sense of separate states in East Asia and the formation of a Japanese subjectivity were related to the decline of the Tang dynasty in the ninth and tenth centuries. Nijishima also points out that because of the conquest of territories by the Khitan and the Xixia, who saw themselves as states equal to that ruled by the Song emperor, international relations in East Asia changed greatly from the times of the Tang dynasty, when the Tang emperor was the only acknowledged sovereign who enfeoffed rulers on the periphery. From this point onward, a new international order arose in East Asia, one in which many did not recognize Chinese dynasties as the sole center.

33. *Qing shi gao,* 1891. Recently an American scholar at Rice University has found a Qianlong-era map, *Jingban tianwen quantu,* which was based on a Kangxi-era official map.

The colophon on the bottom left-hand side is quite interesting and is worth quoting here. The colophon says that in the Kangxi-era version of the map, "every river, mountain, territory, city, district, county, fief, and boundary was placed artfully into an ordered position, like a piece of embroidery." However, by the time the later map was made, "Taiwan and Dinghai were not included in the territory on the map, and offices for registering households have not been established for the protectorate forty-nine banners of Mongolia, the Red Miao, Kangding [also Dardo or Dajianlu], Hami, the Khalkha, Hetao [the upper reaches of the Yellow River] and the lands to the west, and Qinghai Lake." In other words, between the Kangxi and the Qianlong reigns, the Great Qing Empire used military conquest or conversion of peripheral territories into regular administrative regions (*gaitu guiliu*) to grow its territories by "twenty thousand *li*." This expansion was exactly the opposite of the long-term shrinking of state territories that took place during the Song and Ming dynasties. The result was that the territories and borders of "China" would be faced with a host of new problems for many years to come. The version of the *Jingban tianwen quantu* housed in the Rice University libraries was printed between roughly 1780 and 1790 (see http:// exhibits.library.rice.edu/exhibits/show/jingban-tianwen-quantu/history-of-the -jingban-tianwen).

3. Ethnicity

1. Joseph R. Levenson, *Confucian China and Its Modern Fate: The Problem of Intellectual Continuity* (Berkeley: University of California Press, 1958), 103. See also Immanuel Hsü, *China's Entrance into the Family of Nations: The Diplomatic Phase, 1858–1880* (Cambridge, MA: Harvard University Press, 1960).
2. This theory, put forward by John Fairbank and Joseph Levenson in the 1950s, has come under fierce attack for the last few decades. I would argue, however, that although this modernist "stimulus-response" model has many problems, with further revision and elaboration it can continue to have significant explanatory power for historians.
3. If we do not notice the overlap of these two historical processes, then we have no way to understand why "China" today still resembles both a modern nation-state and a traditional empire; we also cannot explain why China is still dealing with dilemmas related to drifting apart from or being at odds with neighboring states, the challenge of Western influence, and internal issues related to the identity of different national groups and geographical regions. We are even less able to explain why scholars and thinkers in China continue to pursue transformation toward a modern state while insisting that the state maintain "unity in diversity" even as they are unwilling to abandon ways of describing China that depend on ideas of Sinicization and acculturation.
4. Regarding this question, see Yoshikai Masato's "Byōzokushi no kindai" [The modern era of the history of the Miao], 1–7, published serially in *Hokkaidō Daigaku bungaku kenkyūka kiyō,* nos. 124–134 (2008–2011), esp. parts 1–3. I learned a great deal when writing a review of this work. See my essay, "Zai lishi, zhengzhi yu guojia zhijiande minzu shi" [The history of nationalities: Between history, politics, and the state], *Nanfang zhoumo,* September 7, 2012.

5. Zhang Taiyan, "Tao Manzhou xi" [Condemning the Manchus], in *Zhang Taiyan quanji* [Complete works of Zhang Taiyan], 6 vols. (Shanghai: Shanghai renmin chubanshe, 1985), 4:190.

6. Zhang Taiyan, "Bo Kang Youwei lun geming shu" [A refutation of Kang Youwei's thoughts on revolution], in *Zhang Taiyan quanji*, 4:173.

7. Zhang Taiyan, "Zhong-Xia wangguo er bai si shi er nian jinian huishu" [Letter written in commemoration of the 242nd anniversary of the loss of the Chinese state], in *Zhang Taiyan quanji*, 4:188.

8. Zou Rong's anti-Manchu tract called for China to "sweep away millennia of despotism in all its forms, throw off millennia of slavishness, annihilate the five million and more of the furry and horned Manchu race, and cleanse ourselves of two hundred and sixty years of unremitting pain." See Zou Rong, *Geming jun* (Beijing: Zhonghua, 1971), 1. Translation borrowed from Tsou Jung (Zou Rong), *The Revolutionary Army: A Chinese Nationalist Tract of 1903*, trans. John Lust (The Hague: Mouton, 1968), 58. Chen Tianhua, "Jue ming shu" [Suicide note] (1905), in *Xinhai geming qian shi nian shilun xuanji* [Collection of political writings from the decade leading up to the 1911 revolution], 3 vols., ed. Zhang Zhan and Wang Renzhi (Beijing: Sanlian, 1960), 1:153.

9. Fan Zuyu, *Tang jian* [Mirror of the Tang] (Shanghai: Shanghai guji, 1981), *juan* 6.

10. Zhang Taiyan, "Bo Kang Youwei lun geming shu," in *Zhang Taiyan quanji*, 2:174. In his "Zhonghua Minguo jie" [The meaning of the Republic of China], Zhang stated that he did not advocate nationalism in and of itself but as a means to an end. See *Zhang Taiyan quanji*, 2:256.

11. Zhang, "Zhonghua Minguo jie," 2:256.

12. Liang Qichao, *Zhongguo shi xulun* [Overview of Chinese history], in *Yinbingshi he ji* [Collected works from the ice drinker's studio], 12 vols. (1936; repr., Beijing: Zhonghua shuju, 1989), *wenji* pt. 6: 5–7.

13. Liang Qichao, "Guojia sixiang bianqian yitong lun" [On changes in ideas about the state], in *Yinbingshi he ji, wenji* pt. 6: 20–21.

14. Guan Yun [pseud. Jiang Zhiyou], "Zhongguo shang gu jiu minzi zhi shi yin" [Traces of ancient nationalities from Chinese history], *Xinmin congbao* 31 (1898), "lishi" section 1–13.

15. Here Liang's ideas about the Chinese nation are slightly different from those found in *Zhongguo shi xu lun*. See Zhongguo zhi xin min [pseud. Liang Qichao], "Lishi shang Zhongguo minzu zhi guancha" [An examination of the Chinese nation across history], *Xinming congbao* 56 and 57 (1905).

16. Guan Yun [pseud. Jiang Zhiyou] "Zhongguo ren zhong kao" [An investigation into the Chinese race], pt. 1, *Xinmin congbao* 35 and 37 (1903).

17. Liang Qichao, "Zhongguo dili da shi lun" [On the general trends of the geography of China], *Yinbingshi heji, wenji* 10:77–78.

18. Many studies have been written about this question. See, for example, Yang Tianshi, "Cong 'pai Man geming' dao 'lian Man geming'" [From anti-Manchu revolution to revolution in unity with Manchus], in *Minguo zhanggu* [Anecdotes of the Republic], ed. Yang Tianshi (Beijing: Zhongguo qingnian chubanshe, 1993), 20; Huang Xingtao, "Xiandai 'Zhonghua minguo' guanniande lishi kaocha—jianlun xinhai geming yu

Zhonghua minzu rentong zhi guanxi" [A historical investigation of the "Republic of China," with a discussion of the relationship between the 1911 revolution and the identity of the Chinese people], *Zhejiang shehui kexue* 2002, no. 1: 129–142; Zhang Yong, "Cong 'shiba xing qi' dao 'wu se qi'—xinhai geming shiqi cong Hanzu guojia dao wu zu gongtong jianguo moshide zhuanbian" [From the eighteen-starred flag to the five-colored flag: The shift from the Han-ethnic nation model of nation-building to the five-nation model], *Beijing daxue xuebao* 2002, no. 2: 106–114; Zhou Jinghong, "Cong Hanzu minzu zhuyi dao Zhonghua minzu zhuyi: Qingmo Minchu Guomindang jiqi qianshen zuzhide bianjing minzu guan zhuanxing" [From Han nationalism to Chinese nationalism: Changes in the late Qing and early Republic in attitudes held by the Guomindang and its predecessor organizations toward nationalities on the borders], *Minzu yanjiu* 2006, no. 4: 11–19, 107; and Sun Hongnian, "Xinhai geming qianhou zhibian linian jiqi yanbian" [Ideas about governing the border regions before and after the 1911 revolution], *Minzu yanjiu* 2011, no. 5: 66–75, 109–110.

19. The multiple translations and reprints of these two essays or speeches show the degree to which people in China followed this issue. See, for example, "Zhina miewang lun" [On the annihilation of China], *Qing yi bao* 75 and 76 (1901), as well as the full-length book *Bingtun Zhongguo ce* [A strategy for annexing China], trans. Wang Jianshan (Shanghai: Kaiming shudian, 1903). The latter essay was reprinted many times, as in *Wai jiao bao* 29 (November 1902) and *Jing shi wen chao,* August 8, 1903.

20. Ariga Nagao was deeply involved in Chinese politics, serving for a time as an adviser to Yuan Shikai. His ideas about China were also influential in Japanese politics.

21. See Sakeda Masatoshi, *Kindai Nihon ni okeru taigaikō undō no kenkyū* [Studies on the strong foreign policy movement in Japan] (Tokyo: Tōkyō Daigaku Shuppankai, 1978), 113; and Banno Junji, " 'Tōyōmeishuron' to 'datsua nyūō ron': Meiji chūki Ajia shinshutsuron no niruikei" [Eastern hegemony or leaving Asia to join Europe: Two theories on Asian expansion in the middle Meiji era], in *Kindai Nihon no taigai taido* [Attitudes toward the outside world in modern Japan], ed. Satō Seizaburō et al. (Tokyo: Tōkyō Daigaku Shuppankai, 1974), 39.

22. Egami Namio, ed., *Tōyōgaku no keifu* [A geneaology of Oriental studies], 2 vols. (Tokyo: Taishūkan shoten, 1992–1994), 1:3.

23. In "Tōyōshijō yori mitaru Meijijidai no hatten" [Development of the Meiji era from the perspective of the history of Asia] (1913), Kuwabara Jitsuzo expressed the enthusiasm among scholars in Japan, using phrases like "annexing Korea," "the supremacy of East Asia," "a nation of the first rank," "exporting culture," and "the awakening of the Asian people" as signposts to describe Japan's rise. See *Kuwabara Jitsuzō zenshū* [Complete works of Kuwabara Jitsuzō], 6 vols. (Tokyo: Iwanami shoten, 1968), 1:551–563.

24. "Baoquan Zhina lun" [Keeping China whole], in *Qing yi bao quanbian* [Complete reprint of the China Discussion] (Yokohama: Xin min she, n.d.), vol. 5, "Lun Zhongguo" section, 7. This essay was translated from the newspaper *Gaikō Jihō* [*Revue diplomatique*].

25. Ozaki Yukio, "Zhina zhi mingyun" [China's fate], in *Qing yi bao quanbian* [Complete reprint of the China Discussion], ed. Liang Qichao (Yokohama: Xin min she, n.d.), vol. 5, "Lun Zhongguo" section, 92–93.

26. In the beginning of the Republican era, the term "Chinese nation" (*Zhonghua minzu*) was widely used, a fact that shows that the idea of "bringing the Four Barbarians into China" gained broad acceptance. See Chen Liankai, *Zhonghua minzu yanjiu chutan* [Preliminary investigation of the concept of the Chinese nation] (Beijing: Zhishi chubanshe, 1994).

27. Lacouperie's *Western Origin of the Early Chinese Civilization* and *The Languages of China before the Chinese,* which came to China via Japan, had a deep influence on Chinese scholars, including Zhang Taiyan, Liu Shipei, Liang Qichao, Jiang Zhiyou, and others. This popularity, of course, was related to other major trends in late-Qing thought, but I will not go into detail here.

28. Gu Jiegang, "Da Liu Hu liang xiansheng shu" [A reply to Messrs. Liu and Hu] (1923), reprinted in *Gu shi bian,* 7 vols. (repr., Shanghai: Shanghai guji, 1982), 1:96–102.

29. See the reports included in Hu Shi's diary, *Hu Shi riji* [Diary of Hu Shi], ed. Cao Boyan (Hefei: Anhui jiaoyu chubanshe, 2001), 380–382.

30. See Kawashima Naniwa, "Qing kan Woren bingtun Zhongguo shu" [A letter on how the Japanese are swallowing China], trans. Gong Debai, *Liu Ri xuesheng ji bao* 1, no. 1 (1921).

31. A relatively early example is "Jingxin dongpo zhi Riben Man-Meng jiji zhengce: Tianzhong Yiyi shang Rihuang zouzhe" [The shocking truth about Japan's policy in Manchuria and Mongolia: Tanaka Giichi's memorial to the Japanese emperor] printed by the Society for Research in Political Thought (Dangyi yanjiuhui) of the Suzhou Middle School in July 1927. Many versions of this memorial were published between 1927 and 1931.

32. Here the author refers to works translated from the Japanese into Chinese, and so the present translation refers to their titles in Chinese. In some cases, there is no direct correspondence between a Japanese title and the Chinese translation, which suggests that some of these translations may have been compiled from multiple sources or were given new titles that differ from the source.—Trans.

33. Beginning in 1920, Chinese newspapers regularly published articles that exposed Japanese surveys of Manchuria, Mongolia, the Hui, Tibet, and the Miao, reminding readers of the ambitions that lie behind these studies. See, for example, "Ri ren tumou Man Meng zhi yanjiu re" [A wave of Japanese studies with an eye on Manchuria and Mongolia], *Chen bao,* November 18, 1920; "Ri dui Hua wenhua ju zuzhi Man Meng tanxian dui," *Shen bao,* August 30, 1926; "Wuwu Longzang fu Menggu diaocha renlei kaogu xue" [Torii Ryūzō visits Mongolia to examine anthropological and archaeological studies there], *Zhongyang ribao,* October 19, 1928; "Riben xuesheng kaocha Man Meng" [Japanese students inspect Manchuria and Mongolia], *Yi shi bao,* August 15, 1928. Another article reminded readers to be cautious: "Kuitan Man Meng, Ri ren shi cha dong sheng zhe he duo" [How many Japanese are observing the eastern provinces as part of inspections of Manchuria and Mongolia], *Yi shi bao,* October 19, 1928.

34. Gu Jiegang, "Yu Gong xuehui yanjiu bianjiang xue zhi zhiqu" [The Yu Gong society's interest in studying borders and frontiers], in *Gu Jiegang quanji* [Complete works of Gu Jiegang], 62 vols. (Beijing: Zhonghua, 2010), 36:215–216. This essay was originally

published in January 1936 under the title "Yu Gong xuehui yanjiu bianjiang jihua shu" [Letter concerning the Yu Gong Scholarly Society's plans for research on border areas].

35. Ibid., 36:215.

36. Fu Sinian, *Fu Sinian quanji* [Complete works of Fu Sinian], 7 vols., ed. Ouyang Zhesheng (Changsha: Hunan jiaoyu chubanshe, 2003), 4:125–127.

37. According to Ding Wenjiang, "The most important reason for the inability to unify China lies in the fact that we do not have a shared faith. The basis of this faith is built on our own understanding of ourselves. History and archaeology study our nation's past, while linguistics, anthropology, and other social sciences study our nation's present. Only by studying our nation's past and present well can we be able to understand ourselves." See Ding Wenjiang, "Zhongyang yanjiuyuande shiming" [The mission of Academia Sinica], *Dongfang zazhi*, January 16, 1935.

38. Fu Sinian, "Yi Xia dong xi shuo" [The hypothesis of the Yi in the east and the Xia in the west], in *Fu Sinian quanji*, 3:226.

39. Ma Rong, "Du Wang Tongling 'Zhongguo minzu shi'" [Reading Wang Tongling's history of the Chinese nation], *Beijing Daxue xuebao* 2002, no. 3: 125–135.

40. For Li Chi's classifications, see *The Formation of the Chinese People: An Anthropological Inquiry* (New York: Russell and Russell, 1928), 254–261.

41. Wang Daw-hwan [Wang Daohuan], "Shiyusuode tizhi renleixue jia" [Physical anthropologists in the Institute of History and Philology], in *Xin xueshu zhi lu* [The path to new scholarship], 2 vols., ed. Tu Cheng-sheng and Wang Fansen (Taipei: Zhongyang yanjiuyuan, 2003), 1:181.

42. See Zha Xiaoying, "Zhengdangde lishi guan: Lun Li Chi de kaoguxue yanjiu yu minzu zhuyi" [Legitimate views of history: On Li Chi's archaeology and nationalism], *Kaogu* 2012, no. 6: 89–92. According to Zha, Li Chi's "ideas about anthropological history were at least as strong as his nationalist sentiment, which led him to argue that certain cultural characteristics were autochthonous and that others were of foreign origin." Likewise, works published by S. M. Shirokogorov (1889–1939) that were based on his studies of physical anthropology in northeastern China, such as *Anthropology of Northern China* (Shanghai: Royal Asiatic Society, 1923) and *Anthropology of Eastern China and Kwangtung Province* (Shanghai: Commercial Press, 1925), were just as marked by nationalist sentiment.

43. Zhang Zhiyu, "Ershi shiji houbande Zhongguo kaoguxue" [Chinese archaeology in the second half of the twentieth century], in Zhang Zhiyu, *Kaoguxue zhuanti liu jiang* [Six lectures on archaeology] (Beijing: Sanlian, 2010), 170–177.

44. Fu Sinian, *Fu Sinian quanji*, 3:235–236.

45. Although we use the term "archaeology" (Ch. *renleixue*) here, the term also includes what later would be called the study of nationalities. For a history of this field, see Wang Jianmin, *Zhongguo minzu xue shi* [The history of nationalities research in China], 2 vols. (Kunming: Yunnan jiaoyu chubanshe, 1991), esp. 1:102–122.

46. Yang Chengzhi, "Cong Xinan minzu shuo dao duli Luoluo" [From the southeastern nationalities to the independent Luoluo group] (1929), quoted in *Hokkaidō Daigaku bungaku kenkyūka kiyō* 130 (2010): 57.

47. Ling Chunsheng, *Songhuajiang xiayoude Hezhe zu* [The Hezhe people of the lower Songhua river] (1934; repr. Shanghai: Shanghai wenyi chubanshe, 1990), 1.

48. Li Yiyuan has pointed out that the publication of *Songhuajiang xiayoude Hezhe zu* in 1934 resulted "not only in the first scientific survey in Chinese nationalities research but also an important example of efforts being made worldwide to gather materials for ethnographic surveys that had been inspired by Bronisław Malinowski's *Argonauts of the Western Pacific* (1922)." See *Li Yiyuan zixuan ji* [Selected works of Li Yiyuan] (Shanghai: Shanghai jiaoyu chubanshe, 2002), 431.

49. See Yano Jin'ichi, "Manmōzō ha Shina honrai no ryōdo ni soshiru ron," *Gaikō jihō* 412 (1922), reprinted in *Kindai Shina ron*, 92–112.

50. Regarding the Bo people, see D. C. Graham, "Ancient White Men's Graves in Szechwan," *Journal of the West China Border Research Society* 5 (1932): 78. See also Rui Yifu, "Bo ren kao" [An investigation into the Bo people], *Shiyusuo jikan* 23 (1951).

51. Li Jinhua, "He wei Tonggusi: Cong bijiao shiye kan Shi Luguo yu Ling Chunsheng de Tonggusiren lishi yanjiu" [What is Tungusic? Examining Shirokogoroff's and Ling Chunsheng's histories of the Tungusic peoples from a comparative perspective], *Wenhua xuekan* 2012, no. 1: 111–115.

52. See the preface to Ling Chunsheng and Rui Yifu, *Xiang xi Miao zu diaocha baogao* [Report on the Miao of western Hunan] (1947; repr., Beijing: Minzu chubanshe, 2003).

53. See Zhang Qiudong, "'Wenhua lie qi' yu 'zhengzhi zijue': Ling Chunsheng yu Shi Qigui de Xiang xi Miaozu yanjiu bijiao fenxi" ["Seeking cultural novelty" and "political self-consciousness": A comparative analysis of studies of the Miao in western Hunan conducted by Ling Chunsheng and Shi Qigui], *Leshan shifan xueyuan xuebao* 25, no. 3 (2010): 108–112.

54. Tao Yunda, "Guanyu Mexie zhi mingcheng fenbu yu qianyi" [On the distribution and dispersion of Mexie names], *Lishi yuyan yanjiusuo jikan* 7, no. 1 (1936): 126.

55. *Fu Sinian quanji*, 3:131.

56. Li Chi, "Ji Xiaodun chutu zhi qingtong qi (zhong pian) hou ji" [Afterword to the second essay on bronze vessels excavated at Xiaodun], in *Li Ji wenji*, ed. Zhang Guangzhi, 5 vols. (Shanghai: Shanghai renmin chubanshe, 2006), 5:134.

57. Li Chi, "Zhongguo shanggu shi zhi chongjian gongzuo jiqi wenti" [The work and challenges of reconstructing ancient Chinese history], in *Li Ji wenji*, 1:354–355.

58. Chen Siyong's article, "Ang'angxi shiqian yizhi" [Prehistoric ruins at Ang'angxi], made reference to Anderson and Torii Ryūzō. Chen rejected Japanese arguments that Manchuria had a separate culture and argued that "the Neolithic culture at Ang'angxi was simply the eastern branch of the Neolithic culture of Rehe in Mongolioa." See "Ang'angxi shiqian yizhi," *Shiyu suo ji kan* 4 (1932): 44.

59. Ma Dazheng and Liu Di's study lists relevant publications on the subject from this period and shows that they were most concentrated in the 1920s and 1930s, making them "a product of the patriotic social movement to save China." See Ma Dazheng and Liu Di, *Ershi shijide Zhongguo bianjing yanjiu* [A study of the borders of China in the twentieth century] (Harbin: Heilongjiang jiaoyu chubanshe, 1998), 77.

60. Liu Yizheng, "*Shidi xuebao* xu" [Preface for *Shidi xuebao*], *Shidi xuebao* 1, no. 1 (November 1921): 1.

61. Therefore, in his preface to *Fundamentals of Chinese History* (*Guo shi yao yi*), Liu stressed the importance of the "rectification of borders, the rectification of the nation, and the rectification of morality and justice" and said that "it is shameful if the borders are not rectified and the nation is not rectified." Liu Yizheng, *Guo shi yao yi* [Fundamentals of Chinese history] (Shanghai: Shangwu yinshuguan, 1945), 65. See also Chen Baoyun, *Xueshu yu guojia: Shidi xuebao jiqi xueren qun yanjiu* [Scholarship and the nation: A study of *Shidi xuebao* and its contributors] (Hefei: Anhui jiaoyu chubanshe, 2010), 113–115.

62. This quotation is a line from a poem written by Lu Xun, "Inscribed on a Small Photograph," written in 1903. In this poem, the young Lu Xun compares himself to the famous poet Qu Yuan, who despaired when being refused an official post by the king. In Lu Xun's case, the analogy spoke to his growing nationalist desire to help his homeland. Translation modified from Leo Ou-fan Lee, *Lu Xun and His Legacy* (Berkeley: University of California Press, 1985), 20–21.—Trans.

63. See Gu Jiegang, "Qin-Han tongyi youlai he Zhanguoren duiyu shijiede xiangxiang," in *Gu Jiegang quanji*, 6:33.

64. Gu Jiegang and Shi Nianhai, *Zhongguo jiangyu yange shi* (1936; repr., Beijing: Shangwu yinshuguan, 2000), 1.

65. *Gu Jiegang riji* [Diary of Gu Jiegang], 12 vols. (Taipei: Lianjing chubanshe, 2007), 2:128–140. The entry for this day (December 31, 1933) includes newspaper clippings that reported on Tan Muyu's research and lectures. For a discussion of Tan Muyu's importance for Gu Jiegang, see Yu Yingshi, *Wei jinde caiqing: Cong Gu Jiegang riji kan Gu Jigangde neixin shijie* [Limitless talent: Understanding the inner world of Gu Jiegang through his diary] (Taipei: Lianjing, 2007), 118.

66. Gu Jiegang, "*Bianjing zhoukan* fakanci" [Inaugural essay for "Borderlands Weekly"], in *Gu Jiegang quanji*, 36:319–321.

67. Gu Jiegang, "Zhonghua minzu shi yige" [The Chinese nation is one], in *Gu Jiegang quanji*, 36:94–108. See also "Wo wei shenme xie 'Zhonghua minzu shi yige'" [Why I wrote "The Chinese nation is one"], in ibid., 36:109–116. For a discussion of the wide-ranging influence of this essay, see Zhou Wenjiu and Zhang Jinpeng, "Guanyu 'Zhonghua minzu shi yige' xueshu lunbiande kaocha" [An investigation into the scholarly debates about "The Chinese nation is one"], *Minzu yanjiu* 2007, no. 3: 22.

68. Fu Sinian, Letter to Zhu Jiahua and Hang Liwu (July 7, 1937), in *Fu Sinian yizha* [Uncollected letters of Fu Sinian], 3 vols., ed. Wang Fansen, Pan Guangzhe, and Wu Zhengshang (Taipei: Zhongyang yanjiuyuan lishi yuyan yanjiusuo, 2011), 2:1012–1018.

69. *Gu Jiegang riji*, 197 (February, 7, 1939).

70. Fei Xiaotong, "Guanyu minzu wentide taolun" [A discussion of the national question], *Yi shi bao*, May 1, 1939.

71. Fei Xiaotong, "Gu Jiegang xiansheng bainian ji" [On the hundredth anniversary of Gu Jiegang's birth], in *Fei Xiaotong wenji* [Collection of prose by Fei Xiaotong] 14 vols. (Beijing: Qun yan chubanshe, 1999), 13:26–27. It was subsequently pointed out that the theory of the "unity in diversity" of the Chinese nation that Fei put forward late in life "nudged his earlier one-sided position to emphasize the 'diversity' of the nation, subtly drawing from a part of Gu Jiegang's thinking to create this more open idea of

'unity in diversity.'" See Zhao Xudong, "Yiti duoyuande zuqun guanxi lun yao" [Major points of debates about unity in diversity in ethnic relations], *Shehui kexue* 2012, no. 4: 53.

72. *Fu Sinian yizha,* 1229 (February 1942).

73. See "Recommendation to Remove Obstacles to National Unity by Correcting Ancient Legends of the Han People Expelling the Miao People from the Yellow River Basin" (Chongqing: Zhonghua minguo jiaoyu bu, 1941), submitted by Gu Jiegang and Ma Yi to the second meeting of the Border Education Committee of the Republic of China. In *Jiaoyu bu shi di jiaoyu weiyuanhui gaikuang* [Status of the committee for historical and geographical education] (Chongqing, 1941), pt. 2.

74. Chiang Kai-shek, *"China's Destiny" and "Chinese Economic Theory"* (1947; repr., Leiden: Brill, 2012), 33, 30.

75. It is worth noting that, after *China's Destiny* was published, Chen Boda and others published *Ping Zhongguo zhi mingyun* [An assessment of China's fate]. Chen's essay argued that Chiang Kai-shek's ideas about "large and small branches of the same bloodline" amounted to a fascist theory of bloodlines. Chen's main evidence for this argument was that (1) the nation was still formed by "shared language, shared geography, shared economic life (the connectedness of economic life) and a shared psychological structure that is demonstrated by a shared culture"; (2) many different national groups existed in Chinese history, and assimilation occurred through brutal conflict, not peaceful coexistence; and (3) even if Chen Boda's argument was marked heavily by Han nationalism, he nonetheless criticized *China's Destiny* for what he saw as its "Han chauvinism and attempts to bully minority nationalities within China" (4–8).

4. History

1. Huntington argued that "blood, language, religion, way of life, were what the Greeks had in common and what distinguished them from the Persians and other non-Greeks." It seems, then, that Han Chinese people are different from other national groups because ethnicity, language, religion, way of life, and other cultural factors. Of course, Huntington is not very clear on the differences between "culture" and "civilization." See Samuel P. Huntington, *The Clash of Civilizations and the Remaking of World Order* (New York: Simon and Schuster, 1996), 42.

2. The difference between Chinese characters and phonetic writing lies mostly in the so-called pictographic elements of Chinese characters, as seen in characters such as *ri* 日 (the sun), *yue* 月 (the moon), *mu* 木 (tree/wood), *shui* 水 (water), *huo* 火 (fire), *shou* 手 (hand), *kou* 口 (mouth), and *dao* 刀 (knife). Many others use more detailed and complicated expressions to reach a new result. For example, by adding one dot to the left of the character *dao* 刀, we get *ren* 刃, which is the edge of a knife. By putting *shou* 手 on top of a tree (*mu* 木), we get *cai* 采, which means to pick, pull, or pluck. When an ox (*niu* 牛) is placed in a stable, we call the stable *lao* 牢; the character shows us an ox with a roof over its head. These characters are known as "compound characters" or "associative compounds" (*hui yi zi*). Compound characters have limited uses, however,

and so "radical-phonetic" or "logographic" characters use sound elements to show differences, as as with characters such as *jiang* 江 (large river) and *he* 河 (river or stream) and *song* 松 (pine) and 柏 *bai* (cypress); in all of these cases, the left-hand element carries an aspect of the meaning, while the right-hand element determines the pronunciation. Because Chinese characters are rooted in the pictographic, however, many of their meanings can be guessed through the elements from which they are made; many were in fact developed through these meanings. For example, if *mu* 木 refers to a tree, and this "tree" is in the middle of the "sun" (*ri* 日), then we have the sun rising in the east, which refers to the character *dong* 東 ("east," simplified now as 东). In another case, *ri* 日 refers to the sun, and the sun is descending into the foliage (*cao* 草) on the horizon, then we have *mu* 莫 (暮), which means "dusk." Chinese characters, then, influence people's thinking and their imaginations and have created a certain habit of literal reading among Chinese people. For a discussion of the way Chinese people revere and place faith in the written word, see Hu Shi, "Ming jiao" [The doctrine of names], in *Hu Shi wenji* [Collection of Hu Shi's prose], ed. Ouyang Zhesheng, 12 vols. (Beijing: Beijing daxue chubanshe 1998), 4, *juan* 2:51–62.

3. Francis L. K. Hsü (Xu Langguang) has argued that Western cultures emphasize self-reliance, while Chinese culture emphasizes mutual dependence. See his "Cultural Differences between East and West and Their Significance for the World Today," *Tsing Hua Journal of Chinese Studies* 2, no. 1 (June 1972): 216–237.

4. "Cultivating oneself" (*xiushen*), "harmonizing one's clan" (*qi jia*), "governing the state well" (*zhi guo*), and "bringing peace throughout the land" (*ping Tianxia*). John King Fairbank said that, although the connection between self-cultivation and ruling the state was an article of faith among Chinese scholars, "from the Greek point of view [it was] a fancy series of non sequiturs." See John King Fairbank, *The United States and China,* 4th ed. (Cambridge, MA: Harvard University Press, 1976), 77. For one translation of "The Great Learning," see Charles Mueller's translation, http://www.acmuller .net/con-dao/greatlearning.html.

5. See also Fei Xiaotong, *From the Soil: The Foundations of Chinese Society, a Translation of Fei Xiaotong's Xiangtu Zhongguo,* trans. Gary Hamilton and Wang Zheng (Berkeley: University of California Press, 1992); and Francis L. K. Hsü, *Under the Ancestors' Shadow: Kinship, Personality, and Social Mobility in China* (1948; repr., Stanford, CA: Stanford University Press, 1971).

6. Song Xiaozong's essay, "Yuan dao bian" [An investigation of the essentials of the moral way], which later was known as "San jiao lun" [On the three teachings]. This essay from the Song dynasty, which is rare because of its direct response to Han Yu, could have easily provoked disagreement because of the prominence of Neo-Confucian thought during the Southern Song. Why would the Xiaozong emperor want to use his authority to write such an essay? This is a question worth considering, as are the responses from Fan Chengda, Shi Hao, and Cheng Taizhi; see Lin Xinzhuan, *Jianyan yilai chao ye za ji* [Notes on the imperial court since the Jianyan period], 2 vols. (Beijing: Zhonghua shuju, 2000), 2:544. Centuries later, the first Ming emperor, Zhu Yuanzhang, also wrote a "San jiao lun," see *Quan ming wen* [Complete prose of the Ming], 2 vols. (Shanghai: Shanghai guji chubanshe, 1992), 1:145.

7. The development of this tradition passed through phases that included the debates over "A Monk Does Not Bow Down to a King" that took place in the Eastern Jin until the point during the Tang dynasty when Buddhism was finally brought under state control and the faithful were required to pay obeisance to their parents and their rulers— or, forced to accept the traditional familial and political ethics of ancient China, filial piety (*xiao*) and loyalty (*zhong*). See the section titled "Buddhist Conquest of China?" in my *An Intellectual History of China: Knowledge, Thought, and Belief before the Seventh Century BC,* trans. Michael S. Duke and Josephine Chiu-Duke (Leiden: Brill, 2014), 350–369.

8. See Ge Zhaoguang, *Qu fu shi ji qita: Liuchao Sui Tang daojiaode sixiang shi yanjiu* [The history of yielding and other topics: Studies of the intellectual history of Taoism in the Six Dynasties, Sui, and Tang] (Beijing: Sanlian, 2003).

9. It is precisely because of the unification of the three teachings that worlds of religion and politics in ancient China were unified and quite different from the absolute influence of religion over politics in the Islamic world. This situation is also quite different from Christianity in the West, which competed with secular powers in the Middle Ages, and with the situation in Japan, where Buddhism and Shinto had great power and authority.

10. Analogies derived from Yin and Yang may include the relationships between the sun and moon and Heaven and Earth and can also be used to understand symbolically the relationship between ruler and official and higher and lower; other relationships derived from Yin and Yang, such as cold and warm, wet and dry, the noble and the lowly, and those of high and low birth, imply a series of techniques for regulating relationships. The Five Elements (*wu xing*) in ancient China referred to the five most basic elements of the universe: metal, wood, water, fire, and earth; but the five elements were applied to a wide variety of things, events, and phenomena in the universe, in society, and the human body, including the five virtues of "benevolence, righteousness, ritual, knowledge, and sageliness." People commonly believed that the Five Elements could be used to understand and order everything in the universe, hence the five colors, five sounds, five flavors, five directions, five internal organs, the five ritual ceremonies, and so on. Without them, people believed society would descend into chaos and the universe would lose all order.

11. There are, of course, many accounts of the origins of ideas about the Five Elements. For a modern account based on ancient sources, see Feng Shi, "Shanggu yuzhou guande kaogu xue yanjiu" [An archaeological study of early views of the universe], *Shiyu suo jikan* 82, no. 3 (2011): 399–491. This article introduces information about Shuangdun Grave No. 1 in Bengbu, a tomb from the Zhongli state (which was destroyed by the Kingdom of Wu in 518 BCE) from the Spring and Autumn period, which was excavated between December 2006 and August 2008. For a report of the excavation of this tomb see Kan Xuhang, Zhou Qun, and Qian Renfa, "Anhui Bengbushi Shuangdun yi hao Chunqiu muzang" [Tomb Shuangdun-1 of the Spring and Autumn period in Bengbu city, Anhui] *Kaogu,* 2009, no. 7: 39–45, 108–110. It is worth noting that (1) the soil of the tomb mound and the tomb fill was a variegated blend of the five colors of green, white, red, black, and yellow, which are all related to ideas about the five elements; and (2) the remains of a fine layer of white quartzite, laid out in the shape of a

jade *bi* disc, was found over the five-colored earth of the tomb mound; this layer could be related to the idea of Heaven covering Earth.

12. In recent years archaeologists have discovered some early materials, such as the *Yin shu* (Pulling book) recorded on Han bamboo slips and unearthed at Zhangjiashan in Hubei, which says that not only that, in ruling the state, "those above [that is, the rulers] must be in accord with the movements of the sun, moon, and starts in Heaven, and those below must live in accordance with the changes of Yin, Yang, and the four seasons on Earth," but also that the people's lives must be in accordance with "Heaven, Earth, and the four seasons." This means that, "In cultivating the self, one must seek accord with Heaven and Earth, like a bellows [that opens and closes]." The laws of Heaven and Earth are like the four seasons, and they, too, influence human life. Therefore, people should also behave like nature and "produce in the spring, grow in the summer, harvest in the fall, and store in winter, for this is the way for one's lineage to flourish." If humans follow the way Heaven sees that "dry and wet and winter and summer follow one another," then they can achieve eternal happiness.

13. In the minds of people in ancient China, anything that could imitate "Heaven" could possess Heaven's mystery and power. The significance of this Heaven, then, had many meanings: during sacrificial rituals, it transformed into a mysterious, dominating force; during divination rituals, it transformed into a mysterious set of corresponding relationships; in the real, lived world, it appears as a mysterious world of desire, one that bolsters people's confidence and helps them resolve a variety of challenges. It is not just the common people, but also the Son of Heaven and the aristocracy who believe that rational evidence and the basis of power come from Heaven. The buildings of the imperial palaces of the Qin and Han were constructed to imitate the structure of Heaven; the ceilings of tomb chambers from the Han were painted with the stars of Heaven; the imperial sacrifices conducted during the Han were directed toward the gods of Heaven and Earth, and the locations of sacrifices were follow a structure that reflected the organization of Heaven. In people's minds, "Heaven" had an incomparably high status: it was the manifestations of nature, the highest realm, the highest of gods, and an unspoken and accepted precondition for and evidence in any discussion.

14. For example, the *Records of the Grand Historian* says that the legendary ruler Yu the Great was the Yellow Emperor's great-great-grandson, and Zhuanxu's grandson. It also says that Emperor Xie of Shang was the descendant of Emperor Ku; that Emperor Ku was the great-grandson of the Yellow Emperor; and that the mother of Houji of Zhou was the wife of Emperor Ku—or a descendant of the Yellow Emperor.

15. In this case, the Xia would be considered as more "Chinese" in today's parlance. The implication, then, is that the ancient Yin and Shang dynasties were not as "Chinese" as previously assumed.—Trans.

16. See Fu Sinian's essay from 1935, "Yi Xia Dong Xi shuo" [On barbarian and Chinese, east and west], *Fu Sinian quanji* 3 (1935): 864.

17. Xu Zhuoyun, *Wozhe yu tazhe: Zhongguo lishi shangde nei wai fenji* [Self and other: Boundaries between inner and outer in Chinese history] (Beijing: Sanlian, 2010), 9.

18. Li Chi, "Anyang zuijin fajue baogao ji liu ci gongzuo zhi zong guji" [Report on recent discoveries at Anyang and an overview of six excavations], in *Li Ji wenji*, ed. Zhang Guangzhi, 5 vols. (Shanghai: Shanghai renmin chubanshe, 2006), 2:280–285. Li Chi

argued that scholars of the history of ancient China should "break down narrow ideas of Chinese culture that stop at the Great Wall. We should use our eyes and legs to travel north of the Great Wall to seek out materials from the history of ancient China. An even older 'old home' is there." See Li Chi, "Ji Xiaodun chutu zhi qingtong qi (zhong pian) hou ji," in *Li Ji wenji*, 5:133. In another essay, "Zhongguo shanggu shi zhi chongjian gongzuo jiqi wenti" [The work of reestablishing the history of ancient China and related questions], Li Chi argued that Chinese culture was not an isolated realm, but rather that its sources came "all the way from the Black Sea to the grasslands of Central Asia, to the Dzungar lands of Xinjiang, to the Gobi Desert in Mongolia, and, finally, to Manchuria" (*Li Ji wenji*, 1:353).

19. The *Zuo Commentary to the Spring and Autumn Annals* records that in the third year of the reign of King Xuan (606 BCE) the kingdom of Chu attacked the Rong tribe of Lu Hun, which was located, surprisingly, in what is now Song County in Henan Province, near Luoyang, the capital of the Eastern Zhou. This fact demonstrated that the Chu and Rong occupied lands that overlapped with one another. Of course, the King of Chu had designs on the Nine Tripods, which symbolized the power of the Zhou Dynasty, and also demonstrated that these various ethnic groups were already part of the same political community of the "Central Lands" (*Zhongguo*) of the Zhou.

20. Some have argued that ideas about Yin and Yang, the Five Elements, and the eight trigrams were derived from three separate techniques of divination, that is, tortoise-shell divination, divination by the *Yi Ching*, and divining by milfoil, which represented the different cultures of eastern, western, and southern China in ancient times. These techniques, it is argued, did not combine with one another until the end of the Warring States period, during which time "a great synthesis occurred within the walls of the palace" that was then endowed with all kinds of moral and political significance. See Pang Pu, "Yin yang wu xing tanyuan" [Searching for the origins of yin and yang and the five elements], *Zhongguo shehui kexue* 1984, no. 3: 75–98.

21. This quotation is from the "Tian-xia" chapter of the *Zhuangzi*, trans. James Legge. See http://ctext.org/zhuangzi/tian-xia.—Trans.

22. Ibid.

23. See Yü Ying-shih, "Zongshu Zhongguo sixiang shi shangde si ci tupo" [An overview of four major breakthroughs in Chinese intellectual history], in Yü Ying-shih, *Zhongguo wenhua shi tongshi* [Overviews of Chinese cultural history] (Hong Kong: Oxford University Press, 2010), 1–20. See also Yü Ying-shih, "Tian ren zhi ji: Zhongguo gudai sixiang shide qiyuan shitan" [Between heaven and man: An inquiry into the origins of ancient Chinese thought], in *Zhongguo shi xin lun: Sixiang shi fence* [New perspectives on Chinese history: Volume on intellectual history], ed. Chen Ruoshui (Taipei: Lianjing, 2012), 11–93.

24. The biography of the Qin Shi Huangdi quotes from "The Faults of Qin" (*Guo Qin lun*) by Jia Yi, who described the Qin unification as follows: the Qin Shi Huangdi "seized the land of the hundred tribes of Yue [in the south], making it into Guilin and Xiang provinces . . . [and] drove the Xiongnu more than seven hundred *li* away" (*Shi ji*, 280). Translation from Watson, *Records of the Grand Historian: Qin Dynasty* (Hong Kong: Research Centre for Translation, 1993), 79.

25. For example, inscriptions on bronze mirrors from the Han dynasty often refer to the "Barbarian Hu" (*Hu lu*) or the "Four Barbarians" (*si Yi*) in relation to the "state" (*guojia*). For example, one mirror calls for "the state (*guojia*) and the people to be at peace and without trouble, the northern barbarians to be wiped out, the lands of the four directions to submit and obey, the winds and rains to come arrive in season and ripen the five grains." Likewise, Sima Qian's *Records of the Grand Historian* includes the "Biographies of the Dayuan" and "Biographies of the Xiongnu," which show the beginnings of a sense of "China" or a "Central Land" (*Zhongguo*) in relation to foreign states and peoples. See Chapter 1, note 15.

26. See "The Basic Annals of the First Emperor of Qin," in Sima Qian, *Records of the Grand Historian,* trans. Burton Watson (Hong Kong: Renditions, 1993), 45.

27. The biography of Dong Zhongshu in the *Han shu* [History of the former Han] includes a memorial written by Dong that recommends that "all that is not within the Six Arts and the learning of Confucius should be rejected and not allowed to develop." His goal was to "make unification possible, make the laws clear, and allow the people to know what to follow." In other words, Dong was calling for the Han Empire to establish a unified politics and culture; see *Han shu,* 2523.

28. Sima Qian, "Basic Annals of the First Emperor of the Qin," 45.

29. *Shi ji,* "Huo zhi lie zhuan" [Biographies of the money-makers], 3261–3270. Translation modified from *Records of the Grand Historian: Han Dynasty,* trans. Burton Watson, 2 vols. (rev. ed., Hong Kong: Renditions, 1993), 2:440.

30. This is as is described in Buddhist canons: "All within the land, each of different type, the Hu, Han, Qiang, the southern barbarians, and the Yue of Chu, each lives in their place, of different colors and types." See *Fa yuan zhu lin,* in *Da zheng zang,* 53:280–281.

31. See *Jin shu* [History of the Jin], 1529–1530. Before Jiang Tong, Fu Xuan argued that "The northern barbarians have the hearts of beasts, different from the Hua [Chinese], with the Xianbei the worst among them. It would be best to establish a commandery in Gaopingchuan and ask the officials there to seek out people from Anding and Xizhou who are willing to move [to outlying areas] and exempt them from taxes and corvée labor. These actions will make it possible to open routes to the north and to populate the frontier regions." Another person, one Guo Qin, argued for policies that would "forbid the Han from living among foreign peoples and gradually drive out the Hu people from Pingyang, Hongnong, Wei commandery, the capital, and Shangdang [now southern Shanxi]." See *Jin Shu,* 1322 and 2549.

32. See Tan Qixiang, "Jindai Hunan ren zhong zhi Man zu xuetong" [Bloodlines of the Man people among modern Hunanese] [1934], reprinted as *Chang shui cui bian* (Shijiazhuang: Hubei jiaoyu chubanshe, 2000), 234–270.

33. See Su Qikang, *Wenxue, zongjiao, xingbie yu minzu: Zhonggu shidaide Yingguo, Zhong-dong, Zhongguo* [Literature, religion, gender, and nation: England, the Middle East, and China in the middle ages] (Taipei: Lianjing, 2005), 237–365. See also *Bei shi* [History of the Northern Dynasties], *juan* 92, which records how an official from Northern Qi named Han Feng (a Han ethnic) "was forced to feed 'Han dogs' and horses. Also, some swords were used only for mowing off the heads of 'Han bandits'

and could not be used to mow grass." This book also often makes statements such as, "The Han dogs are intolerable and are only good for killing," and refers to Han people who claimed to be Hu people, becoming "fake foreign devils" (*jia yang guizi*).

34. According to the "Biographies of the Sons of Taizong" in the *New Book of Tang,* he had a great fondness for all aspects of Turkic culture, enough so to cause conflicts with his family. See *Xin Tang shu,* 3564–3565. It is interesting that during or before the Tang dynasty, studying the language of foreign groups from the north enjoyed some popularity. For example, a chapter on educating children that is found in *Admonitions of the Yan Clan (Yan shi jia xun)* refers to a member of the gentry elite from the Northern Qi who was very proud of the fact that his sons had studied the language of the Xianbei and could play the *pipa* lute, "Because of this [training], they were able to work in service of important officials and were treated with great favor." By the Song dynasty, however, the ability to speak the languages of foreigners from the north came to be seen as a flaw among elites and officials and was even seen as reason to suspect someone of loyalties to foreign lands or be worthy of punishment. In an epitaph for Yu Jing (1000–1064 CE) Ouyang Xiu wrote of how Yu Jing pushed for making peace with the Xixia and personally engaged with successful negotiations with them. But because he "studied the barbarian languages" he was exiled to an official post in Jizhou; he was even attacked by his political enemies and forced to leave officialdom and return to his native place." See *Ouyang Xiu quanji* [Complete works of Ouyang Xiu], 6 vols. (Beijing: Zhonghua, 2001), 2:367. Some time ago, Liu Zijian pointed out that these materials show how "Confucian officials would not pursue such insignificant knowledge as barbarian languages. Usually they depended on interpreters and intermediaries, a practice that reflects chauvinistic attitudes in China and a lack of interest in the affairs of foreign countries. Moreover, those who did understand foreign languages were treated with suspicion or said to have secret or underhanded relations with foreign lands." See Liu Zijian, *Liang Song shi yanjiu lunji* [Studies of the Northern and Southern Song dynasties] (Taipei: Lianjing, 1987), 89.

35. A funerary inscription for a member of the Gautama family was discovered in Chang'an County in Xi'an in 1977. Part of the inscription reads: "This family originally came from central India, but moved to China, setting down roots in China, and across the generations became people of the [Tang] capital. The Guatama family, which had the same surname as the Buddha himself, came to China sometime during the Sui and Tang period. With their skills in astronomy and divination, they eventually became officials in the Chinese court. Their works include the *Treatise on Astrology of the Kaiyuan Era (Kaiyuan zhan jing)* and a translation of the *Calendar of the Nine Forces (Jiu zhi li).*" See Chao Huashan, "Tangdai tianwenxuejia Qutan zhuanmude faxian" [Discovery of a funerary inscription for the Tang-era astronomers of the Gautama family], *Wenwu* 1978, no. 10: 49–53.

36. According to the "Biographies of Persians" (*Xi Rong: Bosi zhuan*) of the *Old Book of Tang (Jiu Tang shu)*, one Peroz, a son of Yazdagerd III, a ruler of the late Sassanian Empire, fled to China after the defeat of the Sassanians by Arab armies. Peroz came to Chang'an in 673 and 675, and some of the people who accompanied him to China established a "Persian temple" or Zoroastrian temple. A large number of the people who

accompanied him eventually took up residence in China. See Fang Hao's discussion in the first volume of his *Zhong Xi jiaotong shi* [A history of relations between China and the west], 2 vols. (Changsha: Yuelu shushe, 1987).

37. The biography of Emperor Ming (*Ming Di ji*) in the *Book of Zhou* (*Zhou shu*) quotes from an imperial edict that said during the Northern Zhou dynasty "Of the ninety-nine surnames of the thirty-six states [that is, including many foreign peoples and clans], those who moved south with the Northern Wei court came to be called 'People of South of the [Yellow] River' (*Henan min* or Henan people). Now that the Northern Zhou court is in Guanzhong [modern-day Shaanxi], the people there should be called 'people of the capital'" (*Zhou shu*, 55). The bibliographic treatise (*Jing ji zhi*) of the *Book of Sui* (*Sui shu*) also notes that "when the Northern Wei moved its capital from Pingcheng [modern-day Datong] to Luoyang, the people who accompanied the court south were from eight principal clans and ten principal surnames, all of whom came from the [larger] imperial clan. There were another thirty-six clans from the various states and another ninety-two clans from various tribes. All of them came to be known as the people of Henan and Luoyang" (*Sui shu*, 990).

38. Chen Yinke, "Li Tang shi zu tuice hou ji" [Afterword to conjectures on the Li clan of the Tang-dynasty royalty], in *Chen Yinke wenji* (Beijing: Sanlian, 2001), 344.

39. Edward H. Schafer, *The Golden Peaches of Samakand: A Study of T'ang Exotics* (Berkeley: University of California Press, 1963); Berthold Laufer, *Sino-Iranica: Chinese Contributions to the History of Civilization in Ancient Iran, with Special Reference to the History of Cultivated Plants and Products* (Chicago: Field Museum of Natural History, 1919).

40. Yuan Zhen, "Fa qu" [Dharma melody], *Quan tang shi* [Complete Tang poems], *juan* 419, Chinese Text Project, http://ctext.org/quantangshi/419/zhs.

41. See Rong Xinjiang, *Zhonggu Zhongguo yu wailai wenming* [Medieval China and foreign civilizations] (Beijing: Sanlian, 2001), 343. [For a study and full translation of this text in English, see Wendi Adamek, *The Teachings of Master Wuzhu: Zeng and Religion of No-Religion* (New York: Columbia University Press, 2011).—Trans.]

42. Qu Dui has argued that "the Tang Dynasty was not a pure China. Because the Tang dynasty was a time when many nations blended together, in places across the Tang state one might see students and monks from Japan and Silla, merchants from Persia, Brahmin monks from India, Kunlun slaves from Southeast Asia, and others who lived side-by-side with the Chinese. So-called Chinese people (*Zhongguo ren*), from the family of the emperor and high officials to soldiers and peasants, all had the blood of various northern tribes from the Han dynasty in their veins. All of their customs were mixed together, and even their speaking and writing had shown signs of change for some time." He also cites the examples of Yuan Zhen (779–831) and Bai Juyi (772–846), explaining that Yuan Zhen was a descendant of the Tuoba people, while Bai Juyi was a descendent of Sogdian peoples. "Because of these racial backgrounds, their poetic styles varied from that of Han people." See Qu Dui, *Zhu'an wen cun* (Shenyang: Liaoning jiaoyu chubanshe, 2001), 129.

43. Valerie Hansen, *The Open Empire: A History of China to 1600* (New York: Norton, 2000).

44. Joanna Waley-Cohen, *The Sextants of Beijing: Global Currents in Chinese History* (New York: Norton, 2000).

45. See Ge Zhaoguang, *Here in "China" I Dwell: Reconstructing Historical Discourses of China for Our Time,* trans. Jesse Field and Qin Fang (Leiden: Brill, 2017), 29–52.

46. Nishijima Sadao, *Chūgoku kodai kokka to Higashi Ajia sekai* [Ancient Chinese states and the East Asian world] (Tokyo: Tōkyō daigaku shuppankai, 1983).

47. This transformation is quite important, because it led to the following changes in traditional China's ideas about the differences between Chinese and foreigners and in the tribute system. Conceptually, the foreigner / Chinese division and the tribute system changed from practical strategies to an imagined order, from a system of ruling over the world to a way of comforting oneself with an imagined version of the world. Politically, the old attitude of the Celestial Kingdom became a real plan for equal relations between states. Intellectually, mainstream ideas among the educated elites concerning All-under-Heaven, China, and the Four Barbarians transformed from an ideas about the boundless territories of All-under-Heaven to a nationalism concerned with the self.

48. See Deng Xiaonan's discussion of the resolution of differences between Hu and Han, *Zuzong zhu fa* [The ancestors' family instructions] (Beijing: Sanlian, 2006), 92–100.

49. Chen Yinke, "Lun Han Yu" [Concerning Han Yu], in Chen Yinke, *Chen Yinke wenji* [Collection of prose by Chen Yinke], 3 vols. (Shanghai: Shanghai guji, 1980), 1:285–297.

50. See my discussion on thought and religious faith from the seventh through the ninth centuries, in Ge Zhaoguang, *Zhongguo sixiang shi* [An intellectual history of China], 3 vols. (Shanghai: Fudan daxue chubanshe, 1998), 2:356–386.

51. Actually, if we start counting from the beginning of the period of Khitan rule, then the "Hui-ification" of Northeastern China lasted for four or five centuries, across the Liao, Jin, and Yuan dynasties.

52. Zhu Yuanzhang, "Da gao xu" [Preface to the grand pronouncements], in *Quan Ming wen,* 1:586.

53. *Ming Taizu shilu* [Veritable records of the reign of Ming Taizu], *juan* 176:2665–2666.

54. One interesting example, discussed by Ping-ti Ho, is a literatus of Xianbei descent, Yuan Haowen, who identified with the Jin dynasty established by the Jurchens. With the establishment of Mongol rule, he collected and edited materials for the *Zhongzhou ji* [Central region collection], a collection that was both marked by the importance of Han Chinese literature and preserved important information about the literary culture of the Jin dynasty.

55. Liu Xia, *Liu Shangbin wen xuji* [Continued collection of the prose of Liu Shangbin], in *Xuxiu siku quanshu,* 1326, *juan* 4, 155.

56. Wang Yi, "Shizhai xiansheng Yu gong mu biao," in *Quan Yuan wen* [Complete prose of the Yuan], 59 vols. (Beijing: Zhonghua, 2001), 55:618.

57. *Ming Taizu shilu,* 33:525.

58. *Huang Ming tiao fa shi lei zuan* [Classified compendium of the Ming legal code], in *Zhongguo zhen xi falü dianji jicheng,* series 2, 4:978.

59. For the preceding, see Zhang Jia, *Xin tianxia zhi hua: Ming chu lisu gaige yanjiu* [Civilizing All-under-Heaven anew: Studies in reforms in social customs of the early Ming] (Shanghai: Fudan daxue chubanshe, 2014).

60. Ge Zhaoguang, "Bici huanrao he jiuchande lishi: Ping Fu Majin *Zhongguo Dongya jinshi jiaoshe shi*" [Mutually revolving and entangled histories: A review of Fuma Susumu's *History of China's Relations with East Asia in the Modern Period*], *Dushu* 2008, no. 1: 80–88.

61. Evelyn Rawski, "Presidential Address: Reenvisioning the Qing: The Significance of the Qing Period in Chinese History," *Journal of Asian Studies* 55, no. 4 (1996): 829–850; Ping-ti Ho, "In Defense of Sinicization: A Rebuttal of Evelyn Rawski's 'Reenvisioning the Qing,'" *Journal of Asian Studies* 57, no. 1 (1998): 123–155.

62. "Idle people wandering about"—those who do not have stable professions or travel between regions to engage in trade—were often viewed with suspicion in traditional Chinese thought. Some traditionally educated scholar-elites would have been troubled by this type of urbanization under the Yuan.—Trans.

63. The lines that separate Classical or literary Chinese and spoken or vernacular Chinese have blurred over time. This development is not solely a linguistic phenomenon; it is also the result of the gradual dissolution of elite society and the entry of marginalized or nonelite elements into the mainstream. Culture (and values) change within language, and thus the elite, elegant, and refined language of the past gradually lost its commanding position in culture, while colloquial language made its way in force into books, onto the stage, and into interpersonal interactions. This transformation is an important aspect of the history of modern Chinese culture.

64. For Fei Xiaotong's comparison of the organization of Chinese and Western societies, see *From the Soil,* 60–65.—Trans.

65. Immanuel C. Y. Hsü argues on the first page that "international society" originally only referred to a group of Western, Christian states. This group later expanded to the extent that its order became equated with the international order, but its arrival in East Asia meant that it came into contact with "another family of nations," which, in turn, resulted in conflict between "two mutually exclusive systems" and the eventual forced integration of the Chinese order into the Western European order. As a result, the "Confucian universal empire" was made into a "modern national state." See Hsü, *China's Entrance into the Family of Nations,* 1–18.

66. Xu Zhuoyun, *Wozhe yu tazhe,* 21.

5. Peripheries

1. For a detailed discussion, see the conclusion to Ge Zhaoguang, *Here in "China" I Dwell: Reconstructing Historical Discourses of China for Our Time,* trans. Jesse Field and Qin Fang (Leiden: Brill, 2017), 187–214.

2. See Chapter 2, note 25.

3. For a discussion of Chinese people's ideas of All-under-Heaven and "the world," see Chapter 1.

4. For a detailed discussion, see Ge Zhaoguang, *Xiangxiang yiyu: Du Li chao Chaoxian Yan xing wenxian zhaji* [Imagining foreign lands: Reading Joseon-era records of embassies to China] (Beijing: Zhonghua, 2014).

5. For further discussion of documents from Korean goodwill embassies, see Ge Zhao-guang, "Wenhua jiande bisai: Chaoxian tongxin shi wenxiande yiyi" [Cultural competition: The significance of documents from the Korean missions], *Zhonghua wen shi lun cong* 2014, no. 2: 1–62.

6. See Yamauchi Koichi, "Kō Daiyō no kaikan ni tsuite" [Hong Dae-yong's perspective on the Chinese/barbarian dichotomy], in *Chōsen gakuhō* [Korean academic bulletin] no. 154 (Tenri: Tenri jihōsha, 1996). See also Ge Zhaoguang, "Cong Chaotian dao Yanxing: Shiqi shiji zhongyehou Dongya wenhua gongtongtide jieti" [From paying tribute to the celestial kingdom to the Journey to the Capital: The disintegration of the East Asian cultural community beginning in the mid-seventeenth century], *Zhonghua wen shi lun cong* 2006, no. 1.

7. See *Yŏnhaengnok sŏnjip* [Selected records of travels to China], 2 vols. (Seoul: Sŏngyun'gwan taehakkyo taedong munhwa yŏn'guwŏn, 1961), 1:338.

8. Wu Han, ed., *Chaoxian Li chao shilu zhongde Zhongguo shiliao* [Historical materials concerning China found in the veritable records of the Joseon dynasty], 12 vols. (Beijing: Zhonghua, 1962), 8:4397.

9. Hayashi Shunsai, *Ka i hentai* [Changing situations between China and foreigners] (Preface, 1674; repr., Tokyo: Tōhō shoten, 1981), 22, 41–45.

10. Jo Hyeong, *Fusang riji* [Japan diary], in *Taikei Chōsen tsūshinshi* [A systematic overview of Korean emissaries], ed. Nakao Hiroshi, 8 vols. (Tokyo: Akashi shoten, 1994–1996), 3:60.

11. Shinobu Seizaburō, *Riben jindai zhengzhi shi* [History of modern Japanese politics], trans. Zhou Qiqian, 4 vols. (Taipei: Guiguan tushu gongsi, 1990), 1:49.

12. Ōba Osamu, ed., *An'ei kunen Awa Chikura hyōchaku Nankinsen Genjun-gō shiryō* [Materials concerning the Nanjing ship Yuanshun, which washed Ashore at Chikura (Awa) in 1780 (An'ei 9)] (Suita: Kansai daigaku shuppanbu, 1991), 29–30.

13. See Matsuura Akira, ed., *Kansei gannen Tosa hyōchaku Anrisen shiryō* [Materials concerning the Chinese ship *Anli* that washed ashore at Tosa in 1789 (Kansei 1)] (Suita: Kansai daigaku shuppanbu, 1989), 351–352.

14. See Tanaka Kenji and Matsuura Akira, eds., *Bunsei kyūnen Enshū hyōchaku Tokutaisen shiryō* [Materials concerning the Chinese ship *Detai* that washed ashore on the coast of Shizuoka Prefecture in 1826 (Bunsei 9)] (Suita: Kansai daigaku shuppanbu, 1986), 108.

15. Yamaga Sokō, *Chūchō jijitsu* [True facts about the Central Dynasty], in *Yamaga Sokō zenshū* [Complete works of Yamaga Sōko], ed. Hirose Yutaka, 15 vols. (Tokyo: Iwanami shoten, 1942), 13:226.

16. Matsuura, *Kansei gannen Tosa hyōchaku Anrisen shiryō*, 357.

17. This is from "Shinzo kukibun" [Oral accounts of Qing Manners], quoted in "Tōsen hyōchaku zakki" [Miscellaneous notes on Chinese ships that washed ashore], in *Kansei jūninen Enshū hyōchaku Tōsen Manshōgō shiryō* [Materials concerning the Chinese ship that washed ashore at Enshū in 1800 (Kansei 12)], ed. Yabuta Yutaka (Suita: Kansai daigaku shuppanbu, 1997), 223.

18. Ai Rulüe, *Zhifang waiji jiao shi*, ed. Xie Fang (Beijing: Zhonghua, 1996), 7.

19. See Chapter 1 of this volume.

20. Zhou Kongjiao, "Yao shu huo zhong ken qi zao e luan meng yin gen ben shu" [Memorial present to request that the emperor move quickly to wipe out root and branch the heretical teachings that are misleading the people], in *Siku cun mu congshu* (repr., Jinan: Qi lu shu she, 1997), *shi bu* 64:126.

21. Anonymous, *Wanguo lai chao tu* [The myriad states pay tribute to the emperor], in *Qing dai gongting huihua* [Court painting of the Qing dynasty], ed. Nie Chongzheng (Hong Kong: Shangwu yinshuguan, 1996), 236–241.

22. See Shinobu, *Riben jindai zhengzhi shi,* 1:49.

6. Practical Questions

1. Samuel P. Huntington, *The Clash of Civilizations and the Remaking of World Order* (New York: Simon and Schuster, 1996). It should be noted that Huntington does not make a particularly strict distinction between "culture" and "civilization."

2. For a more detailed discussion, see Chapter 4.

3. See my discussion in Chapter 1.

4. See Henry Kissinger, *On China* (New York: Penguin, 2011), esp. chap. 2. See also Martin Jacques, *When China Rules the World: The End of the Western World and the Birth of a New Global Order* (New York: Penguin, 2009).

5. See interview in *Chosun Ilbo,* November 28, 2012, A23.

6. For one discussion of the differences between civilization and culture, see Norbert Elias, *The Civilizing Process* (Oxford: Blackwell, 2000), 3–44.

7. See Chapter 1, note 21.

8. *Qing shi gao,* 51:1891.

9. For example, James Hevia's *Cherishing Men from Afar: Qing Guest Ritual and the Macartney Embassy of 1793* (Durham, NC: Duke University Press, 1995), only retells the story using new theory and is not a real history of the time.

10. This phrase is frequently used by diplomatic organizations.

11. This is Huntington's interpretation, which follows arguments made by John K. Fairbank.

12. For example, when the Sassanian Empire was defeated by Arab armies in the mid-seventh century, many Persians asked the Tang dynasty for assistance, but the Tang was not willing to dispatch its troops. The Wanli emperor did send troops to help Korea fight Japan, but only because Korea was on China's border. This is likely the product of a very old mind-set. For example, in his commentary to the *Gongyang Commentary to the Spring and Autumn Annals,* the Han-dynasty scholar He Xiu wrote, "The [true] king does not govern the barbarians or provide them with emoluments. He does not reject those who come to him, and does not ask after those who leave." The outside world, it seems, is not worth mentioning. See *Shisan jing zhushu,* 2202.

13. Zhang Huang, *Tu shu bian,* SKQS 970: 188.

14. Ge Zhaoguang, *Here in "China" I Dwell: Reconstructing Historical Discourses of China for Our Time,* trans. Jesse Field and Qin Fang (Leiden: Brill, 2017), 23–25.

15. This is a major difference with modern Japan.

16. Some people have recently argued that "pacification" was a mode of expansion for traditional Chinese civilization and that, by comparison, "conquest" was a mode of expansion for the civilization of Mediterranean Europe. See Lin Gang, "Zhengfu yu suijing: Wenming kuozhande guancha yu bijiao" [Conquest and pacification: An investigation and comparison of civilizations' means of expansion], *Beijing daxue xuebao* 2012, no. 5, 68–78.

17. "Discourse on Moving the Rong," by Jiang Tong of the Eastern Jin, argues for the belief held by some in ancient China that Chinese and foreigners should simply be geographically separated from one another. The popular belief in the early Song that one should "uphold the ruler and drive out the barbarians" (*zun wang rang Yi*) also expressed an idea widely held among the gentry elites that the north should be divided between the Liao and the Song, and that it was not necessary to exercise rule over Nanzhao or Dali (both in Yunnan). One unusual fact is that the Yuan dynasty did attempt to conquer Japan, but we see that as soon as the Yuan suffered a number of military defeats that they were no longer interested in Japan. The following dynasty, the Han-ethnic Ming dynasty, went so far as to label faraway countries as "lands that shall not be conquered." The interest in Japan shown during the Kangxi and Qianlong reigns (from the late seventeenth century to the late eighteenth century) also shows the degree to which China often did not concern itself with distant lands. Even though Chinese such as Zhu Zunyi, Jiang Chenying, and Weng Guangping discussed Japan, most of their knowledge was derived from other works of history or even from rumors and tales. The most accurate understanding of Japan was found in Weng Guangping's *Wu qi jing bu* [Commentary on the mirror of the East] (1814; repr., Beijing: Quanguo tushuguan wenxian suowei fuzhi zhongxin, 2005).

18. However, because the idea of "grand unification" carries such weight in China, any event that touches on so-called core interests such as Taiwan, the East China Sea, the South China Sea, Xinjiang, or Tibet may lead to intense conflict.

19. China would often refrain from involving itself in matters that did not directly affect it. In the years after gaining the seat in the United Nations as the representative of China, the Chinese government would always abstain from voting on certain important international issues. Huntington's *Clash of Civilizations* argues that Islamic civilization and Confucian civilization would join forces to oppose Western civilization. My view is that, at least in terms of "joining forces," there is little historical basis for this prediction. This is the case in part because, in traditional Chinese culture, Muslim counties close to China have historically not been treated with much respect by Confucian culture, and may have even been seen with lower regard than the West.

20. Huntington, *Clash of Civilizations,* 47.

21. Buddhism is the exception here. Huntington argues that although Buddhism is a major world religion, it has not served as a basis for a distinct civilization because it fell into decline in the places where it originated and spread to other regions. These new regions, however, had their own civilizational foundations, and Buddhism could only be absorbed into their cultures. It could not, however, replace the cultures of those new places and serve as the foundation for a new community.

22. This refers to campaigns against Buddhism that took place during the under Emperor Taiwu (r. 423–452) of the Northern Wei, Emperor Wu (r. 560–578) of the Northern

Zhou, the Wuzong emperor (r. 840–846) of the Tang dynasty, and the Shizong emperor (r. 557–560) of the Northern Zhou.

23. Numerous debates and reversals concerning the primacy of Buddhism or Taoism took place during the reigns of Tang Taizong, Gaozong, and Wu Zetian. During the reign of the Song Huizong emperor, edicts were issued to refer to icons of Buddhas to Taoist immortals and call Buddhist followers "scholars of virtue" (*de shi*). Following debates about the *Hua Hu jing* (Scripture of transforming the barbarians), in the Yuan dynasty, there were cases of orders being given to convert Taoist temples to Buddhist temples.

24. Examples include Tang-dynasty provisions against foreign religions, as well as Qing-dynasty-era bans on Catholicism.

25. For example, some Buddhists argue that "without the support of the sovereign, it is difficult to sustain our practice" (*bu yi guozhu, ze fa shi nan li*), as others hope to achieve the goal of having a "Bodhisattva emperor." Moreover, Chinese Buddhism calls for the propagation of Buddhism (*Fa lun chang zhuan*) while maintaining the stability of the empire (*huang tu yong gu*).

26. Both Buddhism and Taoism understood quite early that "without the support of the sovereign, it is difficult to sustain our practice" and accepted the supervision of the royal court. Since the establishment during the Northern Wei dynasty of official posts to supervise religious organizations, nearly all dynasties have had similar offices.

27. The monk-soldiers of Japanese Buddhism are an exception to the rule in East Asia.

28. Laurence Thompson's *Chinese Religion: An Introduction* begins with the statement that Chinese religion is a "manifestation of the Chinese culture." See *Chinese Religion: An Introduction* (Belmont, CA: Wadsworth, 1996), 1.

29. For example, Taoism as practiced among elites promoted acts of self-cultivation that separated one from society, such as quietly cultivating the body and spirit, or living in reclusion in a temple, in the forest, or in the mountains. Likewise, those influenced by Zen Buddhism sought a life of seclusion and a realm of spiritual calm. None of these practices promote the absolutism seen in so many religions; in fact, what they do promote is a kind of yielding and being at ease with oneself.

30. "The strong eat the weak" refers to the widespread belief, influenced by the importation of social Darwinism at the turn of the twentieth century, that China would be "eaten" or "cut up like a melon" by other countries such as Japan, Russia, England, and other powers.—Trans.

31. Discussions that emphasize "multiple modernities" demonstrate a certain awkwardness. On the one hand, they do not accept the idea that the transition from tradition to modernity was predetermined. On the other hand, they work to maintain the autonomy of thought, culture, and ideas and attempt to use the idea of multiplicity to find theoretical paths for interpreting the self.

32. We can see that in the past decade the term "great nation" or "great state" (*da guo*) has become quite popular as the term has come into use in both scholarship and politics, where discussions of "the rise of great nations," "the rise and fall of great nations," and "the responsibilities of great nations" are all quite common.

33. See Chapter 3.

34. This reference is to book V, part 2 of *Mencius*: "Mencius added, 'Bo Yi was a sage who was unsullied; Yi Yin was the sage who accepted responsibility; Liu Xia Hui was the

sage who was easygoing; Confucius was the sage whose actions were timely. Confucius was the one who gathered together all that was good.'" *Mencius,* trans. D. C. Lau (New York: Penguin, 1970), 150.—Trans.

35. Of course, some people might object and ask, who determines these principles and on what basis do they interpret them? Since the early modern period, hasn't it been the West that determined these principles and demanded that we follow them? Isn't the problem whether or not, when compared with many other undesirable choices, these principles are relatively fair? If we toss out one set of principles, will we have a replacement that everyone can approve of?

36. These works include relative early writings, such as *Tianxia tixi* [The All-under-Heaven system] (Nanjing: Jiangsu jiaoyu chunabshe, 2005), as well as the more recent attempt by Yao Zhongtian to approach the question from a historical perspective in *Hua Xia zhili zhixu shi* [History of the Hua-Xia system of governance] (Haikou: Hainan chubanshe, 2012), esp. the first volume, which concerns All-under-Heaven.

37. These discussions have been very popular in recent years among scholars and thinkers in China. See the "editor's note" (*bianzhe an*) to a special issue of *Wenhua zongheng* on Chinese philosophies of foreign relations and (in the same issue), "Rujiade waijiao yuanze ji qi dangdai yiyi" [Confucian principles of foreign relations and their conemporary significance], *Wenhua zongheng* 2012, no. 8: 17, 45.

38. Sheng Hong, "Cong minzu zhuyi dao Tianxia zhuyi" [From nationalism to All-under-Heavenism], *Zhanlüe yu guanli* 1996, no. 1: 14–19.

39. Immanuel C. Y. Hsü argues that "international society" originally only referred to Western states, but their continuing expansion meant that this "society" became an international order. The arrival of this order in East Asia meant that it came into contact with "another family of nations" led by China. Conflict between these "two mutually exclusive systems" resulted in the forced integration of the Chinese order into the Western European order. As a result, the "Confucian universal empire" was made into a "modern national state." See Immanuel Hsü, *China's Entrance into the Family of Nations: The Diplomatic Phase, 1858–1880* (Cambridge, MA: Harvard University Press, 1960), 1–18. Is it really rational, however, to argue that, because the modern international order came from the West, it should be substituted with a Chinese order that is based on ideas about All-under-Heaven and the tribute system?

40. Zhao Tingyang argues that All-under-Heaven is an idea from the imperial era, a vast, boundless "world" of combined institutions of geography, thought, and society. To bring back this sense of All-under-Heaven, he argues, is to "imagine and attempt to pursue a kind of 'world institution' and a 'world government' backed by worldwide institutions." See Zhao Tingyang "Tianxia tixi: Diguo yu shijie zhidu" [The All-under-Heaven system: Empires and world institutions], *Shijie zhexue* 2003, no. 5: 5. The book he published two years later, *The All-under-Heaven System,* came with the subtitle "an introduction to a philosophy of world institutions."

41. The strategy of "keeping a low profile and biding one's time" is associated with the foreign policy established by Deng Xiaoping.—Trans.

42. The five principles, which came out of China's engagement with postcolonial countries such as India, are mutual respect for territorial integrity and sovereignty; mutual

nonaggression; mutual noninterference in internal affairs; equality and cooperation for mutual benefit; and peaceful coexistence.—Trans.

43. Wang Xiaodong, quoted in Song Xiaojun, *Zhongguo bu gaoxing* [China is not happy] (Nanjing: Jiangsu renmin chubanshe, 2009), 99. See also the chapter on nationalism in Ma Licheng, *Dangdai Zhongguo ba zhong shehui sichao* [Eight trends in social thought in contemporary China] (Beijing: Shehi kexue wenxian chubanshe, 2012), 133–160.

44. See Mo Luo, *Zhongguo zhan qi lai* [China stands up] (Wuhan: Changjiang wenyi chubanshe, 2010), 255. For a discussion of Mo Luo's move from liberalism to statism, see Xu Jilin, "Zouxiang guojia zaitai zhi lu: Cong Mo Luode zhuanxiang kan Zhongguode xuwu zhuyi" [On the road to the states' sacrificial altar: Observing nihilism in China through Mo Luo's transformation], *Dushu* 2010, no. 8: 73–82, and *Dushu* 2010, no. 9: 123–130.

45. Zhao Tingyang, "Tianxia tixi: Diguo yu shijie zhidu" [The All-under-Heaven system: Empire and the world order], *Shijie zhexue* 2003, no. 5: 13.

46. Qiang Shigong, quoted in Chan Koonchung (Chen Guanzhong), *Zhongguo tianchao zhuyi yu Xianggang* [China's dynastic ideology and Hong Kong] (Hong Kong: Oxford University Press, 2012), 87–130.

47. The Gongyang commentary to the *Spring and Autumn Annals* says, "It is difficult to obtain consistent accounts of events, even from those who have seen and heard them; it is even more difficult to obtain consistent accounts of remote events, based on transmitted testimony." (In other words, the records of the times that Confucius's father personally witnessed already show discrepancies, as do the records for the times of Confucius's grandfather and great-grandfather.) The Han-dynasty scholar He Xiu (129–182) later interpreted these words ("seen" and "heard") to mean that, of the twelve feudal lords who ruled the state of Lu during the Spring and Autumn period, the reigns of dukes Zhao, Ding, and Ai had been personally witnessed by Confucius and his father; the reigns of dukes Wen, Xuan, Cheng, and Xiang were conveyed from what Confucius's father had heard about them, while the accounts of the reigns of dukes Yin, Huan, Zhuang, Min, and Xi were based on information passed on by his grandfathers. Because every person's experiences, perspectives, and ideas were different, therefore one would encounter "inconsistent" accounts. He Xiu then further argued that the Gongyang Commentary offered insight into three different kinds of world orders. The first of these was to "treat as foreign the other states of the land of Xia" (that is, to see one's own state as "inner" or central, and treat other states of Hua-Xia as foreign or outside). The second of these was to "adopt the internal perspective of the other states of the land of Xia, they treat as foreign the nomadic Yi and Di." The third of these was to see "everything near and far and large and small in All-under-Heaven as one." The values and hierarchies of these three modes of world order for All-under-Heaven all differ from one another, and, in the hands of so-called New Text Confucian scholars, have become an important starting point for discussing both practical and ideal versions of an "All-under-Heaven order." See *Shisan jing zhushu*, 2200. Translation borrowed from *The Gongyang Commentary on the Spring and Autumn Annals*, trans. H. Miller (New York: Palgrave Macmillan, 2015), 10n10, 180–181.

48. For example, the second issue in 2013 of journal *Kaifang shidai* (Era of openness) devoted space to discussion on "the China moment in world history." A few months later, Yao Zhongqiu published an essay along these lines, also titled "Shijie lishide Zhongguo shike" (The China moment in world history), which argued that "the idea of All-under-Heaven that was followed in premodern China is best suited to Chinese people of the current moment who are facing a world-historical responsibility." See "Shijie lishide Zhongguo shike," *Wenhua zongheng* 2013, no. 6: 80.

INDEX

Qing dynasty, 63; resistance to humiliation and oppression, 146; Song dynasty, 105–106; stages of international understanding, 122–123; traditional approaches, 47–48. *See also* Cultural conflict; Japan; Korea; Western civilization
Islamic Republic of East Turkestan, 75, 86

Jacques, Martin, 136
Jamal al-Din, 41
Japan: All-under-Heaven in, 168n27; attempted Mongol invasions of, 6, 155n9, 188n17; breakdown of relations with China, 5–6, 124–125, 132–133, 155n8; China studies, 12–13, 52–53, 158n29, 159n38, 165n6; Chinese awareness of Japanese imperialist ambitions, 74–75, 89, 172n33; Chinese lack of interest in, 188n17; as context for China, 65–66; development of, 22–23; imperialist ambitions and debates, 70–72, 171n23; invasion of China, 90; Ming dynasty and, 156n10; on Qing dynasty, 127–130, 132; questioning of Chinese borders, 12–13, 52–53; religion in, 178n9; *Shina* term for China, 158n23; state and culture relationship, 112; Tanaka Memorial, 74, 172n31; Treaty of Shimonoseki, 70, 154n2
Jiang Chenying, 188n17
Jiang Tong, "Discourse on Moving the Rong" (*Xi Rong lun*), 40, 102, 188n17
Jiang Zhefu, 82
Jiang Zhiyou, 68, 69, 172n27
Joseon dynasty, 6, 156n11. *See also* Korea

Kaifang shidai (journal), 192n48
Kang Youwei, 10
Kawazoe Shōji, 155n9
Khitans. *See* Liao dynasty
Kim Chong-hu, 125–126
Kissinger, Henry, 136
Konoe Atsumaro, 70
Korea: border with China, 62; breakdown of relations with China, 6, 124–125, 132–133; Chinese assistance against

Japan, 131, 187n12; development of, 22–23; Ming dynasty and, 156n11; on Qing dynasty, 115, 125–127, 132; as source of Chinese information for Japan, 128; state and culture relationship, 112. *See also* South Korea
Kuwabara Jitsuzō, 171n23

Lacouperie, Terrien de, 69, 72–73, 172n27
Language: Chinese, 117, 185n63; Chinese characters, 97, 135, 176n2; study of foreign, 182n34
Later Jin dynasty, 8
Lattimore, Owen, 55
Laufer, Berthold, 103
Leftover Zhou Documents (*Yi Zhou shu*), 37
Levenson, Joseph, 64, 164n37, 169n2
Li Chi (Li Ji), 73, 79–80, 85, 99–100, 173n42, 179n18
Li Yiyuan, 174n48
Li Zhizao, 47, 130
Liang Qichao, 10, 68–69, 86, 88, 93, 172n27
Liang Siyong, 85–86
Liao dynasty (Khitans), 56, 105–106, 138, 168n32
Ling Chunsheng, 81, 82–84
Liu Di, 174n59
Liu Shipei, 172n27
Liu Yizheng, 86–87, 175n61
Liu Zijian, 182n34
Longshan culture, 80–81, 84–85
Loyalty (*zhong*), 108, 178n7
Lü Commentary to the Spring and Autumn Annals (*Lü shi Chunqiu*), 35, 101
Lu Jiuyuan, 42
Lu Rezhen, 34
Lü Simian, 78
Lu Xun, 175n62
Luxuriant Dew of the Spring and Autumn Annals (*Chunqiu fan lu*), 101

Ma Dazheng, 174n59
Ma Rong, 79
Ma Yi, 90, 93
Macartney, George, 48, 132
Manchu. *See* Qing dynasty